THE ATLANTA PENITENTIARY BURNS

THE
ATLANTA
PENITENTIARY
BURNS

The Cuban Detainees take over
the Pen with 121 hostages

Earl Lawson

EARL LAWSON

706 300 4605

LIBERTY HILL

ZETHAN.EARL@GMAIL.COM

Liberty Hill Publishing
2301 Lucien Way #415
Maitland, FL 32751
407.339.4217
www.libertyhillpublishing.com

The Atlanta Federal Penitentiary has a large staff, which is divided between many departments. Most jobs available in a community have a similar type of job inside the institution. Most staff jobs are supervisory, with inmates performing most of the labor.

With the large number of employees, some names in the book may be the same as, or similar to employees who have performed similar jobs. However, for the purposes of this book, names have been changed and any action does not refer to any specific employee(s). Any name given to any individual, inmate, detainee or staff is only a name to place an action in the context of an understandable situation.

Printed in the United States of America.

ISBN-13: 978-1-54564-741-7

The Atlanta Federal Penitentiary has hundreds of employees, inmates, and detainees. Names of any individuals in the book are only names to assist in identifying the event taking place at the time. Any names that I could identify with a specific event were changed. Any such persons who may have held similar positions in the institution are purely coincidental.

TABLE OF CONTENTS

WITH MUCH GRATITUDE:

IN 1987 AND JUST AFTER THE RIOT AND CONTINUING through several years, I was extremely angry. This anger consumed much of my energy. Anger about the fact that the riot had occurred and was completely preventable. Now the anger and hostility come in spurts, without warning or cause. Over the years I have learned to deflect and control the mood swings, but much of the thanks and appreciation goes to other friends.

In an effort to get through the anger, I decided to write this book. I started writing it on a tablet with a pen. As I continued to use this as therapy, a beautiful young mother of two took pity and assisted me. When reading my hand-written transcript become difficult for her, she allowed me to record my manuscript and give her the tapes. She would then type them, print them, and make suggestions where the conversation did not make sense. When the book was completed, she arranged everything into two volumes and bound them for me.

Without the help of LINDSAY LAYTON, a wonderful member of the church that I attended, the book never would have gone beyond the hand-written, paper stage. I can never thank her enough for the time, patience, and Christian love that she showed me, and without compensation for her efforts. With the continued nightmares and night terrors, I did nothing with the book.

When I finally decided to do something with the book, the original would not hold up for publishing. Again, I found a young lady who, along with her work outside the home, being a mother and housewife, took the time to retype the book for me. Ms. Jessica Browning has taken from herself to help me at a time that I needed help.

Without these two young ladies caring for another in need, this book would have never been realized. I want to thank both ladies for the selfless love they have shown me at times when I needed it most. May God add His richest blessings upon each of them.

AN INTRODUCTION

THERE IS A LOT OF INFORMATION, LONG OVERDUE FOR public disclosure, about the U.S. Bureau of Prisons and the U.S. Department of Justice (Just us). The staff ultimately pay for many of the irrational decisions made by incompetent officials who are not held accountable for their actions.

The information contained in this book is accurate. The majority of the names of employees, inmates, and detainees in the book have been changed. Should I use the name of an actual employee or inmate, that person may have nothing to do with actions in the book. The sequence of events may also be out of order. The book will be divided into three actual sections.

- The first section will be prior to 1979, at the U.S. Penitentiary, Atlanta, a maximum security facility for American prisoners.

- The second section will cover the period between 1979 and 1981. This is the time in which the facility was in the process of closing. Inmates and staff were being transferred, and the penitentiary closed, area by area.

- Last, and where most· emphasis will be, the Cuban period. On November 1, 1984, the Cuban population took over cell house B. On November 23, 1987, they took over the entire facility. Efforts will be made to explain why this occurred and who was responsible.

Each of these three separate areas will be broken down into two sections. While they will not be identified as such, hopefully the reader will be able to recognize the relationships between staff (particularly labor-management relations) as well as staff and inmate population relations.

Especially during the period concerning the Cuban population, these relationships will explain how and why twenty-six hostages were held in Oakdale, Louisiana, and, additionally, more than a hundred hostages in Atlanta, Georgia. Only one staff member was injured.

The next aspect of the book, which I would like to explain, is the language and sexual discussions. Many of the books and movies of today have used profanity just to fill up space; in some cases, obscenities are designed to add emphasis to an otherwise nonexistent plot. A maximum security correctional facility is a closed community of individuals who are (at least intended to be) placed under a magnifying glass at all times—this includes their limited sexual life. To remove the conversational style, sexual lifestyle, and attitudes of both staff and the population from the book would result in a "Once Upon a Time" type of story. Once the conversational styles and attitudes have been established within the first few chapters, the language will no longer appear in the book.

At the time I began this writing, there was a great deal of anger, hostility, depression, and mental confusion about the riot. Those strong emotions followed my being held hostage from November 23, 1987 to December 4, 1987. It is with the help and encouragement of my wife Patti, our family, wonderful friends, and others who continually kept my motivation going. While they did not understand what they were prodding along, nor the rampage they were directing, it is with great appreciation that the offers to help, the inquiries about my progress, and the understanding smiles were received. Thanks to all and to God be the glory.

PART ONE

CHAPTER 1

WELCOME TO THE US PENITENTIARY, ATLANTA, GEORGIA

I HAD JUST MOVED TO THE ATLANTA AREA FROM COLUMBUS, Georgia, when I got a notice from the Atlanta Federal Penitentiary about an interview. As I drove into the circle in front of the gray granite, forbidding-looking structure, I was not only uncertain as to *where* I should go, but if I *wanted* to go. The officer in the tower called down through the speaker in the street, asking, "Can I help you?" When I explained that I was to have an interview for employment, he directed me to the visitors' parking lot, which was located just behind me.

After parking, I started walking toward the steps leading into the institution. As I approached a small, glass phone booth-type structure, the officer in the tower again instructed, "One moment, please." As I looked into the booth to see who had spoken, a recording began to play. It was a message notifying all visitors to the institution that the introduction of weapons, ammunition, firearms, drugs, or alcohol into a federal correctional facility was illegal and violators would be prosecuted. After listening to the recorded message, I went up the stairs and into the institution. Once inside the front doorway, I found another officer sitting at a desk. When I explained my presence, he informed me that someone would be out to get me shortly. It was obvious that several other men who waited in the lobby were all there for the same reason.

It was only a short time until someone from personnel came out for us. We each signed in, were issued a visitor's pass, and informed not to wander off on our own. We were to be escorted at all times during this visit. He then instructed the control room officer to open the door into the sally port area and counted us in.

The sally port was an open area with electronically controlled doors on three sides and a wall on the other side. It was located in a bottleneck-type area between the administrative building and corridor. As we went in from the front of the institution, we could see between the bars and into the corridor leading into the interior. We could see one officer standing in the front portion of the corridor. He opened both of the doors to the cell houses and, in a moment, the hallway was full of people. One staff member, identified by their keys and radios, stepped out of each of the cell houses and looked down the corridor.

As we watched the activities in the corridor, our concentration on these activities was lost as a result of the sound of steel striking steel when the door closed and locked behind us. With chills in my spine, I realized that I was locked inside the Atlanta Federal Penitentiary. A set of bars and a door was between me and that crowded hallway.

The personnel officer then motioned for the next door to be opened. The side door leading into a stairwell slowly began to open. Although the view had not been obstructed, we saw the small landing, just through the doorway, with stairs going down and up. We were led up the stairway and into a large hallway with a table. The conference table had chairs on both sides, although it was near the wall on one side. Additional chairs had to be brought in to accommodate the fourteen of us. We were told to have a seat and to complete additional forms. Specific instructions were given concerning any previous arrests to be included in the documentation.

After completing those forms, we were taken to the hospital for a brief physical. As we completed the medical examination, we were escorted back to the chief correctional supervisor's (captain's) office. The captain is the department head for the custodial force (correctional officers). We were taken into his office one at a time for an interview with management officials. I was the last to go in for an interview. While waiting, the captain's clerk, a senior officer specialist (GS-8 correctional officer) told me that I would get the job and to not worry. When I went in, the associate warden (custody), the personnel officer, the captain, and a lieutenant (correctional supervisor) were in the room.

I had a short interview. It had been a long day, for those holding the interviews, as well as for me. I was asked a few questions about my previous work record, availability for work on Sundays and holidays, and so on.

The lieutenant asked, "If you were assigned to work a tower and saw an inmate climbing over the wall, would you have any difficulty shooting him? Since that would be your job."

Without any hesitation I answered, "No."

The captain asked, how could I be so certain that I could shoot someone? I told him that I had been involved in an incident while working as a policeman in Florida, which had resulted in my shooting a man. While taking a human life was not something that I wanted to do, when necessary, I knew that I could. Obviously, that was the answer they wanted to hear, because the next question was, "When can you start?"

I told my wife that I had been hired and was going to start working in two weeks. I told her that, while I thought I would like the work, there would be a shift change each month for a year. After that, I would be changing shifts every three months. I would not be off for weekends or holidays and could not plan family activities until the last minute in most cases.

After about an hour of discussing the negatives of the job, I let her talk me into going ahead and taking the job. After working those hours as a police officer, I knew how she'd hated it. Every time she had a complaint after that, I reminded her that I had been hesitant in taking the job, but she had said that she could deal with my working that type of a schedule.

At 7:30 a.m. on Monday morning October 3, 1973, I reported to work. Thirteen new employees, including me, reported to the front desk and waited. We were soon met by the training coordinator, Mr. Satterling. We were escorted through the gates and, again, the chills went up my spine when the doors clanged together.

We were led upstairs and taken into a room for training. During that week, each of us had to sign for receipt of each policy and form that we received, which was enough to fill a filing cabinet. There were only a few things that I remember about the training. One was Mr. Satterling's introduction to our class.

"You men will find that during your period of employment in this prison, you will be dealing with some of the most useless, cheating, lying, and sorriest bastards ever to breathe fresh air. Besides that, you will have to deal with those damn convicts." While we all laughed, we found that to be the most important and true information given to us.

Mr. Satterling had begun his career at the U.S. Penitentiary, Atlanta, when the inmates marched down one side of the corridor and up the other side. During that time, the inmates did not walk in the center of the hallway—that was reserved for staff. The inmates did not talk to staff without first asking permission. For the most part, an inmate did not want to talk to the staff because others would call him a snitch. Those concepts of correction have long since changed, and Mr. Satterling was teaching the new ideas and practices. Open communication between inmates and staff was a new process. We were learning to listen and understand that the inmates were human beings with feelings.

And problems which could be calmed by talking were now important. Counseling courses were now required for staff, in an effort to promote interpersonal communication skills. Mr. Satterling had appreciated the fact that talking to the inmates was easier than fighting them. He was respected as a training coordinator, since he had a background of experience to draw from and the skills to relate that information to current situations and future trends.

Before he retired, the personnel manager justified downgrading that position from a GS-12 to a GS-11, while upgrading his own from a GS-12 to a GS-13. He retired at a time when affirmative action was being stressed. The position was filled by a woman who had been the warden's secretary; she had never worked in a cell house or with an inmate population. With no negative connotations intended, she was unable to relate events to concepts being taught. Male staff frequently complained about her lack of experience in the subject she was teaching, claiming a lack of relationship between book and actual work conditions.

During training, we had been taken on a tour of the institution. We were shown where to buy meal tickets (then $1.80 each) for the officer's meals. A small dining room separated us from the inmates. We were shown each cell house, the dining hall, the hospital, industries, and the recreation area. This was a totally new and unexpected experience.

As you entered the institution and went inside the second gate, which lead to the main corridor, cell house A was on the left.

Cell house A was, at that time, a cell house with an outer shell, made of granite and steel, with large windows running from shoulder height to the top of the building. They ran all down the front and back side of the building, with a smaller cell house inside of that. There was approximately twenty feet of distance between the outside walls of A block and the cells where the inmates slept.

In the middle of the entire block, there was what was called a *cut-off*. It was a hallway, locked on both ends, that housed the plumbing for the cells on both sides. The floor of the cut-off area was solid cement. The second, third, fourth, and fifth floors were wood with steel crossbeams. The cut-off (or the pipe chases) housed all the air vents for each cell as well as the water and sewage. Each cell had an exhaust vent pulling air out of the cells. Air (heat) came from vents located at floor level on the outside walls. Each cell had two exhaust vents going out and hot water and cold water going in. Water could be controlled to each individual cell from inside a locked and secured area. That was the backside of the cells. On the front of the first floor on both sides of the cut-off there were cells, approximately eight feet deep and sixteen feet long. Each of these cells held four, double bunk beds.

When I first began there in 1973, each cell had the capacity of housing five to eight inmates. On average, there were six inmates, but all cells had the capability of housing eight inmates. Cell blocks A and B were identical, but mirrored. In each case, the office was on the Norton side of the building. Around each set of cellblocks was a walkway (what we called a range). In both blocks, the cells begin with 1 on the Norton side. In cell house A, the first floor was "1 range," second floor was "2 range," third floor was "3 range," etc. The range was a walkway approximately four-feet wide, and when I started working there it had already been enclosed with steel mesh.

We were informed that a year or two prior to that, an employee had made an inmate angry, and the inmate had dropped a five-HP motor from the fifth floor. That motor landed about two feet from the officer and bounced away, just bypassing his certain death. Another officer had nearly been thrown from the third floor. Those events resulted in all the walkways on the outside being screened-in, in order to prevent any further incidents. The mesh screen was approximately sixteen feet from the outer wall. The first floor was the only floor that did not have that screen.

For the last day of training, we were given a different schedule. We learned that the correctional force had seventeen different shifts. They were:

1	midnight – 8 a.m.	9	9:30 a.m. – 6:00 p.m.
2	5:30 a.m. – 2:00 p.m.	10	11:00 a.m. – 7:30 p.m.
3	6:00 a.m. – 2:00 p.m.	11	12 noon -8:30 p.m.

4	6:00 a.m. – 2:30 p.m.	12	12:30 a.m. – 9:00 p.m.
5	7:00 a.m. – 4:00 p.m.	13	2:00 a.m. – 10:00 p.m.
6	7:30 p.m. – 6:00 p.m.	14	2:00 a.m. – 10:30 p.m.
7	7:45 a.m. – 4:15 p.m.	15	3:00 a.m. – 11:00 p.m.
8	8:00 a.m. – 4:00 p.m.	16	4:00 a.m. – midnight
SA	8:00 a.m. – 4:30 p.m.		

The difference between shift 3 and shift 4 was whether or not the assigned post had a lunch relief. If you had a thirty-minute, non-paid lunch break, it was an eight and a half-hour shift assignment. We came in from twelve noon until 8:30 p.m. We were broken up into different areas until 4:00 p.m. From 4:00 p.m. to 4:30 p.m. we went to lunch and then reported back to the dining room. Until 4:00 p.m., we moved from area to area, getting acquainted with the institutional yard, recreation area, card room, and different cellblocks.

We got to the dining hall just before the 4:00 p.m. count was cleared and feeding began. We soon learned why feeding was one of the most disliked assignments in the institution. Working the dining hall during the feeding period was a part of another assignment and not a job within itself. Only the cook foremen remained in the dining area for their entire work shift.

The dining hall was one of the most hazardous areas to have a fight. There were a large number of items such as the hard plastic cups, glasses, bowls, and trays, which could be thrown or broken and used to cut another person. Also, salt and pepper shakers, as well as silverware, were used as weapons. During mealtime you might have four or five employees supervising. With the American population, when two inmates started to fight, everyone in the dining hall joined in the fighting or was running within seconds. In actuality, most of the inmates just wanted out of there without appearing to be a coward or getting hurt. Very few of the inmates wanted any conflict with staff. Most of the inmates were happy to see an officer step up and order them to break it up. Staff stood behind the cafeteria-style buffet and saw that rationed items were issued. Meats were rationed, one per inmate. Many of the inmates did not want the meat of the meal and would give it to someone who wanted more, so this rarely posed a problem.

I had been working in the institution for just under a month, when I was supervising in the cafeteria. Everything was running smoothly when an inmate came through, who did not want his meat. The server asked if he could have it and the inmate in the line said *yes*. The server then made sure that this was okay with me. I did not realize it at the time, but I was being set up. An inmate just down the line asked for an extra piece. The server said, "Sure, you have my piece…is that okay with you?"

It was at that moment that I realized what I'd gotten myself into. I reluctantly agreed. "Yeah, go ahead." By taking the piece from those who refused and giving it to those who asked for more, as well as offering many of his friends extra, he had thirty-nine pieces left for himself when he was finished serving. I also realized that when an inmate was told that he could only have one of a rationed item, he would just go across the dining hall to another of the six serving lines. After that, I did not take the job as seriously as some of the staff.

After the evening meal was over, we were split up into small groups. We had discovered that the main facility was broken down into four cell houses. One of the other trainees and I were assigned to cell house D. This was a smaller unit, containing 180 individual cells. I later learned that cell houses A and B were the more easily-controlled inmates. Inmates in cell houses C and D were the more hardcore inmates. Those were the individuals who could be extremely hazardous, dangerous, and had the tendency to become more assaultive. They were locked in single cells. There were thirty-eight cells on each range. C house had ranges 11 through 15, D house had 16 through 20. Cells 37 and 38 were both combined to make one shower. Showers were provided on each range for the inmates.

The senior officer, Mr. Jackson, or *Jackson* as he was most commonly known, was a fine officer. He was a tall, lanky man of about forty, who spent most of his time sitting in the office. He later explained that from sitting in the office with the lights out, he could observe half of the cell house and know what went on. With the lights off, the inmates could not tell whether he, or anyone else, was in the office. While the theory was sound and I used it on occasion, I found it to be bullshit as it related to him. He has since retired and had no difficulties with his tenure. He was there a long time before I got there and succeeded during a much harder work period than I, so I have nothing but the utmost respect for him.

During the count, every inmate must stand up. You walk cell by cell and count the individuals to get a total of the number of individual inmates in that range. You go to the next range and do the same thing—however all inmates assigned to that housing unit may not be there. Some may be working in the kitchen, while others may be working in the factory. Wherever they'd been assigned to be during count, it must be verified by counting twice. On one occasion, the officer in the cell house and the day watch officer had verified the count. That officer knew precisely who was supposed to be in his range by keeping up with his count on a headcount form. When I arrived after 4:00, I was to start counting. I was given the top floor to count, so I went up to range 20 and counted. When I finished counting, I called down the number of inmates there and I was told that was correct.

The rest of the evening was spent walking the ranges over and over again. When we would see other officers, we would stop and talk with them to get some understanding of what we should or should not be doing. Some officers were friendly and offered suggestions, but for the most part the officers were a jealous bunch. For an officer to be promoted, it required a special act or knowing someone of importance. We had young officers coming to work who were being rapidly promoted, while other senior officers (other GS-7 officers training us) would be competing for the same position that we'd be...in two years. It was believed by some that the more support they'd give us, the more we could show them up at a later time. Thus, help from staff became limited to nonexistent. Very few staff would stop and take the time and explain how to, what to, why to, what not to, why not to do it, and what the policy was. It was the new employee's responsibility to read the books, read the policy statements, read the program statements, see what you can do, what you cannot do, and then use your best judgment and act on what you think is right.

You could stand in front of the institution or on the street and see the stairs leading up to the front lobby. This particular section was the administrative section of the facility. In the front, and smaller, section on the left was the warden's office. On the right was the associate warden of operations (AW-O) office. Across the hall from the warden on the backside was the warden's executive assistant. Across from the AW-O's office was the control center. In the middle of the administrative section was the information desk and switchboard.

On the second floor of the administrative building was the personnel area and credit union. You must go through the first gate and into the sally port to get into the stairwell for that area. The sally port is a section twenty-feet wide by thirty-feet long, which connects the administration building with the rest of the institution. The larger units seen from the outside are cell house A and cell house B.

Looking from the street into A or B cell house, you could sometimes see, through the windows, inmates walking down a walkway (range) around the upper tiers. A grill, which slid to the right, and a commode in the middle were protected by a cubical. The cubical was raised one foot off the floor and was four-feet tall. The door opened to the front of the cell. On each side of the partition was a sink attached to the back wall. After the first five cells, there was a dividing walkway (cut-off) which was ten-feet wide, with a set of stairs going from one range to the next below it. These stair structures were located on the front of A and B units and in the cut-off, in the middle of the range.

There were no stairs in the back, while C and D units had front only. A and B units continued with cells 6 through 10 facing the street and 11 through 15 from the back to the front and facing the institution. Those cells were usually occupied by inmates who had not been in the institution long or were smart-asses. If an inmate wanted to run his mouth or just be hard to get along with, he was moved to one of the two upper ranges, in cells 11 through 15. He had the longest walk to get in and out of his cell and could only see the back of other institutional buildings when looking out of his window. Those areas also demanded more random shakedowns than others.

Cell 16 in cell houses A and B was a shower. The showers had four shower heads and a lip at the front of the cell near the bars, which was eighteen inches high. This was an effort to keep the water in the showers; privacy was not a consideration, but a prohibited act. The position of the staff was that if the inmates were trying to get out of sight, they either wanted to screw, fight, or escape, and all were prohibited. Cells 17 through 20 were identical to the others.

The unit orderlies, the most tidy and cooperative of the inmates, were assigned to the front cells on the floor. This allowed them to be the first going to the dining hall and the least frequently shaken down. While they identified it as a reward for positive behavior, it was also a necessity for staff. When visitors came into the unit, the orderlies' cells were front and center on display. The staff knew that we could depend on their cells to be kept looking presentable. A clean and shiny institution was preferable, but some pigs just would not change their habits. Visitors touring the unit would be shown those few and be told that they were representational of all the units. Once a Congressman insisted on seeing every cell; this resulted in criticism of management and staff.

Cell houses C and D were smaller units with no cut-off. Dorm 2 occupied the bottom floor of cell house E. Dorm 2 was situated below the ground level entrance to cell house E, which was an honor building located outside of the main structure. It was the newest building within the compound. The ground level floor was range 22 and went all the way up to range 25 at the top. This building had an open area in the center with one and two-man cells on the outer walls. Each cell had its own door key.

Cell houses C and D were preferred living quarters because they were single-man cells. These units were used to house only the most dangerous of the inmates. They were the inmates with the highest risk for escape attempts. Sentences of five-hundred years or more were not uncommon. For the most part, as long as they were treated with respect, they were no problem to deal with.

Dorm 1, the Drug Abuse Program (OAP unit) was the smaller of the housing units. It housed inmates who had been required to participate in a drug treatment program by the judge as part of their sentence. This dorm was located under the hospital. Dorms 3 and 4 were occupied mostly by inmates arrested as part of organized crime (Mafia members). Surprisingly enough, most of the contraband found in Dorm 3 and 4 was food. Several of the inmates from organized crime worked in the kitchen. The inmates would steal food from the dining hall and would be assured of having something to snack on. If the staff working that unit were hungry, the inmates would offer them a sandwich if they thought they would not get locked up.

One Mafia leader always had someone with him (his valet) to run errands for him. The valet kept his shoes shined, his clothes ironed, starched, and prepared for him. If a valet was transferred out, someone else would take his place. One of the valets was released on parole but was again arrested and returned to Atlanta. The following day, his cell was wired shut and set on fire with him in it. Although he was burned badly, the staff was able to get him out alive. As soon as he was able to be moved, he was transferred to another institution, where he was stabbed to death two days later. The rumor was that the man for whom he had been the valet, had told him to go by his home and ask his wife for $1,000.00 for his work—his valet service—and she would pay him. When he got out, he went by and asked for $2,000.00, which was paid without question. If the valet would have asked the convict for more, he would have been told to ask for the $2,000.00, but these were the consequences for cheating the convict.

Working that dorm was a great assignment. If you wanted the dorm painted, all you had to do was suggest that it needed painting to the Mafia leader. Before the day was over, someone would be asking permission to paint. This unit was a model unit. Everyone was quiet and cooperative. If someone got too loud or caused a problem of any sort, if the officer even knew about it, he would need only to caution the inmate to restore order. In most cases, the inmate would express fear for his life and request to be placed in segregation or would ask to be moved to cell house A or B with his friends. Despite the inmate never providing a name or a reason for his fear, the request was honored and the inmate moved.

The dorm was not the only area from which inmates requested to be removed and placed in the segregation unit. As a matter of fact, it was a standing joke among staff that we would have lockdown the day following any major sporting event. Inmates would frequently bet more cigarettes than they could pay. Cigarettes were an acceptable means of barter within the prison system. As a result of this, an inmate could have no more than two packs on him outside of his cell and four cartons in his possession in his cell. This meant that a cell with six inmates could have, at most, twenty-four cartons of cigarettes, no matter how many of those inmates smoked. Within the population, many of the inmates had money outside of the facility. Large bets would be paid by asking a family member to send money to a family member of the person owed. Gambling debts which could not be paid would result in transfers, lockdowns, or assaults.

In the basements of cell houses A and B, was an area occupied by inmates who, for the most part, had health problems. It was also an *honor quarters*. Thirteen-hundred to fifteen-hundred inmates were housed in cell houses A, B, C, and D. While sleeping conditions were not much better, the honor quarters were less supervised. One staff member was assigned to the basements on each shift. One floor housed up to three-hundred inmates. This allowed inmates an opportunity to make their own alcohol or meet their lover in relatively safe conditions. Cell house E was a five-floor structure and also had only one officer between midnight and 4:00 p.m. From 4:00 p.m. until midnight, there would be two staff on duty, unless one was needed somewhere else.

The only other housing for the inmates was the temporary quarters. Although some inmates remained in segregation for extremely long periods of time, the segregation unit and hospital units were not permanently-assigned quarters. The hospital was generally short-term housing. Any illness which required prolonged treatment or hospitalization was referred to Springfield, Missouri. An inmate might come into Atlanta from another facility and go directly to segregation, remain there for three years and be transferred to another facility. Yet, he would be assigned to another cell house for accountability and paperwork purposes. The caseworker who would handle the paperwork and check on the inmate would be dependent upon the inmate's assigned cell house. The segregation unit and hospital did not have case managers or other unit staff assigned.

Immediately after orientation, each inmate was assigned a job. New prisoners would most generally start off in food service. The first cook foreman came in at 4:00 a.m., and the remaining inmates on first shift would start as soon as the 4:00 a.m. count had cleared. Breakfast would begin between 6:00 a.m. and 6:15 a.m.; lunch began at 10:15 and ended by 1:00 p.m. Lunch was staggered by job assignment, while dinner, which started immediately after the 4:00 p.m. count, was controlled by a rotation of cell houses. Inmates working the evening shift would be served from 7:30 p.m. to 8:30 p.m. The cooking was done by the inmates working under the supervision of a cook foreman. Inmates assigned to food service generally worked long and hard hours. While the shift was only eight hours, the hours assigned could change, and the work was never considered enjoyable. Those assigned to the dish room had much harder work. From the time that the first inmate entered until it was closed for the night, they had to be cleaning. Floor or utensil, the cleaning never stopped.

The only other job to work after 4:00 p.m. was the industries. The industries had a diversified line of jobs. The mill worked two shifts; first shift began at 7:30 a.m., and second shift ended at 11:30 p.m. Inmates considered to be a security risk could not work beyond 8:00 p.m. The industries made signs for Federal Reservations, brought in raw cotton, made thread, and then made mail bags and mail carts from the thread, as well as mattresses. Industry workers were paid more than the rest of the institution positions and were sought by most of the population. An inmate would work six days a week in food service for twenty dollars a month. The inmate working in industries would earn $150 a month by working overtime.

The next largest employer of the inmates was mechanical services. The institution was maintained completely by inmates. Electrical, plumbing, and additions were supervised by a mechanical services foreman and the labor was provided by the inmate population. The supervisors were skilled in their trade and could teach an inmate who desired to learn a trade. Vocational training was provided for those inmates who wanted to learn mechanical skills, such as electric, heating and air conditioning, plumbing, masonry, auto mechanics, and other skills. An automobile had been donated by the Chevrolet plant next to the institution, and several motorcycles had also been brought in for training. A small quantity of gasoline would be brought in and it was either used or removed from the institution by the end of the day. A TV repair shop and typewriter repair shop were also available under the education department's vocational training programs. These trade schools could be used in conjunction with an on-the-job assignment. Inmates within the various departments were assigned to emergency duty jobs as well. If an inmate broke his sink, the emergency plumber came and made repairs, regardless of what time it was. We also had our fire department, recreation, and sanitation details. Most jobs that are available within the public community were also available to the inmates in the institution. The education department also had classes which could enable an inmate who had entered the institution unable to read or write, to be released with a high school GED. Or even a college degree, earned from a local Atlanta college. While these classes were available and encouraged, no one would be forced to attend.

In 1973, the camp (a low security facility located outside the walls, but on the grounds) did not exist. The grounds of the institution, both inside and outside the walls, were also maintained by the inmates. As many as one hundred inmates, all of which were low custody and security level, would go in and out of the East Gate daily. They were either going to the garage, outside to a receiving storeroom, an outside industries warehouse, or to landscape. In order to be allowed to enter and exit the gate, the inmate must have a gate pass signed by the associate warden (custody) (AWC). A correctional supervisor, senior officer specialist, a senior officer, a trainee as well as two inmate orderlies would work the gate. One inmate had been there so long and was so well trained in the gate operations, that he would break in a staff member or supervisor.

I witnessed one occasion when this inmate jumped on an officer for not doing his job properly. "If you ain't going to do your job, you may as well get your ass out of the way and let someone else do it. You walk around like you're looking for something. You don't even know what you're looking for. Someone could put a machine gun there where you just looked and you wouldn't see it." I never understood how he kept that job for so long without being killed. It was rumored by some that he was crazy, the majority of the inmates were afraid of him. Yet, he was released on parole without harm.

The inmates entering and exiting the gate would be patted down and randomly strip-searched by the staff. During the day shift, the powerhouse crew, firemen, or CMS detail going to work on the staff houses on the grounds would also go in and out through that gate. The East Gate was open from 7:30 a.m. to 3:30 p.m. After 3:30 and before 7:30, inmates would go in and out of the front gate. Along with the inmate traffic, all vehicles entering and leaving the institution would come through the East Gate. At that time, train cars came inside the walls to remove and deliver goods which had been manufactured in our industries department. The East Gate was a sally-port type area with two electronically-controlled sliding gates. One of those two gates had an independently controlled walk-in gate. There was a walkway, which ran the entire length of the gate, and a tower which operated the same hours as the East Gate. The tower officer, instructed by the OIC (Officer in Charge), controlled the outside gate. He also prevented unlawful entrance by force, as the towers were the only place where weapons were allowed. The office at the bottom of the towers was where inmates were strip-searched and paperwork was stored.

The inside gates were key locked and manually opened by the OIC. The gate was long enough to hold a railway engine pushing two railroad cars inside. Most of the time, the train cars were brought in by an institution jeep driven by an inmate. The inmate would be strip-searched and then step inside the gate and out of the way. All the vehicles, regardless of what they were, would be inspected from top to bottom, inside and out. The train cars, usually loaded four to six at a time, would be locked shut and a seal put on each lock to assure that it could not be opened without the seal being broken.

When leaving, the contents of the train did not need to be searched. The exterior was thoroughly inspected to make sure no one had broken in. On one occasion, an escape attempt was made via the train. An inmate had cut a hole in the bottom of the train and after the 4:00 p.m. count. He'd returned to the train and climbed in from underneath. He had someone put putty and grease back into the cracks where the cut had been made. At the 10 p.m. count, it was discovered that the inmate was missing. After a search of the grounds, he was placed on escape status, which was reduced to attempted escape the next day. He was found by the gate staff when the train cars were being pulled out of the institution and inspected.

All towers, including the one above the East Gate, were equipped with a variety of weapons, ammunition, a telephone, and most importantly—an intercom system. The intercom allowed communication between all of the towers, the lieutenant's office, and the control room. Some of the towers also had two-way radios for communicating with other staff. The most boring eight-hour day for three months was working the tower. When assigned to a tower, I found myself eating excessively, smoking cigarettes, and drinking instant coffee. The inmates would spend their time making contraband like an immersion water heater or stinger. We didn't mind as long as they made one for us. The towers, considered by almost everyone to be one of the most important positions to be filled in the penitentiary, became a whipping post. If you made a supervisor mad, it could result in your being assigned to alternating between the towers and the yard during the winter for a year or more. The difficulty was that you could be holding an idle conversation, making a comment about a police department, the City of Atlanta, or any other subject about which a supervisor held strong feelings, and you could be in the outhouse for years.

All the housing units had one man assigned from midnight until 5:30 a.m. A second officer would arrive at 5:30 a.m. and help open the doors and assist in the dining hall. The midnight to 8:00 a.m. shift officer counted the inmates within the unit at 12:00, 2:00, 4:00, and 5:30 a.m. At 6:00 a.m. another unit officer came in for cell houses A and B. At 8:00 a.m., the fourth officer for cell houses A and B, and the third officer for cell houses C and D came in. The third and fourth officers in those units, usually trainees, spent most of their day in the dining hall or running errands for the lieutenant. If someone called in sick or the institution needed an extra man somewhere else, those positions would just be vacated.

The recreation yard opened at 8:30 a.m. seven days a week, unless it was foggy—then everything stopped. Inmates from outside units were counted upon entering and leaving as well as being escorted. Additional staff was put on the yard and outside the wall with other motorized, roving patrols. All inmates were required to work either on weekends or week days. Inmates would also earn vacation time. After working on a job for a year, they could take a week off and get paid for it. Inmates on vacation were permitted to be on the yard during workday hours and return to their unit or assigned area for the 4:00 p.m. count. Inmates not on vacation, or off for the day, who were out on the yard during the workday hours were out of bounds. In the cell house, the officer was to have the unit cleaned, mopped, waxed, and ready for an inspection by 9:00 a.m. From 9:00 a.m. to 12:00, you had nothing for the detail to do but could not let them leave the unit.

Some officers may have enough work to keep five inmates busy for an average of three hours a day. Two hours beginning at 7:30 a.m. and another hour at 12:00 p.m. would be more than enough time for five inmates to do all the work that an officer could find to have done. Yet, he may have fifteen inmates on the detail, and a supervisor might come by and ask why some are sitting down and not working at 2:30 p.m., or why they were not all there. The only person who could release an inmate from a detail was the AWC, except for medical reasons. Most of the officers would allow the inmate to go to the barber shop, look for another job, or whatever destination given, knowing that the inmate was going to the yard. As long as the inmate did not get involved in a fight or serious incident, this was rarely a problem.

CHAPTER 2

ON THE JOB

On a warm October day, the evening meal started at 4:15 and went quickly. By 5:30, only a few stragglers were left. The new class of trainees, thirteen extra staff, walked in and around the tables. They had been reminded that smoking was not allowed in the dining hall. The inmates ate and dutifully went outside for their after-meal smoke. By 5:30, all the regular staff and most of the trainees had been sent to a housing unit or the recreation yard. Four trainees, including myself, and one senior officer remained in the dining hall for another ten minutes. A trainee and I were sent to cell house D and the other two were sent to cell house C.

When we went to cell house D, we found the officer in charge where you could always find him—in the office with the lights out, his legs crossed and his feet on the desk. The back of the chair was leaned up against the wall. During an eight-hour shift, Jackson spent at least seven of them in the office. He might go up to the fifth range in a unit once during a quarter. Other than forced movements from the office, and a weekly tour of the unit, he might go to the lieutenant's office to get a cup of coffee and complain about what the sorry trainees were doing. Or what they were not doing right.

Final yard recall was at 8:00 p.m. Until that time only a few inmates were in the unit unless there were thunderstorms or it was extremely cold. The units were broken down among staff. Regularly, the OIC would be in charge of the flats (first floor), the number two officer would be in charge of the second and third floor, and the number three officer (a trainee) would be in charge of the top two ranges. In cell houses A and B, where four officers were routinely assigned, the number four officer (a trainee) had the top two floors and the other officers had one each.

With two extra officers in cell house D until 8:30 p.m., we were each assigned a range to walk around for two hours. We soon learned that we each were not restricted to that range, but if anything needed to be done on a given range, it was that person's responsibility. We also learned that job assignments were based upon pay grade (the OIC was a GS-8, the number two officer, a GS-7), along with seniority. The number two officer in cell house A might have three years as a GS-7, and the number three officer, also a GS-7 with only two years.

Just in case these systems failed, the post orders for every job called for the number two officer to assist in directing and supervising the number three officer. As a result, the trainee was assigned to do those jobs that no one else wanted to do. When getting into cell house D, Jackson told us that one of us could wear his body alarm. This was a small black box that fit in a small case and was worn on the belt. It was about 3x3" and 1" thick, with a button on the top. If help was needed, you could just push the button, and an alarm would be sounded in the control room. Within a minute and twenty to thirty seconds, additional staff would be there to help you. One officer used the staff bathroom in the unit, which was secured by a padlock. He failed to lock the padlock and left it outside. When he was ready to leave, he had to use the body alarm to have someone unlock the door to let him out. The OIC had a walkie-talkie radio and a body alarm; the other assigned officers had just the body alarm. For communication within the cell house, a bell would be rung to correspond to the post. I was called the number 5 officer for that night. I was told that if a bell rang five times that I was to come to the office. Otherwise, we were to "keep our asses" on the ranges.

As we walked the range we would stop by cells with inmates in them. We would ask how things were going with them, admire their work if they were painting, which many did, or whatever we could think to talk about. Some made it clear that they only wanted to talk to staff if absolutely required. The older, long-term inmates felt that if they talked to staff, they would be considered a snitch. I called out to one such inmate and he came unglued.

He said, "An inmate is a crybaby, a dick-sucking bastard who would snitch on his mother or eat the guard's shit if he thought he could get something out of it. I am a *convict!* I ain't no damn pussy and don't need none of your favors. I robbed a bank, as a matter of fact, I robbed a whole bunch of them and when I get out, I will rob some more. I was man enough to do the crime and I can do the time. Don't come up to me with that *inmate* bullshit."

"As long as you don't beat the government out of a minute's time, that's fine by me," I responded. I walked off, knowing within myself that he had won that conversation. I would never have admitted it, but he had succeeded in intimidating me. I had no idea why I was there or what I should be doing and it was clear he did.

At 7:45 p.m., the final yard recall was given. The door was opened and the inmates began coming in from the yard. After the move had ended, the OIC told me and Big John, the other trainee, to go to the lieutenant's office. The lieutenant called the control room officer on the intercom and told him that he was sending us out, escorted by Butnier. I don't know about the rest of the trainees, but I sure was glad to be getting out of there. This was Friday night and I did not have to be back until 3:00 p.m. on Sunday. For the first month, I would be working cell house C, range 3, from 3:00 to 11:00 p.m. My days off would be Tuesday and Wednesday.

At 2:30 p.m. on Sunday, I went by the control room, which kept up with all of the keys, radios, and body alarms. I gave the control room number 3 officer my chits, a small disk with my name stamped across it, and asked for the body alarm by number and key ring by number that I would need. I got the chits for the officer who I would relieve.

Before going onto any job, each officer is required to read the post orders for that job. The post orders will explain what equipment you will need. The control room officer has a reference for each job, but unless he is a friend of yours he is not going to look up the number for you. After getting the chits, I went through the gates and into the institution. As each of the two gates closed, I was still bothered at the sound of the steel hitting steel and the clank of the lock as the door closed. It took about two weeks for it to sink in that although the doors locked me inside the prison, it opened every time that I came up to go out. Then the sound had less impact and soon became another routine background noise.

After entering the institution, I went to the lieutenant's office to check in. He had a roster and checked each staff member off as they came to work. The 8:00 to 4:00 and 4:00 to 12:00 shifts had what was called a briefing. Those working those two shifts, which were the largest two groups, had to meet in the officer's lounge for roll call. I never knew of any information being given out, but each staff was required to be in the institution fifteen minutes early on their own time for "briefing." (This was later discontinued when the courts ruled that it was overtime.) After being checked in, I went to cell house C to relieve the day-watch officer. At that time, to relieve another officer less than fifteen minutes early (except for 8:00 a.m. and 4:00 p.m.) was like being late for work. Most of the staff was relieved thirty minutes early.

I took Mr. Williams his chits and he went home. I talked with the day watch OIC, Mr. Norton, for a few minutes before going up on the ranges. I later learned Mr. Norton, then in his mid-forties, had once worked in a coal mine in West Virginia like I had. He was a mild mannered, friendly, and pleasant individual who would laugh and joke but did not play. After a cup of coffee and a cigarette, he and I started up the range. When getting to range 12, we met Mr. Elliot, the number 2 officer.

As I had suspected, most of the inmates were out on the yard. The few that were in the unit were watching TV. The recreation center had a thirty-six-inch TV, but because of the crowd, many of the inmates would be in their unit instead. Even though it was no less crowded, it would be quieter in the units. The TV had no speaker of its own on the unit. Instead, it was plugged into a wire with wall outlets. Along the wall was a stack of steel saw-horse-looking objects with a speaker plug-in wire on one end which would fit the wall jack. These would be placed behind a row of seats from the wall toward the cells. It was about twelve feet long with plug-ins along the rail which allowed the inmates to plug in their earphones to listen to the TV. Earphones were also required for listening to a radio in the units. A set of earphones were given to the inmates upon request, but many of the inmates bought their own, which were better fitting and equipped with individual ear volume controls. The TV itself, a twenty-one-inch model, was mounted on a permanent stand attached to the wall and well above head level. Sunday was the only day that

I was not required to go to the dining room at 3:00 p.m. I walked the range until 3:30, when they had the yard call.

By 3:50 p.m., the door from the hallway was closed, and we were told to lock them down and count. Mr. Jackson had relieved Mr. Elliot. He showed me how the lockbox worked. The lockbox was a steel box at the front end of each range, which was locked itself and by a padlock. Inside the box was an arm. This arm was attached to a steel rod which ran above the cell doors and inside the wall. This rod was attached at the top of the arm. Just below the rod, the arm was attached to a spacer, which provided a pivot point. This caused the rod at the top to move inside the wall when the arm was pulled out, unlocking the cells and pulling the rod out, locking the cells when it was pushed in at the bottom. Halfway in, a distinctively marked position called half mast, allowed an open door to be closed, but would not allow a closed door to open. The locking device was not locked into place at half-mast. Cell houses C and D had a crank which turned a long chain (similar to a bicycle chain except several times larger) inside the locking device just above the doors also. From this crank, you could pull all of the doors closed at once. Once closed, the crank had to be unwound to allow the cells to open.

To pull and push the arm two or three times would open and close every lock on the side of the range. If some of the inmates were talking and not paying attention, that sound would give the same effect that the front gates had given me. After pulling and pushing the arm a couple of times, there was a crank which pulled to close any door that was open. The arm would be put on half-mast and the crank would close the door. Mr. Jackson took the left side and informed me to take the right from range 11 to 15. By the time we were on range 12, Mr. Norton had counted one side of 11. As we reached the top floor, I was instructed to count ranges 14 and 15 and call the counts down to Mr. Norton.

In cell houses C and D, this was a quick process. They had only one man in each cell and relatively no place to hide compared to cell houses A and B, with four double bunks and lockers double-stacked. At 4:00 p.m., we would get full cooperation of the inmates, since they wanted to eat and have recreation after the count. The 10:00 p.m. count was the one where they might try to harass staff. When any inmate was caught outside the locked door, being in the wrong place, or in any way interfering with the count, he was taken to the segregation unit immediately after the count cleared. This was equated to an effort to escape. After the unit count cleared, I locked up my body alarm since it set off an alarm for that unit, no matter where the alarm was when the button was pushed.

I was standing behind the chow line, watching the hamburger patties being served. They were being served from a bread tray sitting on the grill to keep them warm. Four of five trays would be set catty-corner on top of each other. As one would be emptied, it would be set under the counter until they got to the last tray. Then an inmate would take the empties away and bring back full trays from the hot cart just behind us. As the inmate served the last patty from the bottom tray, I picked up the empty tray and put it under the counter to make room for the new trays. The metal had not stopped ringing before Lt. JP was standing beside me.

Very low key and quietly he told me, "We have two-thousand convicts in this place looking for something to do. Food service can get all of them that they want. Now we did not hire you to do convict labor or wait on them sorry sons of bitches. If there is not a convict here to serve, and we have something on the line to be served, we pay you to stop the line until the food service gets someone. You can't keep these cock suckers from stealing rationed items—or watch so that you or another officer don't get hurt if these bastards start a fight because you're busy doing their work. Don't ever let me see you degrading an officer's uniform by doing convict labor again."

"Yes sir, boss," I responded. From that time forth, if I needed a gallon of paint, I took a convict to carry it. This was sometimes difficult, but it was a lesson I never forgot. I also learned that no matter what the food was, there would be inmates who would not eat it and would give it to someone who did. When one inmate complained about not getting enough meat, I explained that he could get more bread. He told me that he didn't want bread, but laughed and moved on when I told him that we were trying to make him fat, not strong.

After the evening meal, I returned to house C to find Jackson in his regular position. I let him know that I was going to be taking my dinner break. When I returned thirty minutes later, he had not moved. During the four weeks in house C, working for him, I was told not to do any shaking down and don't get the inmates upset.

"I know the lieutenants like a lot of shaking down, but these convicts work hard and don't want to be fucked with at night. That is what the day watch should be doing while the inmates are out of the unit. If you see something or know that there is something, I mean go ahead and do what you have to do, but don't go into a cell and shake it down, just because you can." I saw him above the first floor once or twice, at the most, during the same period.

The next month I had the same hours, but worked across the hall with Mr. Braxton in house D. Mr. Braxton (also known as Ma) had a very outgoing personality that everyone, inmates and staff, liked. When a job had to be done, he could be depended upon to do it. As long as the convicts would permit, he would laugh, joke, and tease them. When he did so, he made sure that they knew where the line was, but even this was done in a lax manner. He would carry on a line of conversation with the inmates that would have most people fighting mad with him. Everyone would laugh. At the same time, he was not easily offended by mere conversation. During the month that I worked for him, he began to identify particular inmates. "This inmate is that inmate's husband. That bastard is into drugs; watch that thug, he is into everything." He would point out the moonshiners, bank robbers, the violent, and the passive.

He treated all of the inmates in one of two manners; he was either cold, impersonal, and professional, or joking and teasing. He seemed to know what he could get by with and with whom. He would tell one homosexual, "Yeah, let me catch you with his dick up your ass. I will tie you up and take you to segregation (seg) just the way I found you, so everyone knows why you're being locked up."

The convict would tell him, "You're just looking for someone to fuck you since you got too old to get a hard on." They would both laugh and it would be forgotten. The next homosexual to come by, any given conversation would be all business. "Ma" Braxton was not only cautious as to who he teased in this manner, but who was around while he teased. He would never set up a situation where the inmate would become offended or be belittled in front of someone who might exploit that conversation as a weakness. One year, "Ma" Braxton got a Mother's Day card from several of the inmates. Mr. Braxton's initials were M.A. He was highly appreciated and respected by staff and inmates alike.

Mr. Braxton was equally open about some of the staff. The third month I worked C and D relief, two days for Mr. Braxton, two days for Jackson, and one for LoJo in cell house B. By this time, Mr. Braxton had learned a little about me. Between 6:00 and 8:00, I could be counted on to come to the office and drink a cup of coffee at least once, sometimes twice. At 9:30 p.m., we had our first lockdown and count. Those who wanted to stay out and watch TV could…but could not leave the TV area. After the 10:00 p.m. count and every thirty minutes on the hour after until 11:00 p.m., we would have another lockdown. After the count, I would frequently lock down the rest by myself because I was bored.

Between lockdowns, Mr. Braxton and I would sit in the office and talk. He told me that Jackson would go up to the Lieutenant's office and snitch like hell on trainees. A month later, I found that to be true when I went into the lieutenant's office. The one thing that made me so angry was that the useless lieutenant was listening so intently at how sorry a damn trainee was, adding his *wisdom* to the conversation, instead of kicking the OIC's ass for not training his men properly.

Mr. Braxton told me who of the staff to trust and a lot to stay away from. Over time, I found that he had been a fairly good judge of character. Most importantly, he taught me to know my friends. Just because a man comes in and goes out with you, wears the same uniform as you, and will jump right in the middle of a fight to help you, don't ever believe that this makes him your friend. Not only should you know your friends, but never trust them. You will not give an enemy the opportunity to get behind you with an open blade. Any time you get a knife in your back, look and you will find someone you thought to be your friend, about to twist.

In cell house B, I worked with LoJo as the OIC. As the dining hall would be closing, LoJo would have an inmate steal food and bring it to his office. LoJo not only did not leave his office, he really did not care if the rest of the staff showed up, too. Unless the lieutenant came in. On the rare occasion when this would happen, LoJo would start explaining which cell he wanted us to shake down.

One evening, the inmate who had been sent to bring a box of food for LoJo had been stopped by the rear corridor officer. Food coming out of the dining room is contraband, since some inmates would bring food to the units and open up their own business at night, selling the food. Leftovers encouraged rodents and bugs, so the rule was, no food taken from the dining hall. When Mack, the sixty-year-old corridor officer, who had a bad heart and weighed only 160 lbs., took the food from the inmate, John, who was a fifty-year-old, healthy 250 lb. man, threatened to meet him in the parking lot.

The third month, I began to learn a little about my job. In B house, a black officer by the name of William Crooze took time to tell me a little about how my job should be done and why it was done that way. Between him and Mr. Braxton, I began to pick up a little about why I was there. Willie was an outspoken man who knew his job and did it well but made supervisors angry along the way. When a lieutenant would ask him about what another officer was or was not doing, he would respond, "Training these people, keeping up with their progress, knowing what they are doing, that's your job. What in the hell am I supposed to do, your job? Sneak around behind a man and come snitch to you. Fuck you. You collect that big paycheck, so you do your job and you will know what they are doing." No lazy-ass lieutenant liked a smart-mouth nigger; Willie quit after I had been there about three years. He was a well-educated and respected staff member who worked to train new trainees.

The relief job, with one night a week in cell house B for four weeks, was the extent of my working a larger cell house during training. During that month, I was working in cell house D for Mr. Braxton one night. I was walking the ranges after the 10:00 p.m. count. The cell doors had roller glides which sat on a bar overhead. This track, the chain which was controlled by the crank in the lockbox, and the locking mechanism, was all encased in a steel-plated box running from front to back and just above the doorways. On the bottom of this housing was a slot the door went into. The slot was in front of each door and to the right of the door, just far enough to allow the door to clear the doorway. As I was walking the ranges, I stuck my fingers up into the slot and felt something. Pulling it out I found it to be a well-made and very sharp shank (homemade knife). That was the first weapon that I found. I became enthused and went cell to cell and range to range. I found five shanks, a marijuana pipe, and a drug needle kit that night.

The next month I worked the education department, which was a bore. I had both Christmas and New Year's off, but I agreed to work overtime 4:00 to 12:00 on Christmas Day on a tower. Then I learned that working a holiday on overtime was not overtime. My only job was to supervise a detail in cleaning the area, a thirty-minute chore twice a day, and checking on an inmate who did not show up for his class. The first week of the New Year, I had the detail to strip the floor and wax it again, just so I would have something to do. While I was certainly glad to have the holidays off, I sure was glad to see that four weeks come to an end.

My next assignment was the West Yard from midnight to 8:00 a.m. My job was to walk around and check all the locks on the outside doors on all buildings on the west side of the institution. Cell houses B and D and the basement of cell house B, all had a door leading to the compound. Each of these doors had an outside padlock, which had to be checked at midnight and opened at 6:00 a.m. My first and second night on West Yard, I would go down onto the recreation yard and around recreation buildings and inside warehouse area. Tower 8, was being worked by an officer who soon became a good friend, Big O, shined the floodlight located on top of the tower in my eyes. The electronically-controlled light could be moved in any direction, and Big O would keep me in the spotlight. By the end of the second night's rounds, I had gotten tired of the light. I picked up a golf ball from the miniature golf course and spent most of the night gutting the ball.

After the rubber bands were all removed through a small hole, I started filling the ball with match heads. I filled the hollowed ball out with sulphur and even had some matches coming out of the hole for a wick. The next night, when Big O was coming out of the employee's lounge and heading for his tower, I stopped him and gave him the ball. "Enjoy this one!" I said. "If you don't keep that damn light out of my face, you are not going to like the next one!" Big O just laughed at me as he walked off, but he didn't put the light in my eyes again. It was another week as I was checking the yard when I realized that I could have gone to jail for making that fire bomb.

Certain entrances would be used when it came time for the remodeling of the facility. Until the remodeling was complete, inmates used the corridor down the middle of the institution to go to the yard, dining hall, or any other place. After the remodeling, the doors leading to the corridor from each of the cell houses would be welded shut and only those persons who were entering or leaving the institution could use that corridor.

There have always been three concerns with the cellblocks opening into the corridor. First, visitors come down the hallway past cell houses A and B to get to the visiting room. The visitors had access to the doorways to cell houses A and B. This affords the visitor the opportunity to pass something into a cell house. Each of the doorways had a gap, approximately an inch and a half, at the bottom of the doorway that any contraband item could be dropped, then quickly kicked under the doorway with no one seeing it. Not only this, but an item could be accidentally dropped by the doorway or in the hallway, and if an officer did not see this, it could be picked up by an inmate. Introduction of contraband items into the institution was a deep concern at all times, especially from visitors. These persons being family and, frequently being involved in criminal activities with the individual who was incarcerated, left us suspicious of their interest in our security.

Secondly, many of the women—wives, or girlfriends of the inmate population—came into the institution wearing as limited and sexually-appealing clothing as possible. Some females wore miniskirts as short as would be permitted by policy. The Bureau of Prisons does, in fact, have a policy limiting the type of clothing that can be worn. When skirts were too short, the visitor would be denied the opportunity to visit. Shorts were unauthorized for visitation. Also, it was unauthorized for any female to visit braless, but some of the clothing worn showed as much cleavage as possible. As a result of this, we were concerned about the verbal comments or cat calls made by one inmate toward another inmate's family. Such infringement upon visitors would result in a conflict between two inmates and frequently would cause a stabbing or fatality.

The main corridor officer, closer to the front gates, would ask the rear corridor officer closer to the back dining room area, to close down and block off the rear corridor to preclude any inmates from entering the hallway while visitors were brought in or out. Yet the staff was still concerned about the possibility of any inmate taking a visitor as a hostage. During an open movement, an inmate could maneuver himself around to a position that he was not seen until such time as a visitor entered the hallway. He could step out with a weapon and take a visitor as a hostage. The life of a warden, associate warden, or any other staff member had no value once a hostage situation took place. This could not have so easily been the case with a visitor. As a result of the above mentioned concerns, as well as others, it was the desire of the institution many years ago to close off access of the main corridor to either the outside visitors or the inmates. Now with the remodeling this should be easily accomplished at a cost of only a million dollars or so to the taxpayers.

The officer patrolling the West Yard checked the tunnels. Within the tunnels at the steam pipe running from outside the walls, the powerhouse (which heated water to heat the facility) had steam pipes coming through under the ground and into the tunnels. The temperature inside the tunnels was well over a hundred degrees. In one area, a venting system was used to release some of the heat from the tunnel to above ground. This release was covered by a grill and ended in the West Yard. During the winter months and cold hours, when the West Yard as well as the East Yard were open, inmate population as well as staff, would stand over this grill, enjoying the heat. You could stand over the heat vent and remain warm while the temperatures were below freezing.

During the morning hours, after the locks were opened and 7:30 work call, the West Yard officer would stand usually on that grill during the winter months to supervise the inmates entering the work area. One morning I was standing there and the work call finally came over the intercom system, which was a PA system with speakers all over the compound. "Work call, work call, all inmates report to your assigned area for work," came the announcement over the intercom. Inmates then began to mosey toward the factory area.

"Jackson," I called to one inmate, "I don't understand why you are in such a hurry this morning. If you were out on the street you would not get your lazy ass out of bed to go to work. Now that you're working for twenty-five cents an hour, you're trying to rush to be the first one on the job. If you had been that damned excited about your work, you would never have been in jail to start off with!" All of the inmates give a chuckle at this remark. That is, all except Jackson, who responded, "Fuck you, you silly bastards. You do your time, let me do mine."

During the morning watch in each cell house, there was only one officer assigned. This included the honor dorm even though inmates had free movement within the structure all night. The only time any other officer entered the building between midnight and 8:00 a.m., was when the Duckmill Front Officer, who assisted in counting cell house E, or a supervisor. The supervisors did not visit the units other than segregation or the hospital. You soon got to know the supervisors who were going to be out checking the institution just as you knew the staff who would check the unit.

The duck mill front officer was an officer assigned to a small office type area for industry or "duck mill." This officer was responsible for working industries' detail kits. Each supervisor had a crew of inmates working for him. A small book with picture cards of each of the inmates on his detail was to be picked up on a daily basis by the supervisor, officer, or staff, which contained the picture, name, number, and charge of the inmate. These detail crew kit cards also have comments made by staff concerning the individual. They may advise that he is a hard worker, a sloppy worker, an escape risk, or any other pertinent information that a staff member wanted noted for his own or others' information.

Any individual changing jobs put a request on a change sheet, or "cop-out." For example, an individual assigned to the mattress factory may have a request from a staff member signed by his current supervisor as releasing him and a supervisor from the mail bag area as receiving him. Once a cop-out was signed by the current detail supervisor, and a supervisor on a new detail job assignment, the cop-out was forwarded to the case manager. The case manager had the option to either approve or disapprove such transfer in job assignment himself. However, in most cases, the case manager did not interfere with the individual's employment as long as both supervisors were in agreement with such job change. The case manager then forwarded the cop-out memo to the transfer clerk, to place him on a daily transfer sheet for industry details, and the control room checked all other detail kits. The transfer sheet was printed and sent to all departments and all details on a daily basis. The duck mill front officer worked the detail kits in correspondence with the change sheet. If an individual from one job within the factory received a change to another part of the factory, he changed the detail cards from kit to kit. Should the inmate be released from the industries area totally, he would remove the card from the detail kit and forward it to the control center, who placed it in the proper detail kit.

The duck mill front officer went to cell house E shortly before midnight or at midnight, at 1:30 a.m., at 3:30 a.m., and at 5:00 a.m. At each of these times, he backed up and assisted the detail house officer in making the 12:00, 2:00, 4:00, and 5:30 a.m. counts. In the same month, I was on the West Yard, another trainee, who was overzealous, was assigned to the duck mill front. Officer Turnbull was a peculiar young officer who remained within the bureau for an exceptionally short period of time. I believe that he may have completed a year, but if so, not much more than that. The officer working on cell house E was a seasoned GS-7 correctional officer who had been within the bureau for approximately four years. Officer Boyd, a young, black, energetic officer, had a very good nature and disposition. He and I had joked two or three times and talked several times during the course of the two or three weeks that I had been working the West Yard. At 1:30 a.m., I opened the door to let Officer Turnbull into E house to help finish with the count. At approximately 2:00 a.m. the count within that unit had cleared, and Officer Turnbull and officer Boyd were standing at the doorway waiting on me to let officer Turnbull out. Officers Boyd, Turnbull and I were all carrying on a joking conversation.

"Mr. Lawson," Turnbull asked. "You have seen me work now for nearly three weeks on the duck mill front, as well as other jobs within the institution. What do you think about my work?"

"Mr. Turnbull, you should never ask a question unless you are prepared to have an answer," I replied.

"I am serious, I want to know either positively or negatively what you think of my ability as a young officer."

"Well," I responded, "I honestly have no problem with you. It's the captain which concerns me. I understand you work, I just can't understand why in the hell the captain would have a black and a Pollock to make the count of an institution!" At that time Mr. Boyd and I laughed heartily. However, Mr. Turnbull was not amused about this remark.

After that monthly assignment, I was assigned another midnight to 8:00 shift, in the towers. I was assigned a relief job working one tower for two nights and a third tower for one night from midnight to 8:00. On my first night on the tower, I found that it was equipped with an intercom system which worked all towers. This intercom system could be turned off and on, but policy prohibited it from being turned off. It could be turned so that sound from an individual tower could not be heard by other towers, or it could be turned on so that all sounds from within the tower could be heard by all other towers, or it could be intermittently turned on and off for transmission purposes with the sound remaining on. However, this was communication in case of an escape attempt so that the officer in the tower could be talking and shooting at the same time. Since that was the purpose for the intercom, policy prohibited the intercom from being turned off completely.

The purpose for the intercoms as understood by most staff was to afford them the opportunity and assist them in remaining awake. The officers working those hours, from time to time, encountered much difficulty in remaining awake. One could sleep from eight in the morning immediately following getting off work until time to come to work that night. Even with that, most staff could be just as tired as if they'd not gotten any sleep at all. I found that working from midnight to 8:00, my body just seemed to get no rest. I later found that it was just as difficult staying alert on other shifts since they were just as boring. As a result of this, I really appreciated the intercom system to argue with a person over meaningless conversations in an effort to pass the time.

When going into the tower I took a lunch bag, which grew with the first week. It would seem as though I had enough lunch to last two or three meals when entering the tower. However, by 2:00 a.m., I would find myself out of food and starved. On an occasion while working midnight to 8:00 and in the tower, I found myself at 5:00 or 6:00 a.m. with a metal dust pan held in my fingertips behind my head as I set back looking over the wall. It was easy to doze off even accidentally. However, holding the dust pan behind your head in such a manner was uncomfortable, making it more difficult to fall asleep. Should you doze off, or begin dozing off, your fingers would automatically release the dust pan and the sound would immediately wake you up again.

The first month working on the tower I was extremely fortunate. I worked with staff members on the tower such as Big O, Mr. Brown, Mac, and a lot of other talkative individuals who enjoyed the conversation and were not always truthful. We would tell war stories having nothing to do with fact or reality of life. We would cuss or discuss any subject having nothing to do with the amount of knowledge available by members of the tower, and generally having enjoyable conversation at night on the tower. Within the first week, Mr. Brown advised us that he had failed to bring his watch that night. Subsequently, since we all had to check in every half hour on the hour and half hour with control. He wanted someone to notify him of the time so he could call in at the prescribed times. This checking in was for a multitude of reasons; one reason was simply to be sure that we were there and awake. Another was to see that we had not had a heart attack and died on the tower as one staff member had prior to my employment. Another was just to see that an inmate had not managed to climb in and cut our throat, take our weapons and assist others in escaping. While the latter is a little far-fetched, checking in did have its purpose. When Mr. Brown advised us that he did not have a watch, it gave a perfect opportunity for harassment. When we began a conversation, I would about every twenty minutes say "Okay, it's time to check in again." From time to time I could hear Mr. Brown mumbling to himself as he called in early, late, or much too frequently.

While working on the towers, every time that someone from the yard flashes you, you are supposed to return the flash. This is to show him that you are awake, know who he is, and are not going to shoot him. We had one officer on the West Yard that would shine his flashlight at the towers every time he passed (at least every twenty minutes). If a responding flash was not returned, he would start calling on the radio to check on you (try to snitch on you). I saw him come out of the duck mill one night and flash me, I followed him with the light from the duck mill to cell house E. Finally, the lieutenant said quietly over the radio, "Tower 9, get the light off, please." I had not seen the lieutenant go into the duck mill. Everyone had a good laugh at me because of that and also because I did apologize to the lieutenant.

As spring rolled around, time seemed to go by a little more rapidly. I was informed by Officer Lincoln, "Don't concern yourself about getting nothing more than a fully successful evaluation on your monthly evaluations. The supervisor must write a memorandum justifying anything above or below 'fully successful.' If you get below 'fully successful,' he must justify why he is keeping you on the job. If you get an 'outstanding,' he must justify why he is not promoting you. As a result of this, you will never get more than 'fully successful' on your monthly evaluations. Remember, a few months back they had an officer who everybody was very impressed with. The young officer had been employed for approximately nine months and had received two or three 'outstanding' monthly evaluations. All of the supervisors thought he was one of the most outstanding young men who had come to work for the bureau of prisons in several years. However, after approximately nine months they found him bringing drugs into the institution. It was extremely difficult to fire this young man without prosecuting him. The bureau did not really want to prosecute him for bringing in a small quantity of marijuana. He was hesitant in resigning, and they were encountering difficulty in justifying firing him. Since that time, no one will get more than a 'fully successful' mark on their evaluation until the time for them to be accepted as a full-time employee and after the year training."

During our period of training, we had been informed about never giving an inmate a cigarette or a cup of coffee, and equally important, never accepting a cigarette or a cup of coffee from an inmate. We were informed as to how they would give us something or take something from us and then use that to get us to do something for them. We were told how this would end up resulting in us having to bring in drugs, weapons, or something, working strictly for the inmates rather than the institution. At the time of the training, I took this all with a grain of salt. I knew it was their job to impress upon us the security of the institution, but I could not honestly see anybody becoming entrapped into dealing with inmates. Personally, I never hesitated to give or take a cigarette or a cup of coffee from an inmate. Sometimes I might run out of cigarettes and ask an inmate for a cigarette. There were other times, if I had cigarettes with me and an inmate asked me for one, without hesitation or reservation, I would be glad to give them one. I made up my mind early on that should any inmate attempt to threaten me in any way that I would write an incident report on him and take him to the captain's office being ready to admit my wrongdoing. During my first year of employment with the bureau, a total of three individuals were terminated for bringing in drugs to the population. This let me know quickly, they weren't kidding during the annual training.

As spring turned into summer, some of the training class—which had started at the same time as I did, began leaving the training roster. Retired military were the first to be removed from the training roster. At that time, many individuals just retiring from the military and being forty years of age or under or in that area, were coming to work for the bureau of prisons. The bureau and employees were both wholly satisfied with each other. The penitentiary, operating as a quasi-military unit, was always happy to get individuals who would respond "Yes sir, yes sir, yes sir." The retired military, being trained year after year to accept orders and follow blindly, not only received their retirement pay, but an adequate income for their employment. At the same time, most were among the most reliable and dependable employees entering the bureau.

It was September before I went on the quarterly assignment. I was certainly glad to see the one-year training period come to a close. There is a lot of intimidation during that first year, every time you look around someone is running their mouth about not needing a justification to terminate you. They can give you a pink slip at any time. You can be fired for no reason. The Bureau of Prisons functions mostly under intimidation, with limited reward or positive reinforcement for actions. That first year of training had taken its toll upon me, as well as upon most other trainees. I found that inside the institution I was accepting the attitudes and language of the facility. Rarely was I in a conversation for more than two minutes that I was not responding to someone with the term, "Fuck you," "Suck my dick," or calling them such names as "You bitch," "You whore," or other similar remarks. In accepting this conversation within the institution, I equally found it difficult not to use such language at home.

CHAPTER 3

LEARNING THE DUTIES

BECOMING SEASONED, I HAD NOW COMPLETED MY ONE
year as a trainee Correctional Officer and had been promoted to GS-7, Senior Officer. By this time, I had learned most of the institution's policies and procedures. I learned what I could and could not do, what I must and must not do. Any time such situation would arise that I was in question, all I had to do was to think of supervisor JP. When I thought of JP, I immediately knew what had to be done and, without further hesitation, would do the job as needed. During that period of training, I learned an enormous amount from Lt. JP and held a tremendous amount of respect for him.

I came into work as a number two officer in a unit of three officers. As a number two officer, I was working under the direct supervision of the OIC. By this time, I found that there was a lot of competition among staff. The average GS-7 hoping to get promoted had five years' time in grade as a GS-7 before getting promoted to GS-8. Within that period of time, you could make a lot of enemies within the supervisors' ranks or have a lot of competition among younger officers who were energetic and politically oriented within the supervisors' ranks. This could result in an individual being passed over for promotion and a younger officer being promoted. The federal government has never considered seniority for promotion.

The supervisors had a variety of ways of predetermining who was going to be promoted. To begin with, they established the work roster. An individual could be assigned a quarter on a tower and would have evaluation statements such as, "He has limited opportunity to interact with inmates." He could be assigned to a yard for a period of a quarter, a three-month assignment, and would have evaluations such as lack of ability to supervise inmates. With two quarterly assignments in an annual period, it was difficult to become more than *fully successful* on any evaluation. Individuals were being evaluated on the tools needed for promotion instead of the manner that they functioned on their assigned job. As a result of this, supervisors could control your evaluation by controlling your job assignment. The Bureau of Prisons did, and still does, evaluate an individual on the mission of that facility rather than the manner of performance assignment on the quarterly basis period. As an example, you could do an outstanding job, or one of the better jobs of any other staff member having ever worked in the chaplain's area, but still never find any contraband in that area. You could do an outstanding job on the yard, but never break up any fights. As a result of the happenstance or job assignments, your evaluation could very much be controlled. It was and remains my opinion and position that an evaluation as established by the Bureau of Prisons reflects a preconceived notion of the supervisor on the employee and has nothing to do with the functional ability of such employee. One employee received a thirty-day suspension and received an outstanding evaluation for the year.

Another means of controlling the evaluation and promotion system within the Bureau of Prisons was (illegally) falsifying documentation. By this I mean, as indicated earlier, I had found five or six knives in one night in cell house C. However, I made no memos concerning the finding of these weapons. I am not sure who did, in fact, supply documentation of their finding. One employee was called into the supervisor's office and instructed to go look very close to the wall and outside of cell house E between tower 9 and tower 10. He was advised that a rope ladder had been placed alongside the wall. The individual, after receiving such notice from the supervisor, did as he was told. Lo and behold, he did, in fact, find a rope ladder precisely where the supervisor had told him to look. As a result of his diligence and work outside of his assigned area, he was promoted from GS-7 to GS-8 senior officer specialist with only three years' time in grade as a Senior Officer. The young officer working the tower who had spotted the rope ladder along the wall got screwed.

As a result of the variety of manners for getting an individual promoted and an equally high number of means of preventing an individual from being promoted, competition among employees was great. Most staff continued to blame the system or the staff being promoted, rather than the responsible management officials. I am not sure *competition* is the correct word since most of the actions were created by mistrust rather than a feeling of competition. Whatever the proper terminology, there was extremely limited cooperation among fellow employees. Supervisors enjoyed freedom of action while keeping staff fighting among themselves.

Within the GS-7 senior correction officer position, there was even more mistrust and less cooperation than any other place. Many of the young officers realized quickly that they did not have to know how to do a job. All they had to do was watch others and snitch for the lieutenant, and the supervisor would take care of him. As a result of this, the newer employees that you keep up with were those who were visiting the supervisor's office and who were going out to the bars with the supervisors. By the time I had completed my year of probation, I had learned that if I was doing a job and an inmate came up and informed me, "Hey, boss, you really are not supposed to be doing that. You should be doing this, or doing it this way," then I would immediately stop what I was doing and check the post orders or check the appropriate policy to be assured of what I was doing. I never found any inmate to be misinforming me or misleading me. However, if a fellow employee came up and informed me that what I was doing was wrong, I completed the job that

I started, and then went back and checked. I have found in a large number of cases, that some of the officers, either peers or ranking officers, would tell you that you are not supposed to do a specific task and then (as in Jackson's case) go to the supervisor and advise how sorry-assed you were for not doing the job or for doing the job wrong. As a result of fellow employees going out of their way to screw you in this manner, you soon knew to "know your friends."

In each of the housing units was a notebook which contained a listing of every bed in the unit. This notebook, (called the bed book) had every range by number and every cell by number. In the larger housing units (A and B housing units) one page contained ten cells. In the smaller housing units, each page of the bed book contained one range. This was a form made out with lines for each bed within each cell. It was covered by plastic—very much like a photo album. The paper had a space for the last name, number, and job assignment. Each line was filled in by pencil; when the individual received a job change, this was erased from the bed book and the appropriate job assignment placed there. When the individual went out of that cell, he was erased from that cell, leaving it blank for the next person to be moved in. Any change, either in work assignment or orders, came from the transfer sheet. It must be worked every evening on the 4:00 to midnight shift. This book must be accurate at all times since accountability for each inmate was the major job for the correctional staff. This book was used to maintain each count.

Each day there was a count at midnight, 2:00 a.m., 4:00 a.m., 5:30 a.m., 4:00 p.m. and 10:00 p.m. However, the official count each day, which was forwarded to Washington, was the 4:00 p.m. count. This count, which reflected the individuals being on their specific work assignments in many cases, was probably the more difficult of the counts to make up. The 10:00 p.m. count also had individuals still working on job assignments within the factory or other areas of the facility, and again the count may vary. Most of the other counts were not that difficult, since the counts were made while the individuals were within the cell or, early morning, in the food service area.

Any detail supervisor who is going to have an inmate working during any count, counting anywhere outside of his cell, would submit an "out count." This out count would contain the individual's name, number, and cell number and would be submitted for each job work assignment. If the food service was going to work forty individuals during any given count, they had to submit a list with forty different names, broken down by housing units. Cell house A would be separate from cell house B and so on, and such out count would be in duplicate. This out count would be forwarded to the control room officer, to check to be assured that the name corresponded with the number and the housing unit cell assignment was correct. From there, one copy of the out count would be cut up into sections by cell house and sent to the correct housing unit. The OIC would then take the out counts and, with a grease pencil, mark on the plastic to show where any individual on out count would not be in the unit for count. By deducting the number which he had marked off with grease pencil from the total count on that range, he would come up with a correct count. This is extremely simple, once the individual is shown or is given some idea of what was expected. During the beginning of my employment with the bureau, the senior correctional officer specialists would not show a newer officer how to work a count. As a trainee, I found that most of the senior officer specialists seemed to feel that this was too complicated for a trainee to understand.

I came to work one day as the number two officer and found that the OIC of the dorm units had called in sick. As a result of this, I was reassigned from the number two in one housing unit to the OIC of the dorm for the day. During the day, the OIC of the dorm unit stood in the chow line in the dining hall. Additionally, he shook down cells within the unit. However, one of the duties included preparing the 4:00 p.m. count and verifying it with control, prior to 3:00 p.m. While the count was extremely simple after an explanation, I had never been given any information concerning how to make a count.

After standing in the noon-day chow line, I went to the mail room and got the mail for the inmates for the day. I brought it back to the office within the units and separated it by cell so that each inmate could pick up his mail at his convenience. As I was completing this and started to hand out the mail, inmate Noler asked me if I had made the count for the day. I advised him that I had not done that. At this time, he stepped into the office and informed me that he had been the unit clerk. He advised me that, on numerous occasions, he had completed the count for other officers and asked if I would care to have him to do the same for me. I told him, "Yes, go ahead," but watched carefully at all times. He realized that I was a newer officer within the institution and had probably never completed the count, so he explained every step as he went along. As inmate Noler completed the count first for dorm three and then for dorm four, I made up my mind very quickly that, in the future, no officer working for me would have to have an inmate explain how to do his job. After the count had been completed, I called the control room officer (Count Clerk) to verify the 4:00 p.m. count to see that my count and his count matched.

Shortly after becoming a GS-7, I enrolled in college. At that time, I had my associate degree and was working on my bachelor's degree. I enrolled in college courses, taking daytime courses only. At that time, it was the practice of the Bureau of Prisons to schedule hours around the college courses. An individual could take courses and work either 4:00 to midnight or midnight to 8:00 shift and go to class during the day or take evening courses and work midnight to 8:00 or day shift. At that time, I chose to take day classes at college. This had its advantages and disadvantages. Some of the disadvantages while working a full-time forty-hour work week were that I was competing in college courses with individuals who did nothing but go to college. However, while working 4:00 to 12:00 or any hours between 6:00 p.m. and 6:00 a.m., the US government pays a night-differential payment. That is, one receives ten percent above regular salary for working those hours. Additionally, any employee working any hours on Sunday receives an additional twenty-five percent of their base pay. Subsequently, working as a GS-7 junior grade or GS-6, it was advantageous to be working during the night. While attending college, I worked mostly midnight to 8:00 a.m. Additionally, as I indicated earlier, the towers become a whipping post; I had to spend many hours on the tower.

Some of our supervisors never attended college. They entered the bureau at an early age and worked diligently to become a supervisor. They found themselves stagnated at a GS-9 or a GS-11 grade. Many of the officers whom they'd trained had either gone to college while working or had been to college prior to becoming employed with the bureau. Those officers, many times, advanced to an associate warden or warden level. Some of the officers who'd not attended college possessed the skills and knowledge to manage an institution, but they did not have the ability to handle the paperwork required for operating an institution. Even if they possessed those skills, they were unable to be promoted to the level and grade of department head. Some of them resented young officers who were hired into the institution, then attended college—as well as those who already held a degree. They implied that any individual going to college should be a part-time employee and a part-time student. While attending college, that employee was assigned duties which required only limited skills…evaluations reflected those menial duties performed.

Working the tower on the morning watch became a job I was assigned on a regular basis. Come quarterly assignment time, the question was not *where*, but *which* tower I would be working. This did not really bother me drastically, since I was going to college on a full-time basis. I learned to take maximum advantage of the intercom system, picking arguments, and discussing any topic any individual chose. I would advise the employees entering the tower that I would walk all the way around the wall to lie to them before I would sit still and tell them the truth. I would continue on by explaining that I would discuss any topic, any subject, take either side of any argument that they chose and would still beat them because they were a bunch of idiots and had not the ability to hold a conversation. That usually would get the conversation started, and in spite of that introduction, I was always surprised at the things staff would believe.

We discussed Richard Nixon in detail. Many of the world problems we resolved very quickly. Others took us two or three nights. On one occasion, we had a black officer working one of the towers who was racially inclined. He indicated in most conversations that he had been person-ally abused by the white employees for over 100 years. All of the whites in the institution were racists and all of the blacks were mistreated, according to him.

After listening to this for a long period of time, I finally got bored with that conversation. I finally asked him if he had any idea where Henry Kissinger was at that time. He explained readily that Henry Kissinger was down in Africa trying to get those white racists to understand that majority should rule. He continued with the explanation that, "The blacks in South Africa, as in many other places, were not given the opportunity for self-government and self-rule. It is about time that a government comes into power that gives blacks the opportunity to self-govern and self-rule and Henry Kissinger was the first white man to ever stress such a point."

At that time, I asked, "Are blacks in the United States considered a majority and should they, subsequently, be a ruling party?" He hesitated long enough for me to continue with a reminder that, in this country, he was considered a minority. "Minorities in this country want to run the country." I continued, "You are a minority. Just keep your fucking mouth shut. Nobody is interested in anything you have to say, so let the majority rule." At that time, I was a minority on the wall and was soon ganged up on by most towers, including those manned by white officers. That stimulated that conversation until 8:00 a.m.

On another night, I started about midnight trying to get a conversation started and to keep everyone awake. This was one of the nights when I was having an enormously difficult time staying awake myself and was trying every subject possible to get conversation started—but with no success. About 2:00 a.m., I decided that I was not going to keep those bastards awake all night. I then started off with a story about when I was a young lad, standing down at the drug store sipping an RC Cola, eating a MoonPie, as I saw this young man being run out of town. I explained that a young man by the name of Cain had been seen out running around with another man's wife. As a result of his iniquity, he had been sent out to the wilderness for forty years. Continuing with, "Forty years later, and after I'd worked hard all day, I was sitting under a large oak tree, enjoying the cool shade and a cold Coors, when I saw Cain coming back into town."

The poor man had been out in the wilderness alone—no companionship—for forty years. He and his wife and three children came back into town that day…walking down the sidewalk. "By the way, that's where our black heritage began!" It was not quite 2:00 a.m., when I made that comment. At 8:00 a.m., they were still cussing me. I did not have to worry about staying awake that night. Officer Boyd, (known as blackBoyd) used to call me on the telephone. He and I would talk to each other on the telephone, laughing and joking about the comments that were coming over the intercom. We'd stop and ask the other to hold on while we made another racial remark, just to keep stirring up the pot, then get back on the phone with each other.

It was extremely rare when anyone became personally offended by such a remark. When this did occur, any remark that person took personal affront to, I was ready to apologize. I was quick to explain that my job was to get forty hours in without going to sleep with no interest or intent to offend anyone. A couple of our staff members got reported to the captain for some of their remarks, and subsequently had to make a formal response and apology. One of the topics we discussed on a regular basis was religion. I made the mistake, on one occasion, of talking about the Reverend Billy Graham. We were discussing ministers who were on radio and TV (much like conversations that went on in public). When someone brought up Rev. Billy Graham, my opinion at that time, being argumentative of course, was that the Rev. Billy Graham was an excellent minister. While earning extremely limited funds for his efforts, he owned a home and an airplane. All expenses were paid anywhere he wanted to go, all funded by the church. And I made it very clear that, should I have all of my bills paid—all transportation, all living expenses, automobile and gasoline paid for…I would need no income.

I continued with the fact that Reverend Ike was my main man in religion. Reverend Ike, unlike most ministers, told you up front all he wanted was your money. He was not interested in your salvation, your soul, or your small change. The sound of change hitting the offering plate was offensive to his ear; he wanted nothing but the green stuff. About that time my telephone rang. I switched the speaker box off and answered the phone. The individual who had brought up the Rev. Billy Graham was on the other line. He wanted to know if I was serious when I was making negative comments toward the Rev. Billy Graham. I assured him that I was not serious in that or any other conversation I held on the tower. I assured him that if anybody got any indication as to what was actually on my mind on the intercom that it was purely by chance and nothing planned on my part. In fact, nothing could be further from the truth in my opinion of either Rev. Ike or Rev. Billy Graham.

One of my favorite hobbies was to inform other employees working the tower (especially newer employees who were more gullible) on how to use the telephone to get an outside line. In truth, you could not make a call outside the institution from any of the tower telephones. Many of the employees who had been there for fifteen years, and should have known better, but employees were always interested in calling their wives, girlfriends, or both. I would start the conversation off by announcing that I was hungry. Everyone knew this, for the most part, to be true. Then I would indicate that I was going to call McDonald's and see if there was anybody I knew working and have them to bring me some hamburgers over. Of course, there was nobody ever working that I knew. I would then tell them that I was going to call my wife, who would be waiting to be assured that I got to work okay, and I was going to see if she cared to bring me anything over to eat. Of course, she never did. By this time, individuals would be saying that you could not make a phone call from the tower. I assured them that they could, all they had to do was dial 202 to bypass the switchboard and get an outside line. I was amazed at how many of the older officers, who'd been in the institution for a long period of time, would end up calling the warden's home at 1:00 in the morning. All 200 series phone numbers were for institution residences. This worked any time day or night.

One of the antics which made me famous, (or infamous) was that of drawing welfare checks. In a matter-of-fact conversation, I discussed the potential for getting a government subsidy home. In addition to obtaining a check from the government while working and VA benefits for going to college, I assured them that I was getting government-subsidized housing, food stamps, and was paying limited federal taxes. One guy, J.D., who was retired military, particularly wanted to know why I was getting VA benefits. He and I both knew I was going to college and, since he chose not to try to figure it out on his own, I offered the following explanation. "I am getting a for-ty-percent disability check from VA; I was injured while in the military." In questioning this injury, I explained, "This was a result of my disability while in Germany. The strain of being overseas had caused me to have a nervous breakdown."

J.D. immediately became hostile. He explained, "You were not only in the military, but you had a gravy train while you were there! You had a nervous breakdown in Germany! You must really have been a pussy! You really must be crazy."

I responded, "I don't understand such comments coming from you. I spent four years in the military and I get a retirement check from the government. You spent twenty years in the military to get a similar-sized government check. I am getting a disability check, plus VA benefits for going to college to get over my disability. Not only that, I'm working full-time for the same government that is giving me the disability check and a check to recuperate from my disability. I cannot understand how you can consider me crazy."

I continued on with the fact that the government now paid subsidized housing. Another individual from the wall started saying that because of my salary at the institution by itself, I could not draw benefits such as government-subsidized housing. I assured him however, that if he was unable to do so, what he really needed to do was trade and get a bigger house. I assured him that the U.S. government based their system and support to employees based on their need. Their need was determined by taking the income an individual received, deducting shelter (a house payment) and medical expenses, plus the amount of money determined by number of dependents…thus, giving a scheduled amount of need for those dependents. I assured them that between my house payment, my wife, and five dependents (which I explained to be my wife, three children, and two German Shepherds) my income was inadequate to prevent obtaining government subsidy. Additionally, with those dependents and my income (all other disability, VA, and government subsidy being non-taxable) I ended up paying no federal taxes and very limited or zero state taxes.

As a result of this conversation, I was later informed that one individual took three days annual leave to go downtown and attempt to get food stamps. He came back to the institution and required that he get a statement of his income on a monthly basis—without benefit of any night differential, holiday pay, or any other premium pay. Because of his income, this was required by the agency in charge of food stamps. I found it exceptionally difficult to believe that grown men with any experience would believe anything you told them. As a result of my using German Shepherds as dependents, fellow officers told me that I was going to become a federal prisoner. I expressed dismay at their lack of imagination. These pets must be treated very much like a child. Anyone owning a German Shepherd must send them to school to have them obedience trained. Failure to do so would result in the potential for enormous damages created by such animals. Additionally, at least once a year, the animals must be sent to the doctor and on a more regular basis if one really cared for their animals. After all, what more do you do for a child than send them to school, take them to the doctor, feed them, and care for them?

I was working 4:00 to 12:00 West Yard when the 4:00 p.m. count did not clear. It was a short time before they advised over the radio the name and number of the inmate who was out of his cell and could not be located for the count. A search began of the entire institution. After about a thirty-minute search, one of the supervisors informed us that he had located the inmate. The inmate had been located in the business office elevator. They requested that the doctor be notified to come to that area at once. Additionally, they requested that the FBI be called in. He advised the control room officer to clear the count on paper—but leave everyone one locked down until further notice. Being that was in my area I, like most others, went there immediately. My first fatality inside the institution was seeing that inmate in the elevator floor. The inmate had three stab wounds and his throat cut. According to the medical examiner, whichever blow he received first had killed him.

Most murders inside the institution were the result of one of three things: either sex, drugs, or money. A homosexual inmate soon became the property of a male. A homosexual would be taken over by strong arms or love, whichever seemed to motivate the individual, but netting the same results. If the two became lovers, the one playing the role of the husband would become possessive of the homosexual. Any triangular relationship would ultimately result in a fatality. If the relationship was purely monetary, she (the *she* being the homosexual) became a whore in the stable of the male inmate. Any individual who attempted to take over this female or to obtain sexual favors without reimbursement would be grounds for murder.

Drugs usually became a cause of murder as the result of an individual using drugs without means of payment. This same thing would occur on gambling. An individual would get involved in a gambling game, run up a few hundred dollars—or in some cases, a few thousand dollars gambling debt—that he was unable to pay. He would then find a contract had been placed on him. It was the opinion of the inmates that the monies involved were not as important as the need to maintain their own manliness. While many of the reasons for the cause of death inside the institution was what one might consider irrational on the outside, inside it was necessary for the individual (even the homosexuals) to appear strong.

If two inmates were walking down the hallway and accidentally bumped into each other, both individuals must apologize. This was extremely difficult to understand. For example, when an individual, with 1,500 years to complete in his sentence, accidentally bumped into somebody with only 300 years in his sentence, both immediately apologized. I soon discovered that should one *not* apologize, or at least acknowledge that the touch was unintentional, the other would assume that he was making some overt action toward him. That other inmate would rationalize that for this slight to go unpunished, it would leave him appearing weak or unmanly. That would result in the incident escalating rather than diminishing. For self-preservation purposes, an inmate being offended in such a manner would get himself a knife and do his best to kill a person before the act of aggression progressed toward him. This was a defensive move and not an aggressive action.

It was extremely interesting, after a short period of time in the institution, to realize many of the inmates in that facility had no self-respect, respect for their parents, respect for their wives or family—but all demanded respect for themselves be shown from other inmates and staff alike. Subsequently, to call a homosexual "a bitch" or put your hand on an inmate in an aggressive type manner (even in jest or horseplay), one must know the inmate and how he will react to those things. One had to have a base established so that those acts could be accomplished without the individual being of the opinion that his manliness was attacked. The staff member also must know the other inmates around.

It was extremely rare that difficulty was encountered between inmates and staff. One officer was asked to come up on the range by an inmate to check someone in his cell or because someone had broken open his locker. As he started up the range and around the corridor, he was met by another inmate with a knife, cutting him. The inmate did not cut him badly, but jumped back and apologized. "I'm sorry boss, I'm really sorry, I didn't mean to hurt you! It was the sorry mother fucker behind you that I wanted to fuck up!" Another staff member accidentally walked into a fight between two inmates and, calling for both of them to break it up, he stepped a little closer. One of the inmates wielding a knife missed the intended victim and struck the officer on the hand. Again, the inmate immediately stopped and gave the officer the knife. He knew he had already screwed up and was ready to take the consequences.

The only staff member I recall being hurt by an American inmate in the Atlanta Federal Penitentiary was when a recreation specialist walked in on a group of inmates attempting an escape. He was cut badly and almost died as a result of his injuries. However, the escape attempt was foiled shortly thereafter, and the inmates advised the staff of the location of the officer they had cut. This recreation specialist was carried hurriedly to the hospital where he was treated and taken to Grady for further treatment.

The inmates really became dangerous when they were either attempting an escape or under the influence of their homemade brew. The first time I found a can of brew, it was on top of an air conditioning vent in the utility room within Dorm 3. I very diligently attempted to get the container off the air conditioning duct work from well above my head to take it to the supervisor's office. However, in doing so, I spilled the brew on my shirt. This was one nasty aroma, and I ended up wearing it for the rest of the day. That was the last time I tried to remove alcohol from one of the containers.

After getting the brew on my shirt, I decided to make the inmates (preferably those who'd made it) move it themselves. Subsequently, when finding a container of homemade brew, I would get two or three cakes of lye soap, break them up, drop into the container, take something to push it down to make sure it was, at least partially, mixed. Then I let it sit. I decided that if they wanted to drink the brew after it had soaped down good, let them. I never really knew if any was drunk or not, but the next day it would be removed from that area. A lot of the employees used to boast of finding brew. They would tell the inmates that they enjoyed finding a bag or container of brew. They enjoyed opening it up and pissing in it. They would laugh and say they would make those sorry cocksuckers drink their piss if they wanted some alcohol.

While working on the day watch, I found three or four inmates who had been drinking booze most of the day. By then, it was after 2:30 p.m. I started taking the drunkest of the group toward the seg unit. From the building where he was located, he'd have to walk up a set of stairs. He *fell up* the stairs. After getting to the top he decided he didn't want to go up after all. He turned and fell down the stairs again. After getting to the bottom of the stairs, he was ordered, and agreed, to continue with me. Again, he fell most of the way up the stairs. I brought him on in to the rear corridor area without putting my hands on him, for the most part, other than efforts to help steady him. By then, enough other inmates had seen him in this intoxicating condition and were laughing.

The inmate then became loud and argumentative. He decided that he had support and was not going to segregation. Even though two or three of the other inmates decided to help him, to prevent further problems, he still wanted to fight the entire correctional staff. The inmates took him to the segregation door, and an officer took him into the unit. This individual was of no great threat as a result of his intoxication. However, he continued to want to fight, resulting in one of the staff members having to remove his clothing from him for a strip shake. (Every inmate taken into the segregation unit was strip searched, their clothing removed from them and issued a completely new wardrobe from the skin outward.)

The next day when the individual became a little more sober, he called an officer over to the door and asked who the officer was that he wanted to fight with in that unit. He explained that he had gotten drunk and raised a little Cain and showed his ass and wanted to apologize to the officer from the seg unit that he had given such a hard time.

The officer he was talking to was 250 to 260 pounds, six foot, 5 inches tall. He explained, "I am that officer. You said you were going to kick my ass."

The inmate looked at him with a very serious tone and said, "Damn, I must have really been fucked up! I'm sorry boss. I sure appreciate the fact that you didn't hurt me." The officer and the inmates in the cell with him all enjoyed a hearty laugh at this comment.

We did have a few aggressive staff members. Most of this aggression was verbal, and not physical. When the officer treated the inmates in a manner which the inmates considered disrespectful, or harassment, the inmates would retaliate. There were a variety of ways in which the inmates could harass the staff, letting the supervisors realize that the difficulty was only with that specific officer and not any effort to disrupt the institution. One way this was done was to set a fire in a trash can. To go by the book, when a trash can was set on fire it was usually rolled outside of the unit. Additionally, the fire department had to be notified and several reports had to be written by the staff member. Another way was to hide for a count, making the staff count two to three times to get a good count.

One evening, while working 4:00 to 12:00 in the dormitory, I was coming to work when I opened the door to find the trash can already burning. Someone from the next floor up was squirting the fire extinguisher down the stairwell onto the fire. "What in the fuck do you think you're doing up there?" I yelled. "Those sorry sons of a bitches set that on fire, let them live with it." The water from the fire extinguisher stopped momentarily, and I walked on by and started up the stairs. I continued to cuss the silly son of a bitch who didn't have anything better to do but to play with the fire extinguishers. As I rounded the corner to see who was attempting to put the fire out, I found two correctional supervisors (lieutenants) each with a fire extinguisher. I explained to them that putting out the fire would only encourage more fires.

Allowing it to burn, or at least smolder, so that the smoke would fill the unit would resolve that problem. One of the lieutenants said, "Well, we finally got an officer up here to do some shaking down. These bastards don't like it. We've had officers sitting up here in the fucking office so damn long that wouldn't do any shaking down. Now that they have an officer up here on his toes and doing the job, these silly bastards think they are going to run him off. I want this place shaken down every fucking day and you shake down tonight too. These convicts don't run this God damn place. We do." The next week, that young officer was pulled from that unit and reassigned to another unit. During that same quarter I had two fires set on me.

The first one, I really felt to be an accident. While working the 4:00 to 12:00 shift, I always did a lot of shaking down. That is, I would go into the individual cells, go through every locker, every hiding place, every box that I could possibly find. During such a shakedown, I found a hundred dollar bill being used as a pipe filter. I found a container of cocaine being stored in the middle of a sugar bowl (coffee cans being used to hold sugar), and marijuana, as well as weapons. The reason that I shook down so much was because I was bored with doing nothing.

While working in the dormitory, the first fire as I said, I'd thought to be an accident. The trash can was positioned right at the bottom of the stairs. I really felt at that time that, most likely, someone had accidentally thrown a cigarette in there or emptied an ashtray into the trash with a cigarette still burning. At this late hour in the day, this would have resulted in a smoldering-type fire which we experienced. I pushed the trash cart outside, had someone put water on the fire, and when asked about it by the supervisor, explained that it had been an accident. The next evening, when the trash can *again* caught fire, I could not believe that accidents should happen so frequently, especially ones so similar in nature. One of the inmates asked if he could push the trash cart out, and I said, "No." I informed the inmates that I was of the opinion that the first fire may have been an accident, but I felt this to be sheer carelessness. Individuals being so careless must be stopped. I informed the inmates that I had no idea who might be so careless and would never be able to find out. However, the inmates *could* find out should this type of harassment continue.

I allowed the cart to burn for some time. I went into the office, through the office, and outside onto the rooftop. Out of Dorm 3 there was a rooftop over the laundry. This rooftop, being small in nature, gave access to the rooms where the inmates were housed in Dorm 3. I walked around on the roof top there for a short time, just long enough so they saw me out there, enjoying the fresh air, and then went back into the office—which was air conditioned. After a few minutes, someone knocked on the door. I opened it, and much to my surprise, the room was full of smoke! "Can we take the trash can outside now, boss? It's really getting smoky in here and some of us are having difficulty breathing."

I never allowed him or anyone else to know how startled and frightened I was at the situation. I was fully aware of the fact that we did have some older inmates with respiratory problems housed in that unit. Should any of the inmates suffer a breathing problem as a result of my allowing the room to get filled with smoke to that degree, I knew I'd have a problem. I explained in a hostile tone, "You silly bastards don't have anything better to do than build fires, I don't have a damn thing better to do than to evade the smoke. This one is on me. I'll let you get that damn thing out of my house, but this will be the last time it goes out. I don't give a fuck if the damn thing burns all night. At midnight I go home. I don't have to smell this shit when I go home. I don't have to smell smoke when I sleep at night. If you silly bastards can't find out who is setting these damn fires and get it stopped, fuck you. Let it burn. Get that shit out of my house." This was the last time that I encountered a fire in that unit.

A few nights later, while making the 10:00 p.m. count, I counted all of the bodies and came up one body short. I felt reasonably sure that I had made a good count; there was a sporting event on TV and a large crowd sitting in the TV room watching this sporting event. So, at that time, I decided to go ahead and count again and be sure. Again, I counted. This time I was very certain myself that I had not overlooked or misplaced anybody, but again came up one short. It was obvious to me that someone was still dissatisfied with my shakedowns or manner of operating the unit. By this time, they had equally dissatisfied me.

I opened the door from the office into the TV room, and shouted, "Count time, count time!" Immediately there was an uproar. Inmates expressed the fact that they were in the middle of a ball game, and that it was not routine for them to have to return to their cell for count. I explained in no uncertain terms, "Some silly bastard is trying to hide from me or has escaped and I'm going to find that mother fucker if he is in this damn building. I want every swinging dick standing by their bed when I count this time." This time I made the count with a bed book. I knew that if anyone was missing, I would catch them right away in the bed book and know who it was that was missing. However, and much as I expected, no one was missing.

After the count had been completed and I came up with a correct count, I allowed the inmates to return to the TV room to finish the game. One of the inmates came to the office (one of the lieutenants in the Mafia) and asked, "Why do you keep fucking with us?"

"Well, captain," I responded, "I'm doing my time just like you're doing yours. I've got twenty fucking years to do in this place eight hours at a time. I have no interest or desire to harass or fuck with anybody. I walk around this damn place for eight hours with my finger up my ass every five minutes changing hands and get so damn bored that I start shaking down. I am not after anybody or anything, but I still have the job to do, and I'm going to keep on doing it. If those silly bastards don't like that, they are going to have to learn to live with it. Now, every night at the same time we make a count. Tonight, somebody decided to hide from me. I have no interest in finding who in the fuck that was. You and I both know I could not. If you want to watch that fucking

TV set, you find out who the hell is playing games with me and stop it. You don't fuck with me, I don't fuck with you. It's that simple."

That was the last difficulty I had in working with the dorms. The next night when I shook down, I deliberately shook down the individual's cell who I knew was running the kitchen. I found his stove and some of his food, but left it all intact. I shook down three or four cells of the Mafia leaders within the unit and, as very much predicted, found absolutely nothing. I also found some marijuana in a public area which I could not attach to any individual.

Later in the shift, the inmate came to me and told me he appreciated me not taking his stove. I told him, "I don 't give a damn about you having something to eat. I don't even mind you having food there for the other inmates in the unit. Just as long as you don't go opening a restaurant or operating a business without a license. If I find you selling food, I'm going to lock your sorry ass up. Just to have something to cook with, or having some food there, I'm not fucking with you!"

After that, in the evening sometime between 5:00 and 6:00 and usually after the 10:00 count, one of the inmates would come up to me and ask me, "Want a sandwich, boss?"

Even if I was hungry, I would always respond, "No thank you, just had something to eat."

One evening, a trash can was set on fire on all four ranges of E cell house. The unit OIC, Mr. Thomast, was one of the most mild-mannered and calm individuals I have ever had the privilege of meeting. The angriest I have ever seen him, he said something like, "God dang, would you believe that someone would do that?" He was in the office doing some paperwork when an inmate came in and informed him of the fire. He got up and walked out of the office and, looking, could see that trash cans were burning on all floors. At about the same time, one of the towers informed him that there was a fire burning in his unit. He got on his radio and very calmly explained, "10-4, 10-4, I have everything under control here." Then he remarked, for the inmates' benefit, "My, my, isn't that something. It appears to me that someone likes smoke." With this, he returned to his office and continued with his paperwork. This building, being unlike the dormitory, had such ample ventilation that it could not smoke up to the extent of endangering the inmates.

Shortly afterwards, an inmate came into the office where Mr. Thomast was working. He asked, "Can we get those trash cans off the floor and out of the unit, boss? This place is getting awful smoky."

"Oh no," responded Mr. Thomast. "If we remove the trash cans out, he may find something else he wants to burn." Finally, some of the inmates put enough water on the trash cans to keep it from burning. The trash cans were never removed from the building and were never set on fire again.

I was working West Yard, day watch when my *daddy* (a fellow employee who looks after or takes care of me) called me on the radio and asked me to call him by phone. As he answered the phone, I said, "Hey, J.B., what in the hell can I do for you today, sir?"

"Yeah, little buddy, I need a favor. I've got an individual in segregation unit who needs a job before he gets out. He's a sorry bastard who won't work anywhere. He wouldn't even taste pies in a pie factory if they made only his favorite brand. Anyway, we've got to get his sorry ass out of seg unit for a while, and the only we can do that is to find a job for him. Do you have a job you can put him on for me there, little buddy?"

"What's his name and when do you want him to start?"

"Thank you, Lawson, we'll try to get him out of seg tonight and he'll be on your detail first thing in the morning. If he doesn't show up, give me a call so we can run his sorry ass down. He has a habit of not showing up for work."

The next morning, inmate Jackson did not show up as expected. I made a special trip to his unit to get him. He claimed that he did not have any steel-toed shoes and could not work without steel-toed shoes. I took him to the laundry and got him a pair of steel-toed shoes. When we came out onto the West Yard, I took him to the area where I wanted him to be working. We had an area behind the hospital located between the hospital and the wall, which was kind of standing on both ends. We went around the backside of the hospital, around and in between the B and D cell houses. Beside that fenced-in area were cigarette butts thrown from the windows from each of the above mentioned units. I took Jackson inside the fence area and walked around the entire area with him. I pointed out precisely what I wanted done.

I explained carefully to him that anything that did not grow was to be picked up. I then left, locking the gate behind me. Generally, my detail went to lunch at 10:30 a.m. They were not scheduled to go until 11:30, so at that time I opened the gate to let inmate Jackson out. I left instructions with him to return no later than 12:30, the time that I would be back from my lunch break.

When I returned, we again walked back through to check the area which he had policed. I commented about how disappointed I was that he had done so little in that period of time. Again, I expressed my desire for him to work that afternoon and locked the gate. Every few minutes another inmate and/or employee would come and tell me somebody behind that hospital wanted me to come and open the gate for him. Instead, I would make myself visible, wave at him, and continue with other activities. The next day, he showed up for work, and was given the same assignment. Many of the inmates were laughing at him, and all the employees had realized what I had done. When he asked to have me come and get him out, they would respond, "He's busy right now, but I'm sure he will be around shortly."

One of the inmates came out from the unit laughing. He told me, "How silly can that dumb bastard be? That bastard came to the window and informed me that it was against policy to keep him locked up back there. After all, what if a fire broke out—he would be locked in and no way to escape!"

"Well, now what in the fuck does that silly bastard think is going to burn down in the grass between walls?"

The next day Jackson again reported to work on time. This time, as before, he was assigned the same job. At 11:30 a.m. when I opened the gate to let him out, he ran toward the rear corridor.

Instead of going to the dining hall, he went directly to the lieutenant's office. He advised the lieutenant that he was refusing job and quarters. He was not going to work anymore for that crazy bastard on that yard. The lieutenant called and told me to take my man over to the seg unit. Shortly afterward, I spoke with J.B. J.B. told me, "I sure am glad you got rid of that simple bastard again, Lawson. He hasn't washed his stinking ass since he got back into the unit. I was afraid some of the other inmates were going to kill that sorry bastard and I would hate to see somebody getting more time for killing that ignorant bastard."

The only problem was that it was only four weeks until quarter change again. The next quarter, I was assigned into the segregation unit. At that time, I was number 2 officer, the OIC being Officer Nilson. Inmate Jackson, still being locked in the segregation unit, refusing job and quarters, had failed to take a shower during the entire period of his confinement. This was one of the major difficulties with him being housed in the regular housing unit. Protecting inmate Jackson from bodily harm from other inmates in view of his personal hygiene (or lack thereof) or lifestyle was extremely difficult for the correctional force. Inmate Jackson and two other black inmates were housed in a single cell. As a result of the close confinement and lack of ventilation, the cell was developing a bad aroma. The other inmates were complaining on a regular basis about Jackson's failure to take a shower. Finally, officer Nilson and I were forced to join inmate Jackson in the shower, using a brush to clean some of the aroma and stagnation from his body.

While the Atlanta facility was an all-American facility, it housed slightly over 2000 American inmates. In spite of the large number of hostile and violent inmates, only a few difficulties were encountered. I personally am convinced that, should a similar facility or housing unit be developed to house an equal number of ministers of a combination or variety of faiths, tempers would flare and violence would occur on an equal basis. While citizens have the opportunity to leave their homes and go into the community, tempers flare, and aggravation is expressed in most American homes. When you consider the fact that the individuals confined in most correctional facilities are unable to go into the community or escape the individuals they have verbal disagreements with, the frequency of violent explosions between individuals is really not all that great. Even within the institution where, if I recall correctly, an individual was killed once a month for approximately fourteen consecutive months, there was not an overabundance of hostility expressed in view of the population housed in that facility.

There were many unknown or unreported incidents of physical fighting between inmates. Many times, the inmate would come up with a black eye and refuse to make any complaint against any other inmate. He would claim to have fallen in the shower and could produce witnesses to the fall, if needed. Although it was obvious to staff that he had been involved in an altercation with another inmate, we could not prove it, since the inmate did not refuse general population housing. In most cases, this ended the disagreement between the inmates and no additional conflict erupted.

We did have one individual, a black male from the Virgin Islands, who was involved in a massacre on a golf course on the Virgin Islands in the sixties. Inmate Labeach spent much of his time in his original early years of confinement housed in a segregation unit. He was an extreme racist who believed that all whites were blue-eyed devils who needed execution or removal from the face of the earth. As a result of his strong belief, each time he was released from the segregation unit, he would go into the dining hall and a fight would break out. Inmate Labeach would go to the front of the dining hall chow line to get in front of the white inmate closest to the serving line. At that time, a fight would erupt. As a result of his continual conflict, most of his time was in the segregation unit.

On one occasion, when he was released from the segregation unit, when going to the dining room, again a fight erupted. One of our staff, Officer Harmon, a 260-pound white male, found himself in the corner of the dining hall and isolated from other staff members. Once the fight started it spread through the entire dining hall in a matter of seconds. Officer Harmon found himself in a corner confronted by three or four of the militant black inmates who shared the views of inmate Labeach. One of the inmates produced a handmade weapon—a sharpened knife—and threatened to move in on officer Harmon. Officer Harmon, a large man with the frame to carry his weight, reached into his pocket and pulled his own knife. Opening the blade, he motioned with his free hand for the inmate to *come on,* if he so chose. Looking over the situation, the inmate dropped his own knife, and they walked away, leaving the dining hall. These eruptions, for most part, were short-lived, since most of the inmates in the dining hall wanted out and did not want physical violence involved but were protecting themselves on their way out. Staff stuck together and, while going in to get those who'd started the fight, it took them physically out of the dining hall while being protected by other staff. Only other inmates who confronted staff were charged with the fight or confined in segregation as a result of the fight.

During the period of incarceration, an individual finds some person or persons or means of filling his psychological and physical needs. It is during this period of time that the inmate accepts emotional relationships between inmates. Another inmate within the area is one who shares the happiness, joys, sorrows, frustrations, and all the other's emotions. For a sexual release, it is not uncommon for staff to be walking down the range and find an inmate lying on his bed, looking at a *Playboy* magazine, while masturbating. It is during this period of time also that individuals change more from situational homosexuals to homosexuality as a permanent lifestyle. As one inmate expressed when being caught with another inmate's penis in his mouth, "I was not giving him a blow-job, I was just holding it in my mouth until the swelling went down." Individuals initially may come into homosexuality on a situational level, having their sexual needs met by other persons. That is, when he gets tired of having his sexual needs met solely by masturbation, he will find another inmate who will perform sexual acts by anal or oral sex. These individuals soon come to accept a relationship very much as a man and wife in society.

CHAPTER 4

DOING THE JOB

JUST LIKE THE INMATES, THE EMPLOYEE BECOMES MEL-
lowed out by five years. You have learned the policies and how to cover your ass. By then, the inmates know your boundaries and are less apt to create problems for you. As a younger officer or trainee, inmates were constantly attempting to find your limits. The second and third, and even into the fourth year of employment, inmates were attempting to determine how much endurance the staff member would have and what type of molding they could do on the staff member. By attempting to question the moral values of the employee, while portraying their own situation as one of a victim, inmates would attempt to mold staff into persons who were sympathetic to needs of the inmate population. While the inmates clearly identified the fact that the most dangerous employees were those trainees, who were more apt to write more reports than an older officer, they were really aware of the fact that the older officer could do more damage in a shorter period of time with a pencil.

During the early and formative years of employment, if the inmates could convince the employee that the sale or use of cocaine was similar to the era of prohibition of alcohol, they might convince the employee to be less vigilant during shakedown. If the staff could be convinced that the inmate was a victim, he could be used by the inmate to carry something in or out for the inmate. By the time an employee became a seasoned veteran within the facility, he had become aware of the inmate population and the buttons to push to control that population. Some inmates could be easily controlled by a telephone to call the family. Others, having families living in the nearby area, could expect to enjoy a weekend visit every weekend. Some inmates could be controlled with merely a few minutes of TV time per day. By the time one became a senior officer specialist in a federal penitentiary, he usually has become fully aware of the inmate population within each of the major cellblocks. As long as the staff member treats the inmate population with respect, he will encounter limited difficulties while working in that cellblock. If the inmate population does not respect or care for the employee working within the cellblock, one can always expect trouble.

By the time an inmate has been in the institution or system for five years, he has become institutionalized. The following is "Lawson's Theory on Confinement and Recidivism."

An individual who receives a period of confinement within the correctional facility learns what is required to be released. One requirement to obtain the earliest possible release is, in all cases, to display positive behavior while confined. Secondly, all inmates receiving sentences to be served in any correctional facility have learned that it is better to get along with the police than fight them. The correctional staff and staff members within a correctional setting are associated with the police on the outside. While the correctional staff within the facility is well outnumbered on the most part, they control the keys, which divide the inmates into smaller groups. While an inmate may become verbal or physically violent upon one staff member at any given time, within a matter of minutes, the inmate can find himself in an isolated area where he is outnumbered twenty to one.

One of the things which precluded staff from becoming injured on a more regular basis within the Atlanta facility was the staff's response to any threat to a staff member, coupled with the fact that most of the staff were well respected by the inmates. A body alarm, an electronic device worn on the belt which sets off an alarm in the control room, results in an immediate call for assistance over the radio and loudspeakers. This would bring in thirty to fifty staff members responding within the first thirty to forty seconds. When thirty staff members respond to a call for assistance, twenty of the staff members were seeking a fight. These twenty staff members, for the most part, would fight with each other, inmates, or if necessary, start a fight themselves just for their own entertainment. Inmates soon learned not to do anything to require such a response, unless they were prepared to suffer the consequences.

Individuals being housed in a correctional facility for a crime genuinely want to perform acts which appease, or at least create no conflict with staff. Additionally, while they may be extremely violent themselves on the street, they are fully aware that the balance of the population housed within that facility is not there for missing early Sunday morning service. The most violent inmate there readily identifies the fact that he, too, can be killed by members of the population. Subsequently, he is selective with whom he identifies and attempts to identify himself with a group which will offer or support his self-preservation. Additionally, just as expressed with the incidents in the dining hall, most inmates do not want to get involved in any activity which does not directly involve them. As the saying goes, "Do your own time."

Once the inmate has been housed in a correctional facility and desires to appease staff and remain neutral from other inmates, he understands the fact that if he were able to get out of jail at that point in time, he would never return to jail. For the first three years of his sentence, he honestly believes this himself. He means that he would do without monies, do without food, or do with whatever harassment necessary in order to remain crime-free and prevent future incarceration.

However, individuals serving a term of less than three years in confinement find themselves very much like the military staff. Individuals who have been in the military, and in a combat zone, readily identify the fact that they will never go back to combat. After a short period of time the memory goes back to good times shared, friends shared, and he only recalls the fun things that went on and not the conflicts which were encountered. Inmates housed in a correctional facility for less than three years, when released, find that they remember only the good times, the friends, and the funny things which occurred in jail. The long hours of sitting in a cell, worrying about their family, being frightened of other inmates who would take advantage or sexually assault them are soon forgotten.

The inmate has been brought in from the street and placed in an environment that is totally foreign to his nature. He is maintained in that environment at gun point. He readily identifies with the fact that, should he choose to leave that setting, he will be contained even to the price of death. Somewhere between the period of three and five years of confinement, the inmate understands the fact that he is rapidly losing contact with his family, friends, and all things of personal value on the street.

The military assigns their personnel for three-year periods at the maximum. Individuals assigned to any foreign country are assigned up to a maximum of three years and then returned to the continental U.S.A., unless other arrangements are requested by the military personnel. As the individual realizes that he is losing contact with his family and friends, a number of other factors become involved. One such thing is the term "misery loves company." Within that three-to-five-year period, the inmate has developed some sort of friendships or loyalty among other prisoners. As the inmate loses contact with family and friends on the street, the friendships developed within the institution setting are strengthened. Within that three-to-five-year period of time, should the government or any other persons be able to clearly identify that moment that his mindset changes, the individual could be released on the street and would, in fact, remain crime-free for the rest of his life. However, the sentence structure does not allow for this. Criminal behavior demands a specific response, and the response to many of these crimes is well beyond a five-year period. As time passes after the inmate is incarcerated, he finds less and less to talk to his family about. Initially, they talk about the activities and people which they were personally involved with. The topic then turns to hopes and plans for the future while reminiscing over the past. Somewhere between three to five years, the past and future run together. Conversations about Uncle Tom or Uncle Fred's garden or that big party no longer bring the joy they once did. The plans to repair the old or build or buy a new home, visit old friends, or have more parties soon turn to little more than a fantasizing of sexual desires for the spouse and loneliness from being away from other family members.

The time between the relationship with family and the current situation does not lend itself to continuing lasting relationships. Individuals who have their spouse or close family member coming to visit on the visiting days and, as permitted within the correctional setting, soon find that after ten minutes of honest visitation which includes a hug, a kiss, and a concern about other immediate family members, they find themselves sitting there during the duration of the visit with limited conversation topics or nothing to say to one another. The inmate cannot tell the spouse or the one coming to visit that he was propositioned by another inmate or that he propositioned another inmate the day before. The fact that he went to work within the furniture factory industries and made three desks the day before really isn't that impressive to the family. Equally noteworthy is the fact that the crop growth on the farm, too much rain or the lack of rain, is also unimportant to the inmate. The inmate's sex drive is not being fulfilled by either the spouse or any persons visiting. Neither is the sex drive of the spouse or person visiting fulfilled by the inmate. None of the needs, emotional or physical, are being met by each other. There is no dependency and no relationship between those two individuals; there are only fading dreams.

As this becomes more and more apparent to the person housed in the correctional setting, the inmate becomes more and more bitter with society. He looks at the judge no longer as a fair individual, but one who is depriving him of all things of value. Very quickly, the inmate develops the attitude of, "He has done taken my family away from me. He has done taken all my money from me...what in the fuck does this bastard want?" The relationship between the inmate and the staff slowly changes at that time. The inmate develops a more hostile attitude toward staff but limits this hostility to that which will bring only limited repercussion. He must now keep his hopes and dreams alive in himself to maintain his sanity. This bitterness becomes more ingrained, but less expressed. The inmate readily identifies with the fact that he would kill any staff member, if necessary, in an effort to escape—if that staff member was between him and freedom. However, the inmate becomes more friendly and accepting of his role as well as the role of the staff member, and jokes flow freely between the two. The inmate begins to accept the policy of the institution and becomes what one terms "institutionalized." He recognizes that the institution is the authority, sees how the institution is to function, and understands his role within that operational functioning of that facility.

Trouble within the cellblock does not necessarily come in the form of violence. An OIC who is not well-liked by the inmate population may find someone on the fifth range calling for help. Climbing to the fifth floor and searching from there down, finding nothing in the form of an inmate who needs assistance, he returns to the first floor to find a trash can on fire, a broken water pipe, or similar inconveniences. He may get a phone call to find grease on the phone or find a container of shit on his chair. Inmates will find means for keeping the officer running from end to end of the building, solely for the purpose of keeping him off their back. I have only known of one staff member to have a contract placed on him. This correctional officer was taken from the cellblock and placed on the tower for a prolonged period of time in an effort to "protect" him.

Officer Richards was one of the best correctional officers I have ever known or met in the area of detection of drugs. An inmate told me that Officer Richards had come on the range one day, and the inmate in question came about his snitch. Richards told the inmate that he never used a snitch. If any son-of-a-bitch would snitch to him, he would also snitch on him and he did not need that. The inmate responded that no officer could purely—with only luck—find so many drugs. Richards invited the inmate to walk down the range with him. The inmate took him up on it. After walking approximately four or five cells, Officer Richards stopped for a second and said, "There is something in this cell."

The inmate laughed and assured Officer Richards that he was wrong. The inmate had known the person housed in that cell for a long period of time and knew that he wasn't involved with drugs in any way. Officer Richards assured him that there were drugs within the cell. "There were not enough to bring any charges or write an incident report," he said, "but there were drugs in the cell." With that, Officer Richards entered the cell. After about a forty-five-second to one-minute shakedown, Officer Richards ran his fingers on a bottom slide that runs under the door. He pulled out one marijuana leaf and three or four seeds and dropped them on the bed.

He laughed at this, and said, "That's all there is but they are here." The inmate shook his head and returned to the cell.

Officer Richards was always showing up at a place and at a time totally unexpected. As an example, when he was scheduled to come to work at 7:45, he would be on the range and shaking down at 6:00 a.m. Nobody but Officer Richards did this. Officer Richards was laughing about an adventure one day when he advised me that he had been up on the range at approximately 7:30 a.m. Two young officers were also on the range and were semi-shaking down. Officer Richards told them that they may as well quit farting around and decide whether they wanted to shake down or not.

"This is the way it is done," he declared. He walked into a cell with the two young officers following. He looked around for a couple of minutes, put his hand into a small box and pulled out five or six small packets of heroin.

He advised his young trainees, "See? This is how it is done. You don't fart around with your finger up your ass doing nothing." He then left the cell and started down the stairs. He laughed loudly at that time and said, "Damn, I must have been crazy." He named three inmates who were specifically housed in that cell and he said, "Either one of those mother fuckers would cut your throat for one marijuana cigarette. That heroin must have cost them a bundle." Officer Richards, God rest his soul, died of a heart attack as a result of worrying about security within that facility.

Some posts required that an officer have five years (in skills, if not actual years) before they could be assigned. Along with the front gate and east gate, which allowed individuals access in and out of the institution, the receiving and discharge officer (R and D) was in a position that required that the officer knew policy, procedure, and inmates. This is where every inmate who came in or went out of the institution was greeted. Inmates who came into the institution could leave the R and D area with only their body that they brought in, even if they were coming from another institution. Even their body was completely searched. Inmates would come into the institution with dope or money taped under their arms, under their groins, or even under dentures or up their rectum. As a result of this, the officer must be complete from the soles of the inmate's feet to the hair on their head. One new commitment, a repeat offender, attempted to bring a carton of cigarettes in with him from the street. The carton and each pack looked factory fresh. Two or three days a week we would have a bus coming into and leaving the Atlanta facility headed for other institutions. During my period of employment, I have had a large number of inmates who were scheduled for transfer to another facility insisting that they were not going to come out tomorrow morning. They would tell you, "When they come to get me they had better bring help. I'm not going to go no damn place without a fight!" The next morning at 4:00 a.m., when a supervisor and an officer came in and approached the cell, they would ask the individual if he was ready to go and the inmate would respond, "Yeah, boss." I heard a large number of inmates say that they were not going to leave, but I never knew of one that had to be forced out. According to most of the inmates, Atlanta was a good institution in which to do time.

Another post which required those same skills was the visiting room. There, the staff were also introduced to the need for keeping good public relations while being similar in security to R and D. The person visiting the inmate was not searched as the inmates were when visiting the inmate. Once inside the visiting room, a woman would get a balloon with drugs from her bra and put it in her mouth as the inmate came into the visiting room. When kissing the inmate, the balloon would be passed from her mouth to his mouth, and he would swallow it. After leaving the visiting room, he would monitor his next bowel movement to retrieve the balloon. One balloon had a pinhole in it which resulted in the inmate dying from an overdose. Otherwise, the transaction would have gone undetected. Visitors would leave contraband in the restrooms, under chairs or tables for the orderlies. On occasion, a visitor would spill something just to have an orderly (otherwise not present during visitation) called in. It was hoped that the staff would be lax with the orderly since he had been called in from a football game and was not supposed to be on the job.

Drug drops were most frequently made near the fence line by someone either walking or driving by. They would then be picked up by an inmate policing the area or mowing the grounds. They would then either be thrown over the wall if the tower officer could be distracted or carried in during the evening when anything more than a pat shake was an exception rather than the rule. When someone was caught bringing drugs in through this manner, it was the result of a snitch. One inmate working on the landscape had managed to get into a wooded area on the southwest side of the grounds outside the walk and make a bedroom. Every day for some time, his wife came by to visit.

One inmate was reported by a tower to have made a drug pickup. The lieutenant immediately sent Mr. Richards, who was available at that moment, out to shake down the inmate. When Richards approached the inmate out in front of the institution and told him that he was going to be strip searched, the inmate undressed there in front of the institution. He lifted his groins and turned to bend and spread his cheeks in front of the passing motorists, God and everyone. The only one to complain was a secretary from personnel who looked out to see the bare facts.

She was later asked if the call to the lieutenant's office was made before, during, or after the shakedown was completed. The body search produced no drugs, but several memorandums concerning the shakedown were made. The most common evidence of drugs found outside (and sometimes inside) the wall were half-pint or pint whiskey bottles.

CHAPTER 5

INMATE AND STAFF RELATIONS

An individual known as Fast Eddy was housed in D cell house. This individual had several hundred years of sentence. Fast Eddy was a colorful individual who perceived himself to be a high escape risk and a world-renowned bank robber. I am uncertain as to what type of information he was providing to the captain at that time but, at any rate, he managed to get himself paroled. Individual inmates could snitch to the associate warden, captain, or person of authority, and get favorable recommendations at a higher level for parole or release. This reportedly happened within the institution in Fast Eddy's case. Fast Eddy was paroled to work on a farm in Wisconsin, I believe.

Soon after his release, rumors came back to the institution that he had raped the wife of the farmer for whom he was working and escaped. While not incarcerated, he was to report to a parole officer on a regular basis, and when such reporting was not complied with, he was placed on *escape* status. At any rate, a few weeks later, Fast Eddy was heard from. He was located in a bank in Ohio with several hostages. While in the process of robbing the bank, Fast Eddy had a heart attack. After holding the hostages for a few hours and through negotiations, the hostages were released. Fast Eddy was again taken into custody. It was not long until Fast Eddy was again housed in our facility in Atlanta. During that period, the captain had been promoted out of the institution. He had also returned to the institution and was now an associate warden. Something of interest to me was that Fast Eddy was soon placed into an out-custody classification and given an out-custody job and did, in fact, escape from our facility on a walk-off type escape soon after that.

In 1976, I was selected for promotion (actually a lateral assignment) to a case manager position at the Atlanta Federal Community Treatment Center, a halfway house on the grounds of the Atlanta Pen. This was the first time that I came face to face with discrimination on a daily basis in my life. I have known several people who make their personal decisions based upon black and white, and I knew racists within the government that expressed their racial views, both black and white. Prior to the CTC (Community Treatment Center), I had never found an inmate to be guilty or innocent of a charge on an incident report, or a staff member 's decision considered right or wrong based solely on race.

When I went there, I found the CTC director to be a mild-mannered, quiet type, black man. On the surface, he left you believing that he was in charge and on top of everything. On his desk, he had a calendar. When asked a question or told about something, he would grab the calendar and make a note on it as he said, "Good point, Earl. Let me check on that and get back with you." He left the impression that he wanted to be sure before giving the wrong information. No matter how urgent the nature or what the question or information concerned, the next day always brought a new space to check the issues of the day. The director was attending law school and spent his day on school work. He turned his responsibilities over to the senior case manager who had come into the Atlanta Pen for a short time from a GS-7 to GS-9 to GS-11 case manager. He too, was black, but was more racially oriented and less skilled in dealing with people than the director. He developed a core of black staff who made decisions concerning activities of inmates and staff alike, based solely on race.

One inmate was scheduled to be in at 11:00 p.m. one night. He called, claiming his girlfriend was in the emergency room at the hospital and he did not want to leave her alone. I told this black inmate that he could remain with her in the ER. Should she be admitted or released, he was to return to the center.

This was noted in the log book.

When I came to work the next day, the director questioned me about the incident, since the inmate had not come in. When I explained what had transpired, he instructed me to see if I could locate him and get him to the center. "If you can find him, have him come here and then lock him up in Fulton County Jail until we have an IDC (institution disciplinary committee) hearing on him. You write the shot on what happened. If you can't find him, we will call the FBI and report him as escaped." I got him out of bed with my phone call and transported him to jail when he arrived at the center. The next day, the IDC returned him to the center because, "Mr. Lawson had informed him to take as long as he needed."

A white inmate was sent back to the institution on a similar charge by a black staff. When shaking down the cubicle of a black inmate I found a variety of prescribed drugs with several different names on them. I also found a container of homemade brew, which I was shocked to find in the CTC. An incident report was written, and he was taken to Fulton County Jail (used as a segregation unit) pending an IDC. The next day, he too was returned to the CTC.

In 1977, the U.S. Government started cutting back on federal hiring. The Bureau of Prisons started contracting out all the halfway house activities as a means of circumventing the politics. By closing that facility, the bureau effectively gained nine employees. I was transferred to FCI Memphis, Tennessee, but returned to Atlanta early in 1978 for personal reasons. I returned as a GS-7 correctional officer after being a GS-9 case worker. I was personally promised the next available case manager position in Atlanta, but I did not have that in writing—sort of like, "The check is in the mail."

After my return to Atlanta as a correctional officer, I was assigned to West Yard day watch when they were remodeling E cell house. They decided to remove the receiving and discharge area from underneath the rear corridor and place it in Dorm 1. They closed Dorm 1 out completely and began construction in the area. That design was a brilliant plan—besides the East Gate which allowed vehicular traffic into the institution, we also had a West Gate. The West Gate was directly outside of the back door of E cell house. Well before 1978, West Gate had never been opened in over twenty years that anyone knew about. The plan was to build a receiving and discharge (an area where inmates were received into the institution and prepared for release from the institution) in the old Dorm 1 area. This area was to provide a holdover sleeping quarters and a jail-type setting for individuals to be dressed in and dressed out. After laying a large volume of bricks and welding a lot of steel into the area, it was ready to open for use. They built an elaborate fence on both sides of the walkway between the West Gate and the back door of E house, which was to go into R and D. The plan was to bring the bus inside West Gate, unload the bus, allowing inmates to step off the bus and into a R and D section. After spending several hundred thousand dollars on this project, it was discovered that the gate had never been designed for a bus as wide as a newer bus. Subsequently, the gate was never opened or used.

While assigned to the West Yard, bricks were being stacked on the West Yard area on pallets for the construction of R and D. The inmates would take a few from several pallets, leaving the wooden pallets and broken brick all over the yard. I informed the inmates, although they did not work for me or on my detail, that they would start policing up after themselves. I brought several trash containers down to that area and informed them that they could put the broken bricks into that area. I additionally informed them that my detail would get rid of all the wooden pallets that were there at that time, but future pallets would be removed by them. The inmates immediately became angry and told their foremen my plans on disrupting their work. When a foreman came to confront me concerning the taking over of his detail, I assured him, "That was not my intent. However, you and your detail can keep your trash out of my area." After a little more mellow conversation, he understood my goal and agreed that it was viable. When possible, inmates would pit one staff against another and use both of them to get what they wanted. After about a week's period of time I had the entire West Yard area looking very good. I had gotten all of the grass cut, all of the walks edged, and all of the concrete in the area was hosed down on a daily basis.

No matter where I was assigned, I took pride in my work. Even though I had become angry at management and was becoming very active in labor-management relations, as well as becoming active and aggressive in the local union, I took pride and interest in my job. One day shortly after noon, I was called into the captain's office. The captain advised me that he had not seen that West Yard so sloppy in all of his days within the bureau. I advised him promptly that he had no idea what in the hell what he was talking about. "You have not seen a damn thing in my yard. If you have a problem with the way I do my job, put it on paper!"

The captain began to laugh and said, "Just calm down, Lawson, calm down. Really the reason I just called you in here was to tell you that you have been promoted to senior officer specialist."

There was no big difference in the promotion as far as work assignments. One quarter (three months every year) I was still assigned to the morning watch. The only difficulty I had working the morning watch was that while three months out of every year I was assigned to the morning watch, many of the staff on the favoritism basis never worked a morning watch. Work assignments, like promotions, were assigned on a nepotism, favoritism, and racial basis. Some of the "fair-haired boys" remained assigned in posts such as captain's clerk, transfer clerk, and other similar high-profile posts.

The OIC ran the housing units. It was very rare that the supervisor came into the unit to see what was going on. If there were problems within the unit, it was only a short time before the supervisor became aware of such problems. Otherwise, the roster committee attempted to place individuals within housing units that were compatible and cohesive working units and either the OIC to run the unit or an experienced officer to cover for the OIC. Each of the lieutenants attempted to maintain a staff within each unit to preclude the lieutenant having to work. It was much easier to delegate the job to be done than it was to do the job. The only time the lieutenants came into the housing units was when a large number of incidents started occurring in the housing unit or a large number of incident reports started being written.

Every Thursday morning in the housing unit there was an inspection by the associate warden. The inspection included making sure the floors were shined, the bars to each cell were dusted and clean, beds were all made, and cells and the entire unit looked shiny and orderly. Another barometer of the relationship between the staff and the inmates in the unit was the consistency of the inspection report. Should the correctional staff be harassing or be perceived to be harassing the inmates in the housing unit, the inmates would start making their bed very shabbily. None of the cells would be dusted; there would be something wrong in each cell. When the associate wardens came around, this had an adverse impact upon the officers working the cell house. Most of the American inmates living in the U.S. Penitentiary Atlanta enjoyed living there as far as living in a confined facility is concerned. Within many of the correctional institutions, an individual will be given an incident report for things like walking on the grass, failure to have shined their shoes, or within the cell house, not having the shoes aligned correctly under the beds. A lot of the newer facilities are more militaristic than Atlanta ever was.

Within the Atlanta facility, the Atlanta staff was much more concerned about the possibility of the inmate escaping. The American inmates claimed all they had to do in the Atlanta penitentiary was do their time. They did not have someone constantly on their back. To get an incident report or adverse action they had to do something wrong. The inmates housed within the Atlanta penitentiary were all older inmates. An inmate could be assigned to that facility and be under twenty-seven years of age. The average age of the inmate was thirty-five and the next twenty-five years of his life were planned for him. As a result of this, inmates housed in that facility were more stable and mature. There was very limited horseplay, and on rare occasions would there be a physical fight. When a fight occurred, it usually was short-lived and ended in a near-fatality or fatality. One or both inmates would usually be transferred to another facility and placed on a separate list to prevent their returning to the same facility in the future.

It was my opinion that we had the last of a dying generation both in inmates and staff population. One of the older inmates housed in the institution was there for bank robbery. He said that when he got out of jail for this current offense, he was going to retire from criminal activities. He explained that the younger generation went into the banks with a gun waving it around wanting to shoot somebody and hurt somebody. He claimed that they had no pride in their work, no integrity, and no ability to be a criminal. He stated, "These young kids anymore just want to smoke dope and shoot somebody. When I was out robbing banks, I just wanted to get in, get into the safe, get the money and get the hell out of there. I did not want to be seen by anybody or see anybody. I knew if I got caught, it was my ass. I never carried a gun of any type on me because I knew if I got caught, I might be tempted to use it."

Inmate Swinson bragged about being in a "top security" state facility. "While in the facility I was a clerk for the captain. The captain was constantly talking about that being an escape-proof facility. "Nobody has ever escaped from my jail!" the captain would say."

Proud of himself on his ability as an escape artist, Inmate Swinson claimed to have escaped from that facility. "I broke out of the prison and just laid low at a friend's house for a couple of days. Then I decided to break in in the middle of the night and go into the captain's office and steal a swagger stick." The inmate said that the captain would always carry a swagger stick with the bullet head on one end and casing of a rifle bullet on the other. He expressed pride in the fact that, "I must have been the only inmate to ever break in and out of that institution in the same night. Ha, ha, ha."

Inmate Bradley was a loud mouth, know-it-all type of person. He was a long-term convict. From time to time he would try to put staff down for being a "low-life government employee who was too lazy to work for a living." Generally, this would be a lead into a description of his manly feats of crime.

I would usually just tell him, "Bradley, you are nothing more than a professional prisoner. When your mom got tired of doing your laundry, she kicked your ass out. You threw a rock through a post office window and got put in jail because you were too damn sorry to take care of yourself."

One day I was working in the hospital. Several inmates were standing around talking when Bradley started his bull. "This is supposed to be such a bad place. This pen ain't shit. I was in Raeford where you had to be ready to kill or be killed all the time."

"I get so tired of hearing about how bad the other joints are, how bad I am because I was in that joint, and how Atlanta ain't shit. Yet most of the time, this story is coming from a pussy, not a man," I said. Bradley didn't open his mouth—he walked briskly out of the hospital toward his unit. The other inmates didn't open their mouths. We all knew that Bradley could be dangerous.

Just as the inmate population was a more mature population, most of the employees had a more mature nature. Prior to 1982, the Bureau of Prisons hired a large number of retired military. This was beneficial for both military and the government and allowed the U.S. Penitentiary, Atlanta, to receive a lot of employees who were already well-trained and well-equipped for this position. Additionally, a large number of employees in the institution were Atlanta natives. While the bureau required employees to transfer to become a supervisor prior to that time, many of the Atlanta natives were perfectly content with a GS-8 pay grade and would not move. Therefore, we had a good percentage of employees who had spent fifteen or more years within that facility. We had seen the many changes that had taken place during that period of time throughout the Bureau of Prisons, but in view of the fact that they were not seeking promotion, they were much less interested in the change. They resisted change and ignored policies which they did not like.

New employees being run into the institution were being trained the "snitch rule." Basically, this rule is that any individual who observes another employee committing an act which is either unsafe or against bureau policy must report to the supervisor. Failure to report such act would result in the observer becoming a party of the act and equally guilty of whatever charges might be brought. For example, if I as an employee observed another employee taking a fifteen-minute period beyond his scheduled thirty-minute lunch break and failed to report his being AWOL, I could be held accountable for failure to report this AWOL and given the same disciplinary action which he might receive. Again, the Atlanta staff did not concur with such policy. Subsequently, 1973 through 1978, a more cohesive and cooperative employment condition existed. Where older officers would not be supportive in training or helping you, they would be equally uncooperative in assisting lieutenants in catching another officer in wrongdoing. They would be supportive in assisting lieutenants only when the employee was involved in some illegal activity such as bringing alcohol or drugs into the institution. All the employees perceived any such action as placing their own lives in danger.

One employee working the recreation department was strongly suspected of bringing drugs into the institution. As a young officer in the institution I have had convicts coming to me and complaining, "Why in the fuck don't you all do something about that son of a bitch running a drug store? The government is putting people in jail for selling drugs and paying that son of a bitch to come here and sell drugs to us." I explained to them that they should go report to the SIS (Security Investigating Supervisor) or associate warden-custody. I was told that the associate warden had been told on several occasions but claimed that he could not catch them.

I laughed and responded, "Between the FBI, the DEA, and Bureau of Prisons it would appear that some bastard would have sense enough to catch him if he is actually dealing in drugs."

The inmate walked off and said, "Yeah, but everybody's got to get their fucking payoff too." It was about five years later that Mr. Blue was finally caught and prosecuted. As I understood it, he received a three-year sentence, lost his house, family, and all other things of value.

Many of you may have seen the movie, "The French Connection." The individual who was caught as leader of the French Connection was subsequently prosecuted and brought to the Atlanta facility for safekeeping. The rumor was that this inmate could cause a large number of individuals to become prisoners merely by talking. Such conversation would have resulted in an immediate release since the US government was equally interested in stopping the chain as incarcerating the head. As a result of the number of people who could have been incarcerated, reportedly a contract was placed on his life. After a contract was affected and the inmate was killed, officer LoJo was called in and questioned about the possibility of his involvement. LoJo was reported to have brought the money in to pay for the contract. According to rumors at the time, Mr. Logan admitted to this and many other offenses. Mr. Logan admitted to having brought alcohol into the institution, selling a half-pint for fifty dollars on numerous occasions. Additionally, he admitted to many offenses which nobody had previously had knowledge of occurring. Mr. Logan was arrested and was awaiting trial when he attempted suicide. Although he failed in his attempt to commit suicide, he died shortly thereafter of a heart attack and before prosecution.

Two additional employees were charged with bringing drugs into the institution for inmates also. An inmate alleged that he received a drop-off of drugs on a regular basis from the two employees. One of the two-man staff, Mr. Robison, had a loud and boisterous tone in all conversations. He was consistently cursing inmates, claiming the rest of them to be useless bastards. The attorney for the inmate claimed that on numerous occasions he had come into the visiting room to visit with the inmate. While in the visiting room he would be approached by Officer Robison, who would request change for a five-dollar bill. As payment for the deliveries of packages to the inmate, he would receive five hundred-dollar bills for the five-dollar bill. The employee was supposedly taking payment in cocaine from the attorney in the attorney's office. It was the desire of the US attorney to try both individuals together and at one trial. However, officer Robison pled guilty to his charges while the other staff member pled not guilty. They negotiated a plea bargain with the officer who pled guilty; he received a three-year sentence. The other employee was found not guilty but resigned from the Bureau of Prisons. Inmates who reported employees for drug deals were not retaliated against by other employees and/ or inmates.

Inmate Thurmond, a plumber who worked as a plumber on an emergency basis, set up an employee and purchased a lunch box full of marijuana. Immediately following the sale, inmate Thurmond turned over the marijuana to the FBI who searched the employee and found the marked money on him. The employee was fired within six months of his retirement—however, he was not prosecuted for this offense. Inmate Thurmond had been a homosexual who had soon purchased a homosexual. It was humorous to staff, but a week before inmate Thurmond was released from the US penitentiary he held an auction selling his prostitute. Even though inmate Thurmond had turned in an employee, he still maintained a positive and casual relationship with other employees.

PART TWO

CHAPTER 6

TOGETHER WE STAND

PRIOR TO GOING TO WORK FOR THE BUREAU OF PRISONS, I had been in street law enforcement. You can ask police officers why they became policemen and you will get a variety of responses. Many will tell you for the job security, stable employment, retirement benefits, health benefits, and a variety of other reasons. However, most employees are in that line of business because of the activities while on duty. Personally, if I could economically afford to be in street law enforcement I would work as a policeman for no pay. I enjoyed the excitement and continual adrenaline flow as part of the work. While working on the correctional force, and prior to the riot of 1987, I enjoyed the field of corrections for the same purpose. The enjoyable parts of the duty at the institution were those same factors; those factors which kept the adrenaline flowing. While no employee enjoyed seeing anyone lose their life, enjoyed a disturbance, or enjoyed a fight, it was those activities that broke the routine of the day that kept most employees satisfied with the job. For the most part, employees established a relationship with inmates more stable than that with their employer.

After observing the relationship between the policeman and the crook, the employee and the convict, I came up with *Lawson's theory on criminality*. Crooks and cops (employees within the Justice (Just us) department whether it be policeman on the street or correctional officer within confinement) have more in common than either would like to admit. For the policeman, it does not matter if you catch the individual found guilty in court, it is the ability to chase the individual. (The game of cop and robber is more important than the ending of the game.) For the criminal, it too, is the playing of the game.

Criminal Justice (Just us) is sort of like the game of football. Football players play football because they love the sport. They endure the injuries, training, and anything else required, just to play the game. For the moment, serious injuries (getting caught committing a crime) are things which occur to other people. To get a flag in the game of football and a five-yard penalty is roughly equivalent to a five-year sentence within the institutional setting. It hurts, but he still gets to play in the game.

The rewards of the game, positive or negative, become mere reminders of the fact that one played the game. For the law enforcement officer to get a conviction on a large dealer of drugs, a noted criminal, a noted political figure, or other case which gets notoriety, it becomes ego-inflating. However, the policeman will remain on the force even if he never makes such an arrest. The occasional high speed chase or being in the middle of an incident which is roped off to all other persons will motivate him to remain on the job. The more frequent the rate of adrenalin flow, the longer the law enforcement officer will remain on the job. For the criminal to get a big score in his chosen line of criminality is acknowledgement of his skill in that profession.

Comparing these two with the football player again, the football player plays Sunday after Sunday. Winning the Super Bowl is good for the ego and the pocketbook, but that is not a requirement. The football player will still show up at every game. Next year, he will go out and compete for the same job. Winning or losing is not as important as the ability to play the game. The police officer and the crook will have a mutual respect for each other even though they don't appreciate the chosen profession of the other. That is, as long as each continued to play by their appropriate rules. Nobody likes the police officer or prosecuting attorney who falsifies documents, uses false evidence, or who otherwise becomes criminally involved. Nobody likes the criminal who kills the law-enforcement officer. In essence, it is much like a chess game. Individual players who do not take the game seriously and become personal in the game, much like football players when they grab a face mask, break bones, or otherwise play unfairly are not appreciated. During my period of employment of employment at the U.S. Penitentiary, Atlanta, Georgia, I was approached on two separate occasions by inmates with a proposition. On both occasions the approach was both very tentative and joking. The first was made by an older moonshiner from Alabama.

He was a very friendly old codger, and during the first year of training we talked on several occasions while out on the yard. We discussed activities and what I had done prior to coming to the institution, and I mentioned that I had a part-time business washing and waxing mobile homes. After a short discussion about the mobile-home cleaning business, he indicated that that would not be an expensive business to get into, and he could finance someone getting into that business on a more lucrative basis. I explained to him that in order to get into it any deeper than I already was, I would have to resign from the bureau, which I did not choose to do at that time. I later learned that this individual was used on a regular basis by a lieutenant to check out newer employees.

The second incident occurred one evening in the hospital. It was my Friday (it had nothing to do with what day it was, it was merely my last work day of that week) and I made a comment to the extent that I got off in thirty minutes on this Friday and would be headed toward the front door. Two or three inmates were standing there. One of them, Inmate Freemon, said, "Yes, you'll be going out and drinking some Scotch and we won 't have anything at all here. You should bring us a bottle."

I informed him, "Be most happy to. You put a million dollars in a Swiss checking account in my name, and I'll be happy to bring you a pint of Scotch of your choice."

Freemon said, "You can make that kind of money, but you have to bring in something a little more than Scotch."

I explained, "Nope, first thing I want is that million dollars in a Swiss checking account that I can draw monies from, because when I bring you that bottle of Scotch in, I'm going to go up and tell the Lieutenant where the Scotch is located, who has it, and walk out the door. I have no intention of picking up one of these numbers. I will just get my million dollars and leave." We both laughed about it, but he made his point that if I was interested in making extra money, I could contact him, and he would be glad to pay off for me bringing drugs in. And I let him know—clearly—I wasn't interested, and that ended that conversation.

To become involved in inmate drug deals or trafficking in drugs or alcohol in any institution, as I understand it, was reasonably easy. Another young black officer had reputedly been bringing in assorted whiskeys and selling to the inmates at twenty-five dollars a pint. I remember before any investigation got too deep, the staff member resigned and went into the military. This was difficult for me to believe and/or comprehend in view of the fact that this young black officer was on his way up. He suffered a slight setback in his upward mobility when he called in sick to go out on the golf course and play golf with the captain. The captain was unhappy when he found out the next day that the officer had been on sick leave when he was playing golf.

While there was a certain amount of entrapment effort on the part of some of the inmates toward staff who chose to deal in drugs, the relationship between inmates and staff remained consistently at a fairly high level. When a staff member was sitting in the office reading over a newspaper and a supervisor would approach, an inmate would run up and ask for a cake of soap or some other item just to let the staff member know that he should put the paper down. When the staff member would bust an inmate on a legitimate bust, the inmate would generally deny all charges and explain to the lieutenant that the officer must be mistaken or plain lying. When they left the lieutenant's office and headed toward the segregation building, the inmate would laugh and comment, "Well, you got me this time, boss. I'll beat you the next time." Again, these were not taken on a personal basis.

One supervisor (one of the first and better of the black supervisors) in the institution had a problem stuttering. When you took an inmate into the lieutenant's office for an offense, the supervisor would ask the officer to explain what was going on. After a brief explanation, the lieutenant would all the while stare at his feet, with his hands crossed behind him, and would then ask the inmate, "Wha-wha-wha-wha-what happened?" The inmate would generally run a big story on him about how another inmate had planted the marijuana or whatever it was in his pocket.

When the inmate completed his story, the supervisor would say, "Is tha-tha-tha-tha-that all?"

The inmate would then respond with words to the effect of, "Yes sir, boss, that's the truth. That's the gospel."

The lieutenant would lift his gaze from the floor, for the first time during the conversation, and say, "Lo-lo-lo-lock him up."

When an incident report was written on an inmate, he had a trial type hearing before the institution disciplinary committee. This was chaired by the AWC (associate warden, custody) or captain. It usually consisted of the case management coordinator and a manager. Under the leadership of AW Miligan, inmates all seemed to feel the hearing was fair. As a result of the vast knowledge of the inmate population by Mr. Miligan, he could look at the charges of any particular inmate and have some general knowledge as to what had in fact transpired, if anything. He would frequently tell the inmate, "I know you're guilty of this charge, and have done just what the officer has said you did. I'm going to give you thirty days in disciplinary segregation. I'm going to suspend that sentence for a period of six months. If you bring your sorry ass before me for any reason or get another incident report in the next six months, you're going to serve that thirty days before I ever hear the next damn charge." He rarely saw the inmate again and if he did, the inmate rarely complained; he knew he had been caught fairly, tried fairly, and was getting what he deserved.

After Mr. Miligan, there was not that in-depth knowledge or consistency. Lack of consistency made everyone feel cheated. On several occasions I have referred to unit managers. In 1973, there was no such animal. In 1976, when Mr. Jimmy Carter became president, he instituted the regionalization of all government agencies to include the Bureau of Prisons. With 20/20 vision looking back, this appeared to be a means of (1) upgrading and increasing management positions, (2) placing tighter control at a local level, and (3) an anti-union and anti-employee move of limiting the number of options which an employee could take upon termination.

As a representative of the local union, I wrote Senator Herman Talmadge complaining about the regionalization. The Bureau of Prison's regional office in Atlanta, Georgia, was costing the taxpayers in excess of one-million dollars per year. This was an estimated figure on my part as I had no access to cost. For these monies, no one in the regional office ever saw an inmate. It very rapidly had become another little paper-pushing game with each employee assigned to the regional office being responsible for coming up with a new program to justify that position. Between 1976 and 1980, paperwork in the institution multiplied on a daily basis. It very rapidly became necessary for any staff writing an incident report on an inmate to have at least two staff members to write a memorandum to document the truthfulness of the incident report.

It was during this period that management at all levels made an assault on employees. The attitude toward employees was that you were damn lucky to have a job. The decision of management at all levels was, "If you don't like the way you're treated here, get the fuck out; we've got plenty of applicants out on the street trying to get your job." During this period of time, Mr. Blackmon and his organization made the greatest assault on employees. At the same time, the union president was close, personal friends with the warden. As a result of this relationship, getting a grievance filed on the warden was extremely difficult, and getting union cooperation was equally difficult. One of the major difficulties during this era was the appearance of unjust rewards and lack of impartial treatment toward staff. Disciplinary action, like promotions, was run on a racism, favoritism, and nepotism basis.

A black employee caught sleeping on duty would get a letter of reprimand while a white officer would get a three-day suspension with all other things being equal. On the correctional force, black officers were being promoted with less experience or seniority. Outside of custody, in either mechanical services or industries, blacks had more difficulties in being selected to any job. These jobs were wage grade (skilled labor) positions rather than civil service. They were paid at a much higher grade.

In 1973, when I was employed at the Bureau of Prisons, the Atlanta facility employed less than five percent minorities. With the Civil Rights Act of 1976, efforts to increase this number of minority employees (specifically blacks) were made. For a long period of time, when ten employees came into the institution, nine would be black. By 1978, when ten employees would be promoted, five would be black. During this time of the five white employees getting promoted, there would be competition between employees who had five years working for the Bureau of Prisons, while black officers would be competing with other black officers who had been within the bureau for three years.

As a result of the advancement of the minorities, a personnel manager received national recognition for his progress in minority employment. Along with national recognition, he received a check for $1000. This award stimulated his efforts to push minorities at that time. For a long period of time, there was constant conflict between white and black employees; this conflict was not restrained by management officials. Finally, the realization sank in that all the conflict existed between the races; management was screwing both.

At the same time, the ratio of minority (black) employees on the correctional force was reaching an eighty to twenty percent ratio. Running the promotions at the same 50-50 ratio very quickly resulted in white employees being promoted at an earlier seniority than blacks. However, black employees having reached GS-8 senior officer specialists were being pushed into other institutions as GS-9 supervisors at a very high rate (in spite of the fact that many could not write a report) over white staff members. It was a commonly known and accepted fact that the Bureau of Prisons openly and blatantly discriminated in hiring and promotions on an age and racial basis. However, under the anti-union, anti-employee, lack of employee protection established under the Carter administration, there was nothing any employee could do about this. Whether it be right or wrong, the laws merely protected minorities in that era.

During that same era, it always struck me as humorous that J. B. Stoner, a white supremacist, and Hosea Williams, a black radical, would get on their soapboxes and say the same thing. The only difference in conversation was that J.B. Stoner was against all blacks while Hosea Williams was against all whites. Yet J. B. Stoner was considered a racial radical, and Hosea Williams was considered a civic leader. One black employee was found sleeping in an inmate bed in a cell locked in the segregation unit. (No inmate was assigned to that cell.) The black employee was given a verbal reprimand as a result of this. One black officer was found sleeping in a sleeping bag on a tower on a midnight to 8:00 shift. The supervisor bringing charges against him found the same situation the following night. Again, he brought charges and made every effort to terminate the employee.

As a result of this inattentiveness to duty and lack of concern for the security of the institution, the officer received a letter of reprimand in his personnel file. Shortly after, a white employee found sleeping on duty received a five-day suspension, and efforts were made to terminate him. As a result of this disparity in treatment, most supervisors began to turn their heads on any violation, and discipline within the facility became very shabbily run. The officer found sleeping in the sleeping bag on the tower two nights in a row was soon thereafter found to have a six-pack of beer and a TV in the tower while working. As a result of this action, he was terminated. As a result of the disparity in treatment between black and white staff, coupled with the complacent attitude toward employees and their working conditions, many employees stated that if Jack Blackmon was a preacher and was going to heaven, they did not want to be there.

Some young black officers who were promoted to a GS-8, senior officer specialist grade, as a result of the quota promotions were never assigned to OIC positions. As a result of their quick promotion, they had limited experience, and were believed to be unable to handle such duties. When assigned to an OIC post, another officer with greater experience would be assigned as his number 2 and would be expected to carry him.

Working as an OIC in B cell house day watch, I had my number 2 officer go to the break room and buy us a cup of coffee out of the vending machine. Upon his return to the unit, he advised me he had been stopped by a lieutenant and had been written up for being outside of his assigned area. I informed him not to worry about it, that I would take care of it for him. It was only two or three days after that that a labor-management meeting was scheduled, in which I was to participate. When going into the LMR meeting the agenda items were discussed. When asked if any additional items were to be discussed, I advised that there were indeed. I informed the management team that labor was requesting a fifteen-minute lunch break in the morning hours and a fifteen-minute paid break in the afternoon. Mr. Morik, AWC, advised that no way in hell was he to start relieving staff so they could have a fifteen-minute break in the morning and a fifteen-minute break in the afternoon. He advised that it was not only physically impossible, especially with those officers on the tower, but that was just a practice he was not going to allow to get started. I advised Mr. Morik that he obviously misunderstood; the fifteen-minute break was not a request, but a statement of federal law which we were merely asking them to start complying with.

I informed him that the federal labor law required any individual working as much as four hours to receive a fifteen-minute paid break time. Any individual working six hours would be required to be given one fifteen-minute paid break during the early part of that shift, and a thirty-minute non-paid break during the latter part of that shift. Any individual working between six and eight hours would be required to be given a fifteen-minute paid break in the early part, a thirty-minute non-paid break between three and five hours after entering on duty and a fifteen-minute paid break after the non-paid break. I explained to Mr. Morik that we were not trying to get something to which we were not entitled; all we wanted was what was required by the federal law. Mr. Morik still insisted that there would be no way in hell that they would authorize that in an institution, that such arrangement would have to be agreed to upon the master agreement, and there was no way they would agree to that action. Mr. Morik explained that staff had always had the availability to get a cup of coffee and drink it in the unit or take a semi-break on the job. However, he was not going to have anybody relieved.

I had succeeded in bringing Mr. Morik to the stream that I wanted him to drink from. I advised him that we had all been told in the past that there was no difficulty in one man leaving the unit getting a coffee or Coke or something to drink for officers working a cell house and bringing it back to the cell house for others to consume on the job. However, it was obvious that he had failed to notify his supervisors of this in the recent past. I assured Mr. Morik he could make up his mind which of the two he wanted. We were either going to be allowed to drink a cup of coffee on the job or be relieved to go off the job to get a cup of coffee. As for myself, I didn't particularly give a fuck which he decided to do, but we were not going to have our staff written up and disciplinary action coming as a result of their deciding not to decide. It was mutually agreeable by all that the staff would continue the past practice of one staff member going and getting a cup of coffee or Coke or something for additional staff and staff being able to drink a cup of coffee while on the job.

To this day I do not believe that Mr. Morik realized that federal labor law does not apply to federal employees. Even if it did, all of my research was never able to determine that such a labor law as previously explained ever existed. One of the things I had learned while working at the U.S. Penitentiary was that the bureau acted and reacted on intimidation. Fact, truth, reason, or other standards which usually apply, do not apply to the Bureau of Prisons and/or the U.S. Department of Justice (Just us). Mere intimidation is adequate. When becoming an employee of the Bureau of Prisons, maintaining the job for the first year is used as a club held over your head. After completing the training, any future promotions and/or your future career is used as a club over your head for intimidation. The Bureau of Prisons uses intimidation almost exclusively rather than positive reinforcement to motivate staff.

In 1979, the Congress passed a budget which called for the institution to be closed by 1982. When I started to work in 1973, we were told that the Atlanta facility would be closed before we retired. When discussing this with older staff who were nearing their retirement, we were informed, "Shit, they told me the same thing when I came on board." Now, it was law; Atlanta would be closed. The institution was in a state of panic, and everyone was pulling in different directions. Few employees believed that the warden was honest with them (when he did tell them something) and all were concerned about their individual survival. The institution was almost on automatic pilot while all looked for a life raft.

Low level staff were not aware of this decision to close the facility until it was announced by the local news media that the facility would close in 1982. The warden, Jack Blackmon, had a staff meeting with all employees. In the staff meeting, he explained that the institution would be closing and all inmates transferred from that facility. All staff would be required to submit a form requesting their three choices for transfer to other facilities and would be transferred as vacancies opened and our facility closed. Within the form to be submitted we were to give priorities on institutions we chose, first priority, second priority, and third choice. According to Mr. Blackmon, every effort would be made to see that every employee got their first choice. Mr. Blackmon assured us that he would keep us advised of every action as it came about.

In April 1980, I wrote Senator Herman Talmadge a letter requesting that he use his influence to assist in keeping those jobs in Georgia. I explained that not only the salary of the 400-plus employees were going into the local economy, but additional millions of dollars in food, commissary and supplies to maintain the facility. I received the following responses to this letter.

May 12, 1980

Dear Mr. Lawson,

This is in further reference to our previous correspondence regarding the closing of the United States Penitentiary at Atlanta.

Enclosed is a copy of the letter that I have received from Mr. Norman A. Carlson at the U.S. Bureau of Prisons relative to my inquiry on your behalf. I hope this information will be helpful to you.

Again, thank you for letting me hear from you. I hope that you will continue to stay in touch, and please do not hesitate to let me know whenever I might be of service to you in any way.

With every good wish, I am
Sincerely,
Herman E. Talmadge, U.S. Senator

May 5, 1980

Dear Senator Talmadge,

This is in response to your recent inquiry concerning Mr. Earl Lawson's letter on the closing of the United States Penitentiary at Atlanta.

We realize the closing of Atlanta may be a very difficult experience and personally disruptive to some of the personnel in the institution. In an effort to help mitigate the impact, we will offer jobs elsewhere to all employees who wish to remain with the Bureau. In addition, to whatever extent possible, we will assist those employees who prefer to remain in the Atlanta area in finding alternative employment.

It has been a long standing goal of the Bureau of Prisons to close the Atlanta Penitentiary. In addition, the Department of Justice (Just us) Authorization Act for Fiscal Year 1980 (Public Law 96-132) requires that the Attorney General develop a plan to close the penitentiary by September 1984. This plan will be submitted to Congress in September of 1980.

Atlanta is an antiquated, fortress-like prison built in 1902 when prisons were designed to isolate inmates physically and psychologically. Even if extensive renovation were undertaken, we still would have a structure unsuitable for current needs.

The cost of building a new 500-bed facility is considerably less than the cost of renovating Atlanta. For example, the Federal Correctional Institution at Talladega, Alabama which opened in September 1979 had a project cost of $13,700,000 while a staff review of the Atlanta facility indicated it would cost an estimated $44 million to bring Atlanta into compliance with existing standards. Although per capita costs are somewhat higher in smaller facilities, these costs are far-outweighed by the humane environments in which inmates live.

I hope this information is helpful. If I can be of further assistance, please let me know.

Sincerely,
Norman A. Carlson
Director, Federal Prison System

As each staff was required to submit a list of three choices for facilities we wanted to be transferred to, our local union began to fight the closure of the facility. The efforts were poorly organized, poorly directed, and fruitless. As the inmate population began to drop from near 2,000 to
1,000, the number of staff began to dwindle. It was obvious from the way that staff were being
transferred that transfers were being made by the same manner as hiring and promotions. The
only change was transfers were being made in the order of nepotism, favoritism, and then race.
As openings arose in facilities, some of the second or third generation employees would be promoted into those positions. Other fair-haired children would be selected for either promotion or
lateral transfer to a facility of their first choice. When neither of those would apply, a black had
priority consideration for either promotion or lateral transfer to a facility.

Last, but not least, was the get-back list. Many of the Atlanta staff did not want to leave Atlanta.
However, all were required to submit a letter of first, second, and third priority. Some of the officers were afraid not to make a legitimate list for fear of being transferred to a faraway position
such as Wisconsin, California, Minnesota, or a similar place at the last minute. Subsequently,
when the three priority considerations were not available to fill the slot, a person who was not
specifically a favorite of the management would be selected to a first choice even though he
did not desire to move. (Realizing the lack of popularity I enjoyed with Jack Blackmon, my first
choice was the regional office, Atlanta, Georgia, second choice Atlanta training facility, third
choice, any other DOJ facility in the Atlanta area.) It was obvious that seniority, job position, or
other factors were not included in consideration for transfer. Our local union attempted to get
the union president to file a grievance on the warden regarding his selection for transfer process,
but these efforts failed.

When efforts to get the union to file a grievance failed, efforts were made to impeach the
union president. However, these efforts failed. The union president was strongly supportive of
his close friend, the warden, who could muster more manpower in this crisis situation than line
staff. However, at the next election, the union president was voted out of office. As a result of that
election, the union president was promoted to a GS-9 position that was opened for him specifically. After he retired, that position was no longer needed. Additionally, that position maintained
the old union office, and the union was forced into smaller quarters.

To add to the frustration of the employees (and sometimes providing a whipping post to
release hostility) we began to get Cuban detainees. We had seen the tent city on Miami Beach,
heard of the emotional and criminal elements within the flotilla, but that had been Miami and
Ft. Chaffee, Arkansas. We had our own problems. Suddenly, we had fifty grown men who were
aggressive, explosive, uneducated, and to some extent, poorly toilet trained. We were assured
by Mr. Blackmon that this was only temporary; the Atlanta facility would close as scheduled.

During this period of time, it was learned by staff that while the racial statistics on the correctional force were similar to that of the local community, roughly 50-50 population, both races
were flagrantly being discriminated against by age. Management managed to keep screwing

both races and keep staff fighting among themselves. During 1980, CMS and Unicor wage grade employees who were paid higher salaries were primarily (and remain mostly) white. The correctional force which hires a greater number of employees upgraded a larger number of Blacks into management grades. In either position, once an employee reached age thirty-five, his eligibility for promotion was limited. The bureau sought a young work force and used promotions as a recruitment tool. A retired military officer attended seminary and became a Baptist minister. Although he had been a bureau employee for over five years, he received the following letter when applying for an open position as chaplain:

October 18, 1980

Dear Reverend Jackson,

May this acknowledge receipt of and thank you for your recent correspondence concerning the federal chaplaincy.

Your background and credentials are certainly impressive, and you will be a welcome addition to any correctional ministerial department. Unfortunately, due to the fact that you have completed your 35th birthday, the Federal Prison System is unable to offer you employment, either as a staff chaplain or as a chaplain trainee.

Since you have asked about prison ministry in general, perhaps you would be interested in pursuing a career within some state or local correctional system. It is my understanding that the Federal Prison System is the only one that has an age limitation for hiring chaplains. It could prove beneficial to contact the administrators of chaplaincy departments in those locations proximate to your home.

I am disappointed that we are unable to be of more assistance to you. Be assured that the ministry you are seeking is a wonderful apostolate. May you be continually blessed as you work for the spiritual welfare of the incarcerated.

Sincerely,
Richard A. Houlahan, OMI
Administrator of Chaplaincy Services
Federal Prison System

I attempted to get Mr. Jackson to bring EEO charges against the Department of Justice (Just us), but he declined. He lost respect for Mr. Blackmon when Mr. Blackmon made a promise to him that he failed to keep.

In preparation for the closing, E cell house was the first unit to be closed. As inmates were moved from other units for transfer, those housed in E were moved to those bed spaces. After E cell house was completely locked up and secured, B cell house began to be closed. After B cell house was closed, A cell house was closed. The industries were in a transition of being dismantled and transferred to other institutions. Staff, too, was dwindling as jobs were being transferred.

As our population count dropped below 800 American inmates, Fort Chaffee, Arkansas was destroyed in a riot. Initially, we began to get a few detainees sprinkling into our institution (supposedly for a short term) to be held until other housing could be located. When Fort Chaffee, Arkansas, burned, we were advised that we would be getting 300 Cuban detainees. The rumor was that the regional director, Mr. Mckensie, had called Jack Blackmon and advised him that he would be getting 300 Cuban detainees. Mr. Blackmon responded that we had been tearing the beds down, and he was not sure how long it would take to have the beds ready for those detainees. The rumor was that Mr. Mckensie informed him that he *would* have the beds the following day; the Cubans were already on their way to the airport. The next day we received 300 Cuban detainees. Even then, the Cubans were going to be held for a very short time; the institution was closing.

The first Cuban detainees who arrived in the Atlanta facility were violent. For the most part, manners and sanitation among them were nonexistent. They were an ingeniously creative group who could accomplish more with *nothing* than anyone had been aware of to that point. It is extremely difficult to describe the detainee population without one thinking that you are describing each individual. Every emotion and action was magnified in each individual. When they were happy, they were very happy. When they were sad, they were very sad. When they were violent, they were very violent. All of these heightened emotions could be expressed within a five-minute period of time with nothing else having changed. A Cuban detainee could be laughing and joking with you one moment and swinging at you the next, and you would never understand why.

When an assault against staff was made, many times halfway in the middle of what an American would consider the middle of the fight, the detainee would say, "I quit," and for him the fight was over. At that time, he would allow himself to be handcuffed and never raise a finger toward anyone else. He would then say, "I'm sorry, Papa; you got a cigarette for me?" It was extremely difficult for the American staff to become adapted to the Cuban population.

By October 1980, the workload had increased beyond the staff available to fill the posts. As overtime became available, only a few staff were being provided with the opportunity to work overtime. On November 1, 1980 I wrote a letter to the local union president stating that, while some employees were working as many as 104 hours a week, others were getting no overtime. The overtime sign-up roster was being used only to fill sick-call and last-minute posts. The known vacancies were filled on a favoritism basis. As a result of my continued efforts on this issue, management officials made an agreement with the union president that they would give him his choice on the three jobs and shift that he chose on overtime, if he did not fight the overtime issue.

This practice continued until the few officers began to burn out. I had signed up to work specific shifts on particular days. The first time, I was called at 5:00 a.m. to work seg at 7:45 a.m. I came in and worked that post overtime on my day off. A couple of weeks later, I was called on working days and got a call to work B cell house from 4:00 to 12:00 midnight. I refused and informed the lieutenant just to remove my name from the overtime roster. Many of the other staff had done the same thing and as the few got burned out, management could not fill some posts. For a short term, supervisors attempted to install mandatory overtime one day a week on the employee's day off. This resulted in a higher rate of sickness and was quickly discontinued.

As the Cuban population rose, so did the overtime. Very quickly, all staff, even those in CMS and industries, were being asked to work all of the overtime possible. Staff could (and some did) work seven days a week, sixteen hours a day. Employees were not only working long hours but were being physically abused by the detainees as well as psychologically abused by management. Several staff earned more money than the warden during 1982 and 1983.

One of these men was due for promotion. Just before his promotion board, when he was expecting to be promoted, he got a write-up for sleeping on duty. He was threatening to sue, claiming that he had never slept on duty. Six months or so later, I was working 4:00 to 12:00 in the rear corridor. Near midnight, that same officer called to see who the supervisor was that would be coming on duty. When told that the same supervisor was working over he responded, "Good, he will not be out tonight. You can't work both shifts without taking a nap."

The Cuban population made knives (shanks) from items which the American inmates would throw away while trying to find something to make a weapon from. From the third, fourth, and fifth range of each cellblock, we had a 1/8 inch steel mesh screen around the outside of each range. This was to prevent anybody or anything from being thrown over on staff. The Cubans very slowly would tear a piece of that steel wire off in sections of three to nine inches, sharpen a point and have a knife. They would take a rag and make a handle on the other end. They would take a broom handle and very slowly file it down into a point on the concrete floor. Anything that was solid could be converted into a weapon. For the first two years, staff ran from one fire to another fire without time for rest. We started feeding the Cuban population at 6:00 a.m. By the time the 8:00 a.m. shift reported for duty, staff had responded to as many as a dozen body alarms. At the same time these activities were on-going, a majority of the inmate detainee population was desirous of the opportunity to please staff.

The Cuban population did not by any means understand the American form of corrections. In 1982 or 1983, a riot occurred in Indiana. This riot resulted in the American inmate population in that state facility holding hostages for three or four days. The Cubans laughed at this situation and kept close contact with what was going on. They could not understand prison riots; they thought this was the funniest thing they had ever seen. When asked if they had ever had a riot in Cuba, they all responded, "Oh yes, there was one." I asked how long that riot had occurred and was told seven minutes. To that I laughed and informed them that no riot could be considered a riot and last only seven minutes. I was informed that that's how long it took the guards to get the machine guns. *Dat-dat-dat-dat,* and the riot was finished.

There have been no more riots in Cuban prisons after that. I asked this question of a large number of Cuban detainees in different areas within the institution. I got the same story and same response from everyone I asked. The Cubans were willing to cooperate, believing that positive behavior would result in positive consideration for release. Those Cubans who were consistently receiving incident reports. They could not understand how an inmate could throw urine or feces on an officer, assault or cut an officer, or cut another detainee, or commit any other prohibited act and receive a pink piece of paper. It was not until two years later when they began to go to the INS panel and found that the INS panel had a yellow copy of all of their pink forms, that they understood the purpose of incident reports. After that, for a short time, it was quiet and peaceful within the facility and few incident reports were written. Those that were written were usually of more serious magnitude.

During periods of 1982 and 1983, detainees were placed in segregation for a week or two to a month or two without an incident report being written. While such action is against policy, we had so much going that we were unable to handle the activity. Even with staff coming from other institutions to Atlanta for a thirty-day TDY period we did not have enough help. If a detainee committed an act which routinely got them placed in seg for a month (thirty days) we would take them to seg and ask that he be held for thirty days and then kicked out and back to his cell. During that period of time, many of the detainees were literally housebroken and domesticated. As one employee stated, "When you've got the son of a bitch locked in his cell, he stands on his commode and takes his shit. While taking his shit he reaches over to get his tobacco, rolls him a cigarette, puts the hand-rolled cigarette in his mouth and then reaches over and tears a corner off his sheet and then wipes his ass, climbs off the commode, pulls his pants up, buttons them, and then reaches up, gets two electrical wires and holds them together lighting the cigarette from the sparks, what in the fuck are you going to do with him? Within all of that, he exists as happy as if he had his own right mind."

Those Cubans, having newly arrived in the Atlanta facility and having just rioted in Fort Chaffee, Arkansas, were militant by nature. Initially, they were opened up at a quarter range (five cells per quarter range) every time to go to the dining hall. This was approximately thirty detainees all fighting to be first in line. These detainees would fill a cafeteria-type tray running over on all sides with rice. Those who could not eat it all in one sitting would take the rice and put it in their pockets. They would then transport it to their cell house where they would take it out of their pockets and put it in their locker. In a short time, getting rid of the roaches was extremely difficult. The roaches, flies, or other insects did not affect the rice; the detainees still ate it when they got hungry. One associate warden got extremely excited when he went into the dining room looking around and found the floor feeling rather greasy. As he looked around and went into the dish room, where pots and pans and trays were being washed, he found a Cuban detainee taking a shit in a number-ten can.

Another difference between the American inmate and the Cuban detainee was the desire to touch. With the American inmate, there may be an occasional pat on the back from either the staff or the inmate, if an appropriate basis had been established. The Cuban detainees had not been permitted to come within reach of the Cuban guard. According to the detainees, and the Cuban penal system, the guards did not enter the cellblock. The strongest of the Cubans became the cell house boss. The guard told him what he wanted and accomplished the goal. When the guard did, in fact, walk through the cell house, he carried a machete with him. If any prisoner got within reach of the machete, he got cut. Most of the Cuban detainees housed in the Atlanta facility had scars on or about their body. Most (whether it be true or not is unknown) claimed that these cuts had been inflicted by guards of Cuban prisons. Initially, the detainees remained on lockdown status for the most part. We were still in the process of shipping out the American population. I was in charge of C cell house, which was to be the last cell house to cell house American inmates.

As we began to build up the Cuban population, the legal minds determined that it would be necessary to maintain American inmates as long as we had Cubans there. The logic behind this was that it would not be fitting and proper (legal) to shoot a Cuban detainee for escape. However, as long as there was one American inmate housed in that facility, the officer was not expected to be able to identify whether it was an American inmate or a Cuban on the wall. Keeping American inmates housed in that facility justified keeping the towers open and preventing the population from escaping. As a result of this decision, the inmates were transferred to the dorm units, and additional American inmates were brought in.

While feeding one quarter (five cells or up to forty detainees) approximately twenty staff members formed two lines funneling them down into one line feeding into the serving lane, to control the crowd being served. As one quarter range got fed, a second quarter range would be let out. This continued until the one complete range was in the dining room. As a result of the aggressive and assaultive behavior, no more than one range was allowed out at a time initially.

One of the things that fascinated the American staff was when a fight broke out in the dining hall. When Americans were there and a fight occurred, the entire dining room became involved. When the Cubans were there and a fight started, it rarely expanded beyond the two individuals fighting. One detainee eating would jump back out of the way grabbing his tray, watching the fight while continuing to eat. When his table was cleared he would sit back down at the table and continue eating and watching the fight. For the most part, when staff broke in and stopped the fight, both detainees were prepared to stop. On occasion, one would be still quite angry and would continue fighting, even with staff. Even with that, others would not join the fight.

CHAPTER 7

WELCOME TO THE HOTEL ATLANTA

WHEN THE CUBAN DETAINEES FIRST ARRIVED IN ATLANTA, they claimed they were going to take over the Atlanta facility just as they had Fort Chaffee. The American inmates and Cuban detainees were separated at all times. The detainees indicated they were going to take over the unit where the American inmates were housed, come down and rescue the American inmates. The detainees claimed they were going to break into the American housing unit and release all Americans from their cells. The American inmates informed staff that staff needed to get the hell out of the way if the Cubans ever came into their cell house. They claimed that they would resolve the problem. They were not going to be part of the Cuban take-over; they were going to kill every one of those bastards. I explained to the American inmates that I was not going to do an excessive amount of shaking down for weapons. In view of the hostile nature of the detainees, I could not blame the American inmates for wanting to protect themselves.

However, I did request that any American inmate with a weapon in his possession or any-where where he had access or knowledge of such weapon, to leave the weapon in open view so it could be picked up and destroyed before Cubans were moved into the housing unit and upon release of the American inmate from that unit. American inmates felt slighted because of the limited access they had to the dining hall, restrictions on the recreation area, and the fact that the Cuban detainees would steal from the American population at every available oppor-tunity. In the beginning, the American inmates were very good to the Cuban detainees. They would stand around their rear quarter area and outside the locked bar type gate as the detainees would go to their lunch. They would give the detainees cigarettes (the detainees had no money in the commissary account and could not purchase cigarettes at that time) and generally be friendly to the Cuban detainees. However, some of the Cuban detainees would be walking by on the way to the dining hall, reach over and grab a watch off the wrist of an American inmate. The inmates would be standing by the bars, and detainees would walk by and spit on them. As a result of this negative behavior, it was only a short time until the American inmates became openly hostile toward the detainees.

Many of the daily activities and routine activities within the institution were extremely frustrating for the employees. While a majority of the Cuban detainees had a desire to please the officers and were willing workers, getting them directed to completing a task in an appropriate manner satisfactory to staff was difficult. Simple tasks like mopping the floor in a housing unit were extremely frustrating. The mop bucket, an eighteen-inch by four-foot cart on wheels, was divided into two sections. The American inmate would put hot, soapy water in one section and clean water in the other section. With several inmates mopping, a group would take the hot soapy water and mop the floor with soapy water. Another group would take the clear water and rinse the floor. As the mop water got dirty, the soapy water would be emptied, and the clear water would have soap added. Clear water would be then placed in the empty tank. They would repeat this process three or four times to mop a large cell house. All efforts to train the Cuban detainees to do this failed. The Cuban detainees would fill the bucket (both sides) with soapy water. One detainee would then take his hand and splash water onto the floor. All others would mop the floor dry.

The detainees had to be directly ordered and closely supervised in order to get them to change the water no matter what size area they were mopping. If not ordered and supervised, the mops would never be washed. Immediately upon their arrival into the Atlanta facility, English-speaking detainees were pulled from the cell and made orderlies. If none of the detainees in the area spoke English, those who displayed a more positive attitude (more manageable) were used as orderlies. I am mostly convinced that, if at that time the U.S. government had established a prerequisite of walking around the institution on their hands without falling, promising they would then be released, we would have had all our detainees walking on their hands. Although there was a cultural difference and language barrier, most detainees generally wanted to appease staff. The Cuban detainees would work much harder, much longer periods of time, and expect much less in return than their American counterparts. Those who were not assigned as orderlies or to other details spent much of their time locked in a cell. As a result of the large number of hours on lockdown basis, the detainees had to be run down and secured in their cell after being let out for any meal. When we opened them up to go to the dining hall, they went with no difficulty. They would return from the dining hall to the unit with no difficulty either. However, upon reaching the cell house they would run the ranges, visiting with friends.

Again, staff were working sixteen hours a day and as many as seven days a week when possible. While the staff had been reduced during the planned closure of the facility, the destiny of the U.S. Penitentiary, Atlanta, Georgia was still in question. Subsequently, there was no major drive to reinstate employees or reinforce the complement of staff. While there was consistent hiring going on, dealing with the Cuban population was much more draining. As a result of these efforts and coupled with the low salary for such hazards, Atlanta was suffering a high turnover rate. Shortage of staff resulted in a large number of hours by staff, a large turnover resulted in a larger number of unskilled guards, and Cubans on lockdown status a large number of hours with no means of releasing their energies all came together to build an explosive situation in the compound. As the detainee population continued to climb, it was evident that the Atlanta staff could no longer maintain control of the institution. Subsequently, correctional officers from other facilities were brought in on a thirty-day period TDY from other institutions.

The Atlanta management staff, in its typical high-handed manner, attempted to ride rough shod over the TDY staff from their first entry into our institution. Those officers were out in a motel away from the institution and with limited transportation. As a result of this, they had to be prepared to leave the motel one to one and a half hours prior to time to report to work. Additionally, after getting off duty, they had to wait until the last man was relieved before returning to the motel via institution carpool van. Additionally, management insisted that they be housed in rooms two or three employees to a room, whereas this is not authorized or ordered by bureau policy. Many of these employees were not volunteers. They were ordered to be in Atlanta and away from their family. The sleeping arrangement was unsatisfactory in view of the fact that some working different shifts and being assigned to the same room would not permit anyone to get any sleep. When complaints were lodged by some of the employees, our management staff, in their infinite wisdom, ordered three different staff members to return to their home institution and made efforts to bring charges against them. These efforts failed as a result of complaints being lodged by all other employees. After a very short time, the employees were housed in single rooms as directed.

On a thirty-day basis, the employee could not become aware of the culture of the Cuban population. The Cuban population did not become familiar with the temporary officers and insisted upon Atlanta staff members being there to issue orders. While this would have caused limited difficulty with an American inmate, the Cuban population had no *carrots* which we could dangle over their heads. They were basically sentenced to life imprisonment with no parole, unless returned to Cuba. Subsequently, if they, as a group, decided they did not want to do something, we could not lock them all up. They were disrupted by the fact that staff coming from other institutions were coming and expecting difficulties as per stories returning to the institution via other returning TDY staff. When one enters any correctional facility expecting trouble, it is rarely long before he finds it. Atlanta was no exception, especially with the Cuban population.

The Cuban population, being more highly strung, was more susceptible to exploding. Staff working all the overtime hours they chose, being tired, TDY staff being hostile because of being forced into an environment which they were uncomfortable with, made staff to be almost as explosive as the detainees. Additionally, as if this was not enough, there was still no resolution as to the status of the Atlanta facility. As far as the Atlanta staff knew, they would be transferring to other facilities, and the Atlanta facility would be closed. It was a matter of merely relocating the detainees to other institutions. After Mr. Blackmon had promised he would keep us abreast of any decisions made concerning the closure of the facility, we never heard anything else from him. All other information came via the inmate grapevine, which for the most part was rather accurate.

As a result of all the aforementioned difficulties, the detainees assaulting staff and/or staff overreacting to situations was commonplace. One officer stepped into a rest room in A cell house to take a leak. While standing there, taking a piss, a detainee reached over from the outside and cut him in the back. By the time he could zip up and look out the door, nobody was there. When a new group of detainees arrived from another facility, (usually as a result of a major disturbance at the other facility) our staff made it very clear that we would not tolerate such behavior in our facility. The Cuban population, not unlike the American population, was not familiar with and did not approve of being strip searched. For them, to take off all their clothes, bend over, spread their cheeks for someone to look up their ass, was an attack upon their masculinity. Since this was the policy and procedure of the Atlanta facility (and all other federal facilities) to search all body cavities of any inmates leaving or entering the facility, R and D was a hot staff.

When Cuban detainees were being received in R and D, every effort to make adequate staffing available was made. When the detainee bucked at being strip shook, there was no hesitation and reservation in tearing off every stitch of his clothes. He was ordered in his native language to remove all clothing, and it was explained why the strip search was taking place. When he refused to comply, all force necessary was used to get immediate compliance. Usually, only one detainee per busload had to be strip shook manually. While there was no desire nor effort to harm or injure the detainee, this was used as an opportunity to allow him and others to see that any order of staff would be followed. As a result of this method, many future difficulties were resolved in R and D. One of the things the Cuban population learned early was how to count. When a Cuban detainee became aggressive or assaultive toward the staff, it was only moments before he was well outnumbered. The Cubans were never treated in a brutal manner by staff. However, they were treated in a more physical manner than the American inmates because that was what they responded to, and the potential for civil lawsuits at every corner were less prevalent.

Some of the American inmates who spit on the staff would then run to the courts every time the staff retaliated for being spit on. (When the older convicts acted aggressively toward staff, they expected physical reprisal. The inmates, usually on short sentences, acted as though they were the victim because they were in jail. Their aggressive acts toward staff were defensive, and staff were being paid to take it.) Subsequently, the Bureau of Prisons expected staff to resolve all difficulties without physical contact of any type, which might be conceived as a retaliatory action. You were not to put your hand on the inmate unless absolutely necessary and at that time you were only to restrain movement of the inmate. The Cuban detainee (much like the old American convict) expected to get the hell slapped out of him when he spit on you. Failure to take such action would mean permanent loss of control of the detainee. Any staff who failed to display "manly attributes" received no respect and had no control over any of the population.

Equally, when you said or did something that the detainee felt to be unfair, he perceived it to be his manly obligation to retaliate. As a result of the cultural difference, many of these assaults took place. Once this aggressive act (protecting of the manhood) was accomplished, the Cuban detainee held no hostility or bitterness toward staff.

One stocky detainee, who had long hair and a full beard and was called Jesus, had strong emotional difficulties. As a result of this, he was on strong medication and anti-depressants. Realizing that Jesus was having emotional difficulty, I made it a point every time I saw him to stop and talk to him. This would be a very short simple conversation such as, "How are you today, everything okay with you, are you getting enough to eat?" or similar conversation. After a short time, he accepted me as a friend. When seeing me coming, he would come out of his way and say, "Hey, amigo, how are you today?"

On one occasion I was in the cell house and encountered difficulty with another detainee. Although this was before AIDS was prominent, I was convinced the man was dying with AIDS. This man was approximately ninety-pounds soaking wet. Every time he came back from the dining hall we had to physically force him into his cell. On one evening when my temper was not as strong as usual, I started taking him physically to his cell. With this, the detainee turned and grabbed, with both hands, under my throat. He started pushing and squeezing as hard as he could. This effort and pressure equated to a little less than the average five or six-year-old would use. For some unknown reason, his useless effort struck me as funny and I started to laugh. However, Jesus came by and saw this. Jesus did not think this was funny at all. If I had not stepped up and stopped Jesus, he would have killed that man. Even after I calmed Jesus down, he still made it very clear to the detainee that I was his friend and that he did not allow anybody to assault his friend. The detainee then went on to his cell without further difficulty. After that, I never had any more difficulty from that detainee.

When the Cuban detainees first arrived in the Atlanta facility, there was limited to no educational or vocational training available (we were still in the process of closing the facility). After the number of detainees reached 800 to 1,200 and continued to climb, it was obvious that we were going to have detainees for some time. At this time some educational programs were developed but not required. When vocational programs started for the Cuban detainees they consisted of various activities such as landscaping. Landscaping was, in fact, how to push a lawn mower. They taught them how to wash pots and pans and clean floors in the food service area. There was no effort to prepare any detainee for potential release.

Not only did we limit the number of training programs available, we cited no purpose for such training, showed no usefulness for any participation on the part of the detainees. Basically, the Cuban detainees seemed to understand and accept their plight. Those who were criminally insane (and there were many) understood their potential for release was limited. Others recognized the fact that they must prove themselves worthy of a release. They were willing to stay in the institution and do whatever was necessary to effect a release. They identified their behavior and ability to participate in programs with a better opportunity for release. However, after two to three years, they found this not to be true. We taught them the American philosophy that the squeaky wheel gets the grease. Some of the more hardcore convict-type inmates became more manipulative. There would be kingpin leaders and every illicit activity going on in the unit. At the same time, they would be very supportive of staff and give the appearance of doing what staff wanted at all times. Additionally, they would become snitches for supervisors or the OIC.

Detainees who were strong-arming other detainees and were creating problems within the unit were being released. Those detainees who were doing those details they were assigned, doing all that was asked, and were working on their own time to prepare themselves for eventual release, were not being released. After two or three years of realization as to what was happening, we again started encountering difficulties. The detainees maintained their culture even inside our regulations. While we had a laundry to wash clothing, they found that was not dependable, and their personal clothing would be either lost or taken. Subsequently, most of their laundry was done in the cell. The detainees would take their bedding, pants, shirts, and underclothes and put it in a five-gallon bucket. They would go to the shower dressed to wash their clothes. They would then make a clothesline by stretching a rope (torn sheet) across the cell and hang their clothes on it to dry. This was against bureau policy because it blocked the views.

Since it was against policy, disruptive, and left us concerned about the potential of activities going on behind the clotheslines, we would go in and cut them down. However, after finding the same situation in every cell, cutting down the clotheslines in every cell, only to find that they were put right back up and the clothes still hanging, this was given up as a wasted cause. The detainees continued their practice of hanging their clothes. They would take their bath from the commode and mop the cell with the soapy water they spilled on the floor. Another practice commonplace with the Cubans was hanging a blanket between the upper cot and lower cot on their bunk beds. This was prohibited also, and initially brought immediate response. However, after cutting them down fourteen times per day per double bed and the realization that you can't put everybody in segregation, this became an acceptable practice. Subsequently, they continued to make their bedrooms on the lower bunk.

Prior to late 1981, in early 1982, the Cuban detainees could not understand the American system of corrections. They had the understanding that should one follow the procedures as outlined by the staff and follow all regulations. Then they stood a much better chance of being released into society. This was the extent of their understanding; most attempted to comply with this understanding. As best as I could understand from the Cuban population, in the Cuban correctional facilities the officers or staff entered the housing units only to get a person out. The staff carried a machete on their hip, and any detainee who got within reach of the Cuban guard with the machete got cut. In the dining hall, food was put on the table for all of the inmates. It was served on a first come, first served basis. Those who were unable to get to the table before they ran out of food were left hungry. In many cases, the physically stronger (called the "Jefe" or *boss* in English) controlled who went first to the dining hall and who did not. While allowing some of the weaker to go first, the cell was rewarded by having their chow brought to them, along with work and sexual favors. By controlling such favors, they maintained control of the housing units.

In the American facilities the stronger wanted to be the "Jefe" for the officers, that is, wanted to run the unit with the officers' blessings. Officers would only allow a "lead orderly" within the unit. The lead orderly, *Jefe*, ensured that the entire unit was clean. The Jefe then supervised the other inmates and checked over each of the areas, a job which staff was supposed to do. As a Jefe, they were given special privileges by these officers. The special benefits were not much different from those in Cuba. For instance, they were allowed to bring food in from the dining hall and store it in their cell. They were allowed to stay out later than other detainees and have special TV privileges. They could then convert the extra food or TV privileges by moving the TV to a particular angle or to a particular channel and convert these favors into sexual favors or other benefits such as carrying weapons for them. Not only the lead orderly, but all other orderlies would transport weapons from one cell to another for their friends. In return, friends would hold their weapons for them. Any orderly caught with a weapon in his possession or any cell which housed orderlies possessing a weapon would result in all orderlies being terminated immediately.

By late 1981, and early 1982, the detainees expected to be rewarded. By this, they were expecting to be released to the street for positive behavior. However, this did not come to pass. Many of the orderlies would strong-arm other detainees, use their position to steal from other orderlies in the unit while the other orderlies were on the job, set up other detainees (or have other detainees set up another man) by placing a weapon in their bed and then reporting such weapon to the OIC. Subsequently, those individuals, by setting up other detainees or strong-arming other detainees, were forwarded privileges which did, in fact, include early release. They followed the principle that the squeaky wheel gets the grease. In many cases, those who created the most problems were kicked out of the institution the earliest.

By 1982, the detainees were going before a panel. Such an appearance was limited to a mere sham. The panel had before them a packet which included any documents which the detainee could obtain from outside the institution. It also included an annual progress review of work and confinement. This review, in many cases, was made without benefit of input from the detainee, the detainee's employer, the unit officers, and was made in the comfort of an air-conditioned office. It also included the incident reports, if any, that the detainee may have received. Not only did the case managers preparing the progress review (in many cases) not contact the detainee, but they concealed themselves in an area where the detainees could not contact them. The detainees were informed of the review on a call-out sheet, that is, on Monday afternoon, the call out would come out for them to appear at 9:30 a.m. or 9:00 a.m. the following morning for the panel. Even in spite of his limited knowledge, the detainee could not take a witness before the INS panel with him. Even a staff member such as myself was unable to go before the panel with any of the detainees who may have slept in the quarter, was working or worked on my detail.

Many of the detainees were harassed and joked with or were teased by the immigration panel. The panel was not conducted in a professional manner, and the detainees did not feel that the panel had the slightest bit of concern that it was their life and future at stake.

Once getting by this hurdle, the problem then began. When the hearing was concluded, the chairperson for the panel or the hearing judge for immigration would inform the detainee that he would be getting a notice back from Washington with a decision. After a few weeks, the detainees would, in fact, get a response back from Washington. In many cases the response would state that the individual would be released on a particular date, which would usually be two to three months in the future. However, as this date got nearer, they would be advised that they would be unable to be released at that time. One of the conditions of release was that each detainee be released to a halfway house. No halfway house space was available to the detainees. A limited number of halfway houses providing for release of the Cuban detainees had sole choice whether to accept or not accept any detainee. Additionally, space was extremely limited in these facilities as a result of the demands placed on the facilities by government regulations.

One Cuban detainee working for me on the Labor-1 detail advised me that he was supposed to have been released in July 1983. (These dates may very well be far from correct and are unimportant as far as accuracy within the month or year.) The contact with Fendora was made in September 1983. He explained to me that he was supposed to have been released in July, but then it would be early October. Early in October, he advised me that they had again postponed his release and that it would be November. In November, Fendora advised me that he was growing very angry and was afraid he was going to do something drastic. He would not again be released in November and had no idea when he might, in fact, be released. The contact in immigration concerning the November date said he would not be released at that time because they could not find a place for him. At that time, I went to INS on behalf of detainee Fendora.

I spoke to the panel who explained that they were trying with two or three separate halfway houses to get him released but had been unable to find one that would accept him. However, they assured me he would be released by early December. I went back to Fendora and explained to Fendora this information. In early December when he was not released, and no contact was made with him, he again went to INS and was unable to obtain any information. Subsequently, he again came to me. I then went back to INS and questioned them concerning the information they had given me. They advised me that as a result of the upcoming holidays they would not be able to get him out before until after the close of the year, probably the middle of January. I expressed my dissatisfaction with their passing on erroneous and false information to the detainees in this manner. I explained they were placing not only their lives, but the lives of other detainees and the staff in jeopardy by continuously providing false and erroneous information to the detainees.

In early 1984 I received another job assignment. However, when walking through the compound I saw the detainee still on the same job. I called him aside and asked him what happened concerning his release. He informed me, "I don't know. Immigration say they got no place for me!"

"You mean they still have no place to release you to?"

"I don't know. I no got no problem with no officer, but sometimes I think if I get a knife I go kill a Immigration. Sometimes I think maybe I kill myself. I don't know. I just want to get out of jail and go to my family." This time I understood his aggravation thoroughly and shared that aggravation. During the period of working at the penitentiary I learned one thing. Never lie to an inmate. I have found in working with the inmates that you can slap them, cuss them, or whatever, but don't lie to them. That is the one unforgivable sin that you never live down.

Again, I returned to the immigration officer that informed me of release. I informed him in no uncertain terms how useless he was in my opinion. I explained to him that they were programming all of the detainees to fail, allowing none of them an opportunity to go onto the street and be successful. By the time a release became available, frustration by the detainee created hostility toward all forms of authority. I explained to the INS that at least he could have the guts to tell the detainee that he was not going to be released. The fact that he was planning to lie to the detainee was bad enough, but lying to staff and lying to me was even worse. I explained that I would write to Washington and the immigration office and express my dissatisfaction with the manner in which they were handling the job. I explained that I felt sure they were probably not really concerned about my overreacting and did not give a damn about my views, but such a complacent attitude on the part of the government representative was in my opinion inexcusable.

"You sit here and tell the detainee that there is a chance for a release to the street. Washington then sends him a letter that he is going to New Orleans on October 15. On October 30 you tell him that he could not go to New Orleans, make a joke and send him back to his unit. Then you take your sorry ass out of this protected area and go home. When this all builds up and explodes on an officer, you're not around; you wind the bomb up, turn it loose, and then go hide under your blankets. We end up fighting with these bastards because INS plays these silly ass games. The more that I talked, the angrier I got. It finally dawned upon me that I was making an ass of myself about something that he probably had no more control over than I. He was very apologetic for misinforming me, but these conditions were beyond his control. He did state that he was sure he would be able to have Fendora out of the facility within the next forty-five days. I never did write the letter to the INS, but Fendora was released. Three of the detainees who knew Fendora talked to me while he was detained in our facility and maintained contact with Fendora, showed me pictures they had received of him.

Fendora's case is not unique. During the period between 1980 and 1987, this was a regular practice for most detainees. As a result of the release pattern, many of the detainees who had been released were returned to our facility. Several of the detainees who had been released to the street from our facility should never, in fact, have been released on any street anywhere in the world. However, many of the detainees could have been released onto the street and then trained to be productive citizens.

Because of difficulties during that period of time and, especially the riots on November 1, 1984 and November 23, 1987, a major problem was the lack of effort by the U.S. government to distinguish between those inmates. Additionally, during that period of time, no effort was made to train the detainee in the development of a suitable release plan.

In 1983, when the hearings began full force, only a few of the detainees were openly and frequently displaying negative behavior. Those individuals who, as previously indicated, should never have been released on any street in the world, should never have been housed in a correctional facility either. However, as a result of their status within the US, coupled with their extremely aggressive behavior, there was no place else for them either. When most of the detainees had become Americanized through the correctional facility, realizing that the pen was used to control rather than the stick, our jobs became easier. Additionally, we made our jobs easier through accepting those behaviors within the Cuban population which we could not change. The staff began to accept the transvestite and homosexual behavior of the detainees, while the detainees became less assaultive toward staff. In 1984, the frustration was again beginning to build in the population.

In 1984, we began to receive several of the detainees who had been released on the street back into our facility. For the most part (and for the most part correctly) the detainees who blamed their plight on the street on society, had become aware of their constitutional rights. Many of the detainees became aware of the fact that they could step up in our face, start running their mouth, and we would legally be unable to respond. Additionally, in 1982, physical response to any situation became aggressively attacked by management officials. Between late 1981 and early 1983, staff were encountering many new problems just as the Cubans were. When the warden finally realized that Atlanta was not closing, he attempted to gain control over a tired, hostile, belligerent, and frustrated group of employees. Yet, with affirmative action and fear of racial discrimination claims, he only created more problems. During that period of time, Atlanta suffered more assaults on staff by inmates than the rest of the bureau combined. During that same period, we also suffered more disciplinary action than the balance of the bureau.

Warden Blackmon established a pattern from his first position as warden. Every other captain would be promoted, and every other captain busted out of the facility. When Mr. Blackmon retired, the captain in Atlanta was on the pattern of being busted. We all laughed at the fact that his record was finally broken, but after he retired, he got the last laugh. His record stands; one up and one down. Mr. Blackmon came into a vibrant penitentiary as warden. Three years later, he was working out the process of closing that facility. Two years later, he had a mostly Cuban population and an inadequate staff. Staff coming in from other facilities were not as controllable as those from Atlanta.

As a result of the time in one facility, and changes taking place in that facility, it is my opinion that Mr. Blackmon burned out. He allowed other subordinate staff who were inept, power hungry, and ruthless in their dealings with other persons to start running his job. As a result of this, GS-9 correctional supervisors were making irrational decisions which affected the total correctional work force. These decisions resulted in adverse action taken on employees without basis but were totally supported by "high level personnel." When the captain would not allow correctional staff to dictate the actions of his staff or made effort to support staff, he was reduced in grade and replaced by a "yes" man.

It is only poetic Justice (Just us), but the last captain brought in by Mr. Blackmon fit the desires of the Blackmon administration. It was Blackmon's retirement that made his record stand. By 1982, the Correctional force had eighty-percent minority with less than five-percent Hispanic, despite the fact that we had a Cuban population. At the same time, they were still promoting on a racial quota (50-50) basis. Between the hostility of management, the frustrated and hostile population, the lack of fairness and equity in promotions, the lack of positive reinforcement toward their efforts, the Atlanta staff was expressing their stress-related problems in several ways. Some vented their anger at home and had marital problems; some vented their anger at either the detainees or staff; some coped with the use of drugs or alcohol; and others had emotional or heart problems. I used a pen to take my hostility out on management and became known for my poison pen.

CHAPTER 8

A CHRONOLOGY OF EVENTS

IN PREVIOUS CHAPTERS, I HAVE ATTEMPTED TO LAY A
foundation of how the institution operated and relationships within that setting. I have gone
back and forth in time, especially between 1978 and 1983, with a background for events. In this
chapter, I would like to begin a more orderly and chronological approach to events within that
background. Efforts will be made to express what happened, rather than how or why.

Between October 1973 and November 1976, I had been a correctional officer in Atlanta.
When I went there I was unsure of myself and my role; an old convict was sitting at a desk (waiting
on the OIC) with his feet on the desk while we were waiting to be issued our uniforms. He was
telling us what we needed to do, and what would be expected of us. I thought he ran the place
until the OIC came in. Even with a law enforcement background, I was as green as they came.
Between 1973 and 1976 I received some excellent training from the old, hardcore convicts and
hard line staff. During that same period, I completed a BS degree in sociology.

In November 1976, I went to the CTC, which was located on the penitentiary grounds and
three houses east of the main facility. I kept contact with the facility and what was going on in
the institution during that period. It was during that period that thirteen inmates were murdered
in a similar number of months. The negative percent of minority, less than five-percent Hispanic,
despite the fact that we had a Cuban population. At the same time, promotions were made on
a racial quota (50-50) basis.

After the murders within the institution and the negative publicity, the bureau decided to
transfer a large number of the inmates to other facilities, breaking up the leaders and agitators.
During the late afternoon one summer day, three buses were brought out on the circle in front
of the institution. Because of the problems, all inmates were being pot shook as they came into
the cell house. One inmate became verbal about being shook down after getting off work at
3:30 p.m. "You mother-fuckers are going to quit this shit when we take this damn place over," he
commented in a loud and intimidating tone to the officer.

After all had come in and they were locked down for count, he cried like a baby when the officer came to his cell and said, "Now, smart ass, pack your shit. The next thing that you take over is a seat on that bus out front. Your ass is going to Marion." He and ninety other inmates made the 4:00 p.m. count on the buses out front. After that, the institution was quiet; nobody wanted a transfer.

In September 1978, the CTC was closed. I transferred the last inmate to the Salvation Army in Atlanta, which got the contract for the halfway house, locked the door and transferred to Memphis. I enjoyed FCI Memphis, even though I had difficulty with the fence around the institution after years of having the wall. While I was at CTC, two inmates climbed out on the ledge near the top of A cell house and were held at bay by a tower until a fire truck came with a ladder to get them down, and another came over the wall. Even so, I had just gotten familiar with the wall. The detainee that came over the wall did so behind the hospital, which was an isolated area. After he got over the wall, there were still two fences just like these in Memphis and a tower close in both directions. When he landed on the outside, he hurt his foot. When the carbine was pointed toward him, he lay down just as he was asked. An AW came out (more commonly known by staff as an *idiot*) shouting, "Shoot the bastard! Shoot the bastard! Here, give me the gun down here and I will shoot him."

Almost immediately after leaving Atlanta, I discovered that I needed to return as a result of personal problems. I documented the need and went to Mr. Ernie Moore, the assistant director. I was informed that I could return to Atlanta immediately as a guard and would get the next open case manager position, or I could wait in Memphis until there was an opening. In April 1979, I returned to Atlanta as a guard, a correctional officer.

In October of 1979, it was announced that the facility would be closing by October 1, 1982. Each employee was to give a list of their three choices of institutions to be transferred to. As vacancies arose in the bureau, Atlanta staff were going to be transferred out. Inmates were to begin being transferred immediately. Even after Congress had acted, I never really believed that the institution would close. Many employees who had no desire to leave Atlanta submitted their three choices. A vacancy came up and they either had to move out or take a chance on getting sent to a fourth or fifth choice facility later. Later, when the institution did not close, Mr. Blackmon refused to accept them back in the same capacity even though a vacancy would exist. My request was any bureau position outside the walls, or a lockdown setting, such as a halfway house.

When I returned to Atlanta, I met a changing staff. The older supervisors who had learned the job by doing the job had diminished in numbers, and those still there seemed only to be marking time until their retirement. The employees all seemed to be doing as little as they could get by with, and even that was begrudgingly. The white officers (GS-7's) with three years as a GS-7 were not being promoted to GS-8, while some black officers with eighteen months as a GS-7 were getting promoted. In many cases, the white officers were complaining that they were expected to do the work while the blacks were getting the pay. The black officers complained about being given an assignment without proper training on what was to be done or how it should be done, being assigned a racist bunch of rednecks who would neither help or support him, and never really being given the authority to do the job. In spite of these facts, they were being held accountable for the job and the employees. On the racial issue, management's ploy to divide and conquer was effective.

In the frustration for economic survival, employees were frequently reporting persons of the other race for wrongdoing, even though the action was frequently commonplace. The newer supervisors were happy to document this and encouraged such practices. On occasion, when the supervisor confronted an employee about a nonsignificant infraction he would add, "Don't worry about this bullshit. I have you covered this time, but you had better watch that son of a bitch." This would usually result in prompt retaliatory information. The more experienced officers who were not part of the problem were just trying to stay out of the crossfire and, "Let the kids play their games." Those employees knew who they could trust, how far to trust them, and protected each other.

Those older, hard-working employees who just wanted to do their job and go home kept the institution operating during those periods when all else was on automatic pilot. They had learned that the supervisor who'd say, "As long as you are right, I will support you 100 percent," was a useless bastard. When you are 100 percent right, you don't need the support. It is when you are only 75 percent right that you need the support. Those few staff that just wanted to do the best possible job were put in the position of when you are only 75 percent right, lie about it. If the supervisor (through his snitches) pushed the issue, staff brought two good witnesses and made them look like the asses they were.

As plans to close were implemented in 1980 and positions opened, positions with promotion were given to the "fair-haired boys." Lateral positions would go to a fair-haired child who wanted a particular facility having nothing to do with the closure. When posts became available that an employee who was not in good terms with management really wanted, the warden would claim that we did not have enough manpower and would ask that the staff be allowed to remain in Atlanta. The local union attempted to get the union to file a grievance and arbitrate that issue but could not accomplish the goal. The union did employ an attorney to assist in developing an approach to preventing closure or fair and equitable transfers. This proved to be a waste of funds since the local administration and the institutional administration had agreed not to disagree. While the union president was voted out of office in 1982, the relationship with the Blackmon administration continued to deteriorate until he retired in July 1986.

The American inmates had been a part of the institution from the beginning of the career of the employees. There was a base of respect; additionally, most of the inmates did not want Atlanta to close any more than the employees. Atlanta was a good place for convicts to do their time. Contrary to an image displayed by many of the news media, when you put 2,000 inmates in one place, 500 or more of which are known killers, you will have killings. This is just as factual as stating that you will have prayer in the Southern Baptist Convention. In spite of the killings, the inmates claimed that for any inmate who'd leave the gambling, drugs, and sissies alone, Atlanta was a safe and good place to do time. "The hacks (guards) don't bother you on this nit-pick shit; you can do your time without being harassed. Now if you fuck up, they will get you; they are going to do their job." This comment by inmate Hall was a common attitude displayed by American inmates. The Cuban detainees they did not enjoy that base relationship.

In 1980 when the first detainees, a total of fifty arrived, staff was seeking a release for their frustration and hostility. Those detainees had become disruptive and unmanageable in the institution that they had come from. When they came into our R and D section, they had not become comfortable with the strip search. Instructing them to take off their clothes, and bend over and spread their cheeks was asking for a fight in many cases. Our staff, having worked with other uncooperative persons in the past, were always prepared for that occasion. During this period of time, overreaction was more commonplace as a result of staff frustrations.

When the fifty got to R and D, they were put into a holding cell to be processed one at a time. When the first detainee did not want to strip, his clothes were torn off him. (The Cuban detainees saw being stripped as an assault on their manhood.) The next forty-nine were more coopera- tive. Once the detainees were through R and D, they were taken to A cell house. They were met by a large number of staff, led by a Spanish-speaking officer. The expectations of the Atlanta facility and the results for non-compliance were made clear by the officer who was leaning on a broom handle. While there was no effort to touch any of the detainees, the intimidation was clearly present. The detainees were then assigned their cell and issued their goodie bag which contained toothpaste, toothbrush, comb, soap, toilet tissue, pencil and writing paper. They were then taken up to their new home. They were let out of the house only to go to the dining hall for meals. They were not alone long; it was only a short time before we received another 300 who had incited a riot in another facility. As problems began in each of the institutions who had detainees, the troublemakers were pulled and sent to Atlanta, even though verbal commitments were continuing about Atlanta closing in 1982. As a result of the insecurity about the future, staff had shorter fuses.

While interpreters were available to overcome the language barrier there were several other problems. Many of the interpreters had a bad image from staff; officers never believed that the detainees were being told what they were saying and were uncertain as to the conversa- tion of the detainees. In other cases, even some of the Spanish-speaking staff complained that the detainees had such poor use of the Spanish language that they didn't know what they were saying.

I likened it to my talking to a group of high school students. I know the words that they used and the meaning of those words (according to Webster) but I have no idea what is intended by the conversation. The biggest problem was the culture.

Once the detainees found that they could touch staff without "excuse me," (as they frequently pronounced "quese me") as a right to start their conversation no matter where you were in a conversation with someone else. If you were in the middle of sentence, in a conversation initiated by someone else, you might hear, "quese me." and the detainee start his convrsation while holding onto your shoulder to get full attention. While there was no respect shown for others, they expected full respect to listen to their concerns.

As a result of the shakedown procedures, (and I never was certain as to how much of the protest was an effort to manipulate) they displayed an impression that they thought staff were gay. In fact, some of the sissies were reported to have given sexual favors to some staff. One employee's name became commonly associated with this hearsay. Rumors from the orderlies, who earned money and bought cigarettes from the beginning, were that anyone could have sexual favors performed for five cigarettes. The blatant homosexual activities and transvestite appearance was also a cultural difference to us as it related to inmates. We were told that this was a result of Castro's laws against homosexuality resulting in large numbers of homosexuals being put in jail.

Other differences which created difficulty, was the loud tone used in conversation coupled with the use of the hands. Two friends engaged in cordial conversation would lead staff to believe they were about to fight. The most difficult element to deal with initially was their snitching. An American inmate may drop a note on your desk or come in and whisper information to you, but not the Cubans. They would come and grab you by the arm and say, "Come on...mucho problems up here!" as they pulled you. When you got to the cell, they would point to another detainee and say, "This man no fucking good, he mucho problems, he got a knife under his bed! Lookie (look) go ahead! Lookie!" The detainee that he was talking about would drop his head. You would go in and get the shank from under the mattress and place the detainee in seg, wondering if they were not both lying to you.

Finding shanks in Atlanta was commonplace. I went into a cell that housed six detainees in A cell house, and had the detainees go to one side of the cell while I shook the other side. I found three shanks and then traded sides, only to find two more. I am sure that I missed one, but after I left the cell I realized how stupid I really was. There was no other staff on the range and I'd gone into their cell raising hell.

Another of the difficulties in handling the detainees was a combination of their mental or emotional instability and their low boiling point. With some, you could be holding a conversation and all of a sudden be in a fight with him for no known reason. This added to the staff's existing overreactions, if one would consider efforts to maintain self-preservation an *overreaction*. Other detainees would ask for a cell change to move two cells down or into another cell house. When told *no*, they would get angry and cut their wrists. One enjoyed pushing a wire about three inches into his belly, while another would eat screws, nails, or broken glass. Staff were neither emotionally equipped nor adequately trained in dealing with this type of mental patients. The end result was that we developed a merry-go-round.

One of the mental patients (*crazies*, as the Cubans called them) would assault staff. We would send them to seg. When he'd calmed down a little they would send him to the hospital F ward (the mental ward) for treatment. After a couple of months locked down in F ward, he would be well enough to go to A and B ward, an open unit in the hospital for medical patients that was used for mental patients. If they did not assault staff there, they were returned to C cell house where the only change was that they could go to the dining hall for meals. After a short time, the detainee would assault another staff. While Atlanta had a high rate of assaults, a relatively few number of detainees were involved. The problem was that this provided the worst possible conditions for the emotionally ill and staff. We did not treat them as sick, even though one evaluation of the detainees had revealed that all the 2,000 detainees, except 132, needed psychiatric help. We could not treat them like convicts, because you could not hold them accountable for their actions. We were both caught in the middle of a political war game.

Between 1980 through 1982, we never knew quite what we were dealing with. We would begin breakfast by 6:00 a.m. It was commonplace for staff to respond to a body alarm call for assistance three or four times before being relieved by the day watch at 8:00 a.m. Limited overtime was available in 1980, but by early 1981, everyone could get more hours than they wanted. By 1982, TDY staff were coming from other facilities. As a result of all of these factors, the staff emotionally remained in a "fight or flight" response mode at all times, when on duty. That is, the mind told the body that it was in imminent danger and must be prepared to defend itself or run—at all times. Between 1980 and 1982, the body reacted to that response quickly. When the detainee swung his arm as he did in normal conversation with another detainee, he would find himself in a fight in many occasions. When the staff was not in the fight-or-flight response, he would find that one of the "crazies" had gone off on him. In either case the staff were becoming exhausted—mentally and physically.

At the same time staff were having difficulty dealing with the new population, they were also having difficulty with relations between themselves and management officials. While many of the detainees were not yet housebroken, one AW demanded that the floors would always shine like a mirror. As a result of his insistence on a having shined floor and the desire of the safety manager to become warden at any cost, wax was put on the floors. In the past, as a result of the danger of staff falling on a wet, slippery floor when responding to an emergency, the safety office refused to allow any wax on the floors. They were required to be spotless, but no wax. While it could not be proven, it was always suspected that some accident reports were never filed to make the warden look better at operating a facility without trouble while making his record of a facility with limited number of (preventable) accidents. While this could not be proven, the local union had difficulty in getting copies of the accident reports, although the Master agreement required that one be provided.

Even many of the low level supervisors were caught in the middle of a struggle. One supervisor put me in for a quality step increase. After the captain informed him that I was a good man, and would get the QSI, he told me, and thanked me for my hard work. A few days later, the captain told him that I was not going to get a damn thing as long as I was there, as per Warden Blackmon.

Another supervisor was working the morning watch when the AW came in and sat in front of his desk at 5:30 a.m. He told the lieutenant, "You should put your paperwork in for captain. You would make a good captain."

"No," the lieutenant responded. "If I was to get to be a captain and some damn AW came in and started telling my men what to do, I would kick his ass. I'm better off right where I am!" The AW got up and walked out.

Between 1980 and 1982, there were many small disturbances. Even though there was a constant conflict between staff and a few detainees, most of the detainees were working to establish positive relationships with staff in an effort to secure their freedom. While the detainees were the most frustrating population to deal with as a result of their total disregard for policy, they had no difficulty in assuming the consequence for their actions. A detainee would not blame his actions on anyone else. When a detainee had a conflict with a staff, the other detainees got out of the way. The detainees, reacting to their own frustrations, would burn sheets and break sinks and commodes, from time to time, between 1980 and 1982. At any time, these events would only involve a few cells; not all of the detainees would become involved in any single disturbance. These events occurred after lockdown and while they were in their cell. Other than the individual assaults on staff, the detainees did not attempt to hurt staff. Once I stepped in between two detainees fighting (one slapping the other). It was not until I pushed the aggressor back that I realized that he had a single-edge razor in between two fingers and had been cutting the other detainee. He was very careful not to push back on me and gave me the blades.

The detainees had difficulty understanding our correctional system. Following any negative actions, they got a pink piece of paper. Throwing urine or feces on a staff, hitting an employee, or cutting an employee or another detainee, they'd get a pink sheet of paper. They were more accustomed to immediate reprisal. Several of the detainees collected the papers and prided themselves on who had the most. It was not until they went to the panel and were told to come back in two years without an incident report that they understood our power of the pen as a controlling device. Even knowing the power of the pen, they showed more respect to a "respond for assistance," which brought from thirty to fifty staff who were looking to vent their anger. Some of those staff would have fought with each other.

In 1980 or early 1981, the administration decided that staff was getting too aggressive with the population. All of a sudden, several staff had charges brought against them. The captain and several lieutenants were busted, but they took all responsibility. The new captain was told he did not have to come to Atlanta, but that was where his paycheck was going to be. He was further advised that he had a year to clean the place up and, either be promoted out or busted out. He was the up-swing captain. During the year that he was present, several employees had charges brought against them. Four staff, which included a supervisor and a mill foreman who had been working overtime, had to go to the Merit-System Protection Agency for a hearing to prevent being busted and transferred. For a while, staff were being taken advantage of by the population, who had realized the lack of response to any situation.

In 1982, the detainees had their first serious riot. The detainees had come to the U.S.A. seeking a new freedom. Some had (according to the detainees) been told that they had an option; they could leave their jail cell and go to America or be shot! I am certain that some drugs were used, but Castro's mental institutions were opened up and his patients put on a boat to American health! While we scream about Castro's tactics at reducing his national budget, I am amused by our society's disassociation with the social budget cuts. Ronald Reagan had a National Day of Prayer and emptied our mental institutions onto the street.

Almost immediately after being placed in our modernized correctional facilities, the detainees began a *seek and destroy* mission. I am reminded of a company of GIs, having been out in the field for months and then being brought into a hotel and told, "Have a good weekend, you are shipping overseas Monday!" The Cubans were told, "You are being kept here pending your deportation back to Cuba!" While idle conversation was that they may…eventually, they *were* being held pending deportation. Many of our necessities were luxuries to them. The new and modern institutions were not designed for that clientele. After Ft. Chaffee was burned, Atlanta began getting the worst of the group. As it had been discovered that Atlanta could keep them with fewer difficulties than other facilities, they began to ship them all to one facility.

Just as a point of humor, the bureau's thinking, initially, was to spread them into all of the institutions and "Americanize" them. As the detainees realized that they were in American jails for Cuban crimes and had no parole or end of sentence in sight, they had nothing to lose. Their frustration led to severe property damage in every facility that they were placed in. Instead of seeking a fair and equitable set of standards for the detainees to reach for a release, we sent them all to Atlanta. We changed our thinking to "Placing them all in one facility so that we might have specialized programs for this unique group." Beginning in 1980, and while the staff was extremely hostile about being uprooted and the underhanded manner in which the administration was handling these changes, the worst of the Cubans came. Immediately, two frustrated and hostile groups met. While we were outnumbered, we were better trained, better equipped, better organized (only because of the training and knowledge of the older line staff) and responded to any challenge quickly and in force. The detainees enjoyed limited freedom through 1980 and 1981. By the end of 1981, we were letting them go to the yard once a week for recreation and out for meals; otherwise only a few were out of their cells.

By late 1981 and early 1982, it was evident that the institution was not going to close (even though the warden never told staff) as scheduled. Our population was up to 2,000 Cubans and climbing with few jobs and even less of the specialized training for this unique group. By 1982, they were developing panels to determine who would and who would not be released. In all of this, no clear-cut measure was used by which the detainees could see or understand where they stood in relationship to a potential release. Educational participation, vocational training, or compliance with institutional regulations seemed to do little toward a release. Completing the time to be served for the crime committed in Cuba had nothing to do with their release. The only thing that assisted at all (and that was not guaranteed) was community ties. Even there, the government resisted the Catholic Conference as a "bunch of do-gooders," which was the only source of developing community ties.

In 1982, the frustration level of the detainees reached a boiling point. It was humorous to staff at the time, but as time went by, it is more understandable. The Cubans had a riot, but it was not until after they were locked in their cells. Many remembered the riot in Cuba when they were ordered to their cell and took too long to get there. Many broke the sinks from the walls and water pipes and threw the pieces through the windows. Some burned their bedding and mattresses. By the second day of this, they were tired and ready to quit. During that period, the ringleaders were pulled out, with shields protecting staff, and a fire hose kept other detainees from charging when a cell door was opened.

During the riot, our associate warden had some of the detainees out of the cells to police up cigarette butts from the yard. After the riot, the same AW made a survey of damages. While walking through three inches of water, broken porcelain from commodes and sinks, ashes from burned bedding, and a tired, but angry population, he insisted that staff open a cell and remove the *Playboy* centerfold of a nude woman taped to the door of a wall locker.

During the riot, every time a news media vehicle would come across the street, a new flurry of fires from burning sheets would appear. Water was three inches on the floor and running down the hallway (corridor) day and night. Fortunately, the institution was designed so that the water could be cut off cell by cell. Because of the sporadic action from one area to another, you would think that the problem was resolved only to find a pipe broken somewhere else. Extra staff were kept over to help in controlling B cell house.

While all eyes were on the flurry of fires and activities in B cell house, a detainee busted a hole in the side of the seg unit, E cell house, and escaped. At the hearing for the charges brought against the employee, we claimed that E cell house was not and could not be converted into a secure segregation unit, but the administration claimed it to be safe. (This is the same building about which management claimed that the doors were so dilapidated that security could be breached as an excuse for their not locking down on November 1987. It was still a seg unit.)

For a couple of months after the disturbance, the detainees were left on lockdown and fed from paper bags three times a day. They were escorted to a locked area on the yard for exercise five cells at a time a couple of times per week. During this time, the OIC of B cellhouse had a larger population and more staff that he was supervising than most of the newer and smaller institutions. When they did begin to open them up slowly, all detainees were on their best behavior. Most wanted to get out of their cell—they would volunteer to clean windows, scrub floors, or anything else just to get out of their cells. For the most part, the Cubans were a high-strung population who needed to release their energy. Being an orderly or being out of the cell gave the detainee prestige and a commodity to sell. He could run a delivery or floating communication system.

Frequently, he could convince the officer to let a friend, "Be friende for me! Good man, mucho worke, you see—you likee!" they would say. I always thought that it was funny! You had a one-hour job for ten not being done in two hours by twenty, but one more would make the difference. But what the hell was one more, as long as they weren't creating problems.

During this period, I was working A cell house 4:00 to 12:00 as OIC. The detainees started bringing their TV over in front of their cell as we would start to lock down and count. I stopped that one the second night I found that they didn't want to clean until after their program was finished. One detainee became very verbal and said that one of them would work. "No problem," I responded.

When I opened the door they all sat still, the one ringleader insisting, "No worke for you."

"No problemo, no necessito worke, necessito officino. Now! Do you want to bring your sorry asses to the office or do you want me to get enough staff to bring you down?" I told them.

"We go to office. We no worke!" As we got to the office I pulled out a stack of incident reports, got one and laid the others aside. I got the picture cards out for all orderlies. While I was getting the papers together, the ringleader had been joined by another leader. In Spanish, they were telling the others that I could not lock them all up, and when the cell house wasn't clean, I would have problems. I wrote the two incident reports for refusing to work and encouraging others to participate in a work stoppage. They were still out there standing, but a couple in the back were leaning on their brooms.

When this was completed, I asked a Spanish-speaking officer to ask them in their own language, "Ask them if they are going to work!"

"No," they responded, "No worke!"

"Are you telling the other orderlies not to work?"

"Si, nobody no worke for you!"

I then gave the bilingual officer the picture cards and incident reports. "Take them to the lieutenant's office and have their asses put in seg." I turned to the number two officer and demanded, "I know that we have somebody in here who will clean this shit house. Find me two more orderlies." I then slowly pulled the rest of the picture cards up. By then, the two in the back had their brooms moving. There had been three others close to the front who had insisted that they were not going to work, but that they spoke only for themselves. I then asked the next one of them, "Worke? Si or No?"

The three looked at each other and then to me, "Si, we worke, U," they all responded. Within a couple minutes they were all at work.

The next day when I came in, the two sent to seg were back in their cell. When I opened up to clean, they started out but were ordered back. "Me orderly!" they claimed.

"You are not my orderly and will not work for me again, stay in your cell!" I responded. The next day when I came in I was approached by the unit staff who gave them their jobs back and turned them out of seg.

"What is the problem with the orderlies?" he asked.

"No problem. I had two who refused to work and had talked the others into not working, but I handled that. I still don't understand why they were kept on, with jobs as orderlies," I responded.

"Well, they said that all they'd wanted to do was to watch the news from their cell after they finished, and you wouldn't let them," he explained.

"You had my statement in writing! I remember when my word was as good as an inmate's!" I responded angrily and walked off. He was promoted out shortly after that event.

PART THREE

CHAPTER 9

RIOT OF 1984

AFTER THE RIOT IN 1982, THE DETAINEES WERE LOCKED down (by their choice). After the riot had ended, the damage was slowly repaired, and the detainees remained on a lockdown status for several weeks. When staff began letting the detainees out, the detainees were interviewed by unit staff individually. During these interviews, the detainees were questioned about their involvement in the recent riot. Most readily admitted they did not want to become involved; they'd gone to bed and hadn't seen a thing. They also had to promise to return to work, work hard every day, and create no more problems. The detainees were tired of their cells and would have agreed to anything.

Only a few refused to return to work. Some of the detainees saw their work as justification for keeping them locked up. In the mail bag factory, the institution had made a contract to produce so many mail bags for the Post Office. Should we release the Cubans, some of the detainees felt that we would be unable to fulfill the contract. The same with all the other factories; we must have manpower to work our factories. The detainees started to work in industries for twenty-two cents an hour, a salary which was top pay for any part of the institution and topped out at $1.10 per hour. As a result of the pay incentive, the industries jobs were a highly sought after job. Yet, in spite of the pay, many saw industries as their slave master. For the most part, the detainees were excellent workers on any job. During that period of time, I was assigned to labor one, a job responsible for getting the trash picked up from each unit and the kitchen. I operated the compactor while my detail emptied trash from all over the institution.

After the trash was emptied, we also cut all the grass inside the walls, except for the recreation yard. We picked up trash, swept and hosed down the area. When any other area had a need for manual labor, my detail was also frequently used. While my detail worked hard seven days a week (they were split up and worked every other weekend), I could not get the money to pay each of them twenty-two cents an hour. In addition to not being able to acquire the most highly motivated crew, there was also supervisor problems.

My supervisor, a lieutenant, evaluated me based upon my accomplishments in following his orders. His evaluation was based upon his following the captain's orders, who reported to the AW-C. The AW-O, who had nothing to do with custody, had developed the habit of calling me direct to do something that he wanted done. When bringing this out in the Labor Management Relations did not resolve the problems, I finally would ask if he had brought this request to my supervisor. At first, he started with an intimidation speech. After a few times of explaining that I was tied up at the moment, but by the time that it got to my supervisor I should almost be free, he got the message. Especially when I never got free until the lieutenant told me to do it. This put the AW to calling the lieutenant rather than AW-C, but it got him off of my back.

In late 1982 and early 1983, some of the detainees were being released to the street. For the most part, those who were released had been programmed to fail. A large number of those going out were the strong-armed type who had been around a penal system and knew how to manipulate the system. They were not prepared emotionally, scholastically, or vocationally. During their period of confinement, our assistance in preparing them for society had been a deficit rather than an asset. We had taught them to butcher the English language at best. We taught them to use the same word twice; instead of teaching them, "It is necessary to get the job done," we would say, "Necessary worke-worke." When I got home, at the supper table I would tell my kids "Eate, eate!" The most common use of the English language again was, "Suck my dick," or "Fuck you in the asshole, bitch." The vulgarity was the first of our English lessons in our daily working with them.

The Cubans had been given nothing but bad press (not necessarily undeserved) since their first arrival. Now we had taken ill-mannered men and placed them in a hostile environment. These men knew very little about the American culture; for instance, when you ask a stranger on the street for the time, you don't put your hands on him and succeed. Additionally, the unemployment rate was high during that period of time. A lot of citizens held the attitude, "Why are those damn foreigners coming over here to take my job?" This, coupled with the memory of the tent city in Miami, stories of shoot-outs on the streets of Miami by rival drug gangs, the burning of Fort Chaffee, and their having very-limited community ties or support, meant legitimate employment was extremely difficult to find. Along with these negatives, hanging over their head also was the fact that any legal charge would result in their immediate return to Atlanta.

While the detainees were free and, on the street, they became street-wise, American style. They had their civil rights; staff had to afford them every judicial prudence and had to work with them much in the same manner as policemen are supposed to deal with any U.S. American citizen during a formal investigation of a crime. Even the American inmates do not get this. The judge had already deprived the offender by placing them in jail. Our actions were merely administrative in fulfilling the Order of the Court. The Cubans who had been released to the streets returned with exaggerated accomplishments. The news media, TV programs, and to a large extent, movies, showed the average American living in a comfortable neighborhood, driving a late model car, dressing very nicely, and having few concerns about paying their bills.

For the most part, the detainees returning from the street boasted of obtaining those things plus having all the sex, booze, and drugs that they wanted. Many of the detainees who had never been on the street became excited about the opportunity to have these things and depressed at the perception that, after doing everything within their power, they were still facing life imprisonment with no parole—having never gone to court. In addition to the frustration of those detainees who had never been released to the street, those who returned from the street were equally frustrated. They told stories (true or untrue was not important as it left the same feeling in the minds of those who had never been released) of continual harassment by the immigration officers. Some claimed they were stopped for a misdemeanor within the state, tried and sentenced within the state, and upon release from the misdemeanor, were sent to the Atlanta Federal Penitentiary to serve the rest of their life.

Those detainees who had committed crimes, misdemeanors, or felonies within the state had two major complaints about being in the Atlanta Federal Penitentiary. The first major complaint was that of the immigration staff who picked them up at the state line. They alleged that the immigration authorities informed them that they would be brought to the Atlanta facility for a short term for processing and then returned to their families or returned to the streets. The second major complaint was that they had committed a crime, just as any other American, and had served their time just as any other American on the street but were still being housed in a federal facility pending deportation.

Personally, I am of the opinion that, had a process been in place for deportation and the detainees been deported immediately, they could have understood this process. However, being housed in a correctional facility pending the enactment of something that did not exist became extremely frustrating to each of them. As a result of the frustration and apparent endlessness to the current situation, most of the Cuban detainee population was becoming more militant.

Not only were the detainees frustrated with their plight, but staff, too, were suffering from a self-serving management that cared nothing about either the employees or the population. Employees were harassed at home as the story about a warden who'd been arrested—for shoplifting a hairbrush from Kroger—hit the press, as well as at work by young, inexperienced, and inept supervisors. Just as all other things reproduce themselves, so does incompetence within management. The difficulty with such a system as was used in promotions was that incompetence within the institution rapidly became ignorance at the regional and central office level.

Back in 1973, when I began employment at the U.S. Penitentiary, Atlanta, three or four black staff members at most were employed. In 1976, with the enactment of the Civil Rights Act of 1976 and President Jimmy Carter's desire to increase minority percentages within government leadership, rapid changes were made. Very quickly, when the federal penitentiary began to hire ten employees, nine would be minorities. In 1978, a promotion would result in one black and one white being promoted equally. Whether equally or functionally qualified, the institution continued hiring and promoting on a regular quota system. In 1981, the correctional forces in the Atlanta facility was in excess of seventy percent black. The facility continued to promote on a 50-50 ratio.

With the bringing in of the Cuban population, efforts to recruit Hispanics were also made. A chief correctional supervisor (captain), the personnel officer, and associate warden made a trip to Puerto Rico on a recruitment trip. As a result of this effort, several Puerto Rican staff members were brought into the institution. However, as they explained, the personnel officer had made them a lot of promises that were not kept; many of them quit very quickly. While returning to the promotion system, when this occurred and ten employees were being promoted, five would be black, one Hispanic, and four white. A Hispanic may be black or white but was determined to be Hispanic.

In 1977, when the board of promotions initially began, the ratio of minorities within the institution was quite small. Some minorities were promoted, having been employed for one year as a GS-6, (trainee), and a year as a GS-7 (promotion between GS-6 and GS-7 was automatic after one year). So, after having little more than a year as a GS-7, minorities were being promoted to GS-8—determined by their race rather than experience or skill. Minorities were being promoted with fourteen or fifteen months as a GS-7, while at the same time whites were being promoted with thirty-six months or more as a GS-7.

In 1982, the rule had changed drastically. By that time, the ratio was less than thirty percent white, but the quota system of promotion continued. Subsequently, white officers were being promoted after limited time as a GS-7 and blacks were being discriminated against. The trouble was that the promotions based on race did not end at that level.

GS-9 correctional supervisor was a management position. The young officers who were felt to possess the training and/or skills to work the most responsible positions in the institution were supervising other, more experienced, staff.

Charges were being brought against staff, who were caught in the middle, due to inexperienced supervisors. When a young supervisor told an older officer to do something that was wrong, the officer got a charge brought against him. If he did as instructed, high level management officials would claim that the supervisor was just learning his job, but the officer had been around long enough to know better. If he did not do as instructed, but attempted to explain that it was against policy, he would be charged with refusing to obey the order. This aggressive action did not end with the immediate supervisor.

The warden, Mr. Blackmon, once charged an officer with sleeping on duty. During the purported incident, an employee just around the corner was painting a cell, and another employee on the other side of a wall working on plumbing. Despite both employees having written an affidavit that the three were involved in an ongoing conversation at the time, the individual was suspended on the charge.

During the early spring and summer of 1984, there was an extreme amount of tension in the facility. The staff was expecting a long, hot summer from the detainees and did receive that. On a couple occasions on weekends, the detainees became angry as a result of frustration while on the yard. They attempted to bring demonstrations on the yard as a matter of releasing those frustrations. Efforts to prevent those demonstrations resulted in increased frustration. One Sunday afternoon when a demonstration was in process and staff began to break it up, the detainees overran the staff. They threw objects at the staff and busted some windows out of the metal detector. No one was injured as a result of this altercation, but this was a result of the detainees' desire not to hurt staff. In retrospect, it was obvious that the detainees were functioning much as the US government. There was what political science called "muddling their way through". They proceeded in one direction until striking an object; they hesitated, turned direction, and continued on until hitting another object.

After the extremely tense moments when the staff were vastly outnumbered, the detainees went on in to their units. Other than this and other demonstrations occurring during the summer of 1984, nothing happened. No staff was injured, and no lockdowns occurred. Frustrations were extremely high in the Cuban population and tensions high among staff during that period.

As the fall came about, there was continuous rumors about an impending riot. In any event occurring in the federal facility, either by the American inmates or the Cuban detainees, staff were usually advised well in advance. This is a result of a variety of factors. One being that individuals who have long sentences to serve or perceive themselves to be in the institution for a long period of time have decided that to be their home. They want no problems in their home any more than any other individual in society. Another is those individuals who perceive release in the not too distant future really do not want to take a chance of having bodily injury to themselves prior to their potential release. The most common, however, is that individuals become fearful for their own life and safety and inform some staff of impending action to protect themselves and maintain self-preservation.

In middle October, rumors were rampant all over the facility about an impending riot within the Atlanta federal penitentiary. Staff were advised to keep their ears open and contact their better snitches in an effort to locate the time, date, and leaders of any such riot. In October, it was learned that a riot was going to take place in the immediate future. Names of the leaders surfaced, and information leading staff to believe that a riot was not only going to be inside their situation, but a disturbance would also occur outside the institution, in conjunction with the riot in the facility. Sufficient information was obtained that management was sure that families of some of the detainees were going to hold a demonstration on the street in front of the institution. They planned to have megaphones to call to the Cubans inside during their speeches and to block McDonough Boulevard just in front of the facility. When police began making arrests on the street, leaders within the institution were going to incite the masses to riot.

On November 1, 1984, information was strong enough to lead management officials to believe that a specific group of individuals was planning a riot for the following weekend. Two of the leaders were brothers. On the evening of November 1, 1984, a decision was made to lock up those individuals. That evening a young officer was instructed to bring one of the two individuals to the lieutenant's office. Lou arrived in the lieutenant's office. Lieutenant Bone and the unit manager, Mr. Morgan, were present. Lieutenant Bone informed the individual that allegations had been made against him and he was being locked in segregation unit pending investigation.

Over objections of the unit manager and in violation of bureau policy, when the detainee asked to return to his cell to pick up his own personal property and return to his unit, B cell house, prior to going to the segregation unit, Lieutenant Bone allowed him to do so while being escorted by the young officer. When the detainee entered B cell house, he took off running from the officer. The officer was unable to locate him immediately and found that he was not in his cell where he was assigned. Moments after, the detainee and a large number of other detainees located the officer and taunted him, pushing him toward the front of the institution. The inmate had gone and gotten his brother and a large number of other individuals who had planned to be leaders in the major disturbance, and they started pushing staff toward the front exit of the unit.

One case manager, Mr. Price, had been in the receiving and discharge unit for the screening of the Cuban detainees being admitted into the institution. When entering into the cell house he saw several correctional staff in the office area but thought nothing of it. He went on by and toward his office which was located in the back half of the flats. As he passed the first cell, a detainee whom he did not know personally called to him, "Price, don't go back there!" Mr. Price took a couple of steps further and stopped to review the situation. As he visually looked over the unit, he saw nothing out of place. Just in front of him and against the wall near the cutoff was a large number of detainees, which was commonplace. They were just standing against the wall, one foot raised against the wall, and talking. Mr. Price decided that he would go on back to his office, pick up some papers he had on his desk, and leave the unit. He had continued back toward his office for a few feet when a large number of detainees rounded the corner to cut him off. Seeing Mr. Price, one of the detainees picked up a mop bucket and threw it in the direction of Mr. Price. There was no effort to hit Mr. Price with the bucket, but it was intended merely as a warning for Mr. Price to change directions and not enter that crowd.

The detainees had started to back up each range including the flats and had pushed every staff member back against the door. While making no effort to injure or assault staff, they had weapons such as mop handles, broom handles, clubs, table legs and a few knives. Additionally, B cell house housed at that time between 575 and 600 detainees. Staff pressed on as a result of the call for assistance in B unit. There were approximately a dozen staff which included the four employees assigned to that unit. Staff realized their situation immediately and were happy to vacate the unit. As the main corridor officer opened the door and staff started coming out of the unit, one Cuban detainee with a personal grudge toward a supervisor swung a table leg at him.

Mr. Jordon, a correctional officer, raised his hand to stop the blow and prevented serious injury to the head or skull of the supervisor. As a result of this, the officer received a broken arm. Excluding this incident, the detainees allowed the staff to leave the unit and the door to be re-locked by the main corridor officer. This not only allowed the staff to be locked outside of the unit but isolated the size of the disturbance to that unit. Immediately following the door being locked, the detainees began to put beds, mattresses and other objects in front of the doorway on the inside as well as the side door leading to the yard. This was an effort to prevent staff from entering. A group of detainees had blocked both doorways, others began to ransack unit officers' and unit staff's offices.

Some of the detainees began to start small fires all over the unit. The fires, consisting mostly of mattresses and sanitary supplies, were initially and chiefly built in the offices to destroy all documents and computers within the offices. As additional staff was called in for assistance and the press notified, fires began to spread with the development of press vehicles across the street.

I was scheduled to work from 8:00 until 4:00 p.m. that day. At about 7:30, I got a phone call to come to the institution, there were problems. When I got there, police, fire trucks, press, and a street full of spectators were already there. I jumped out of the car (leaving the headlights on and killing my battery) and went inside to be told to go toward personnel; we were going to take the gun range. We were given batons and WW-2 gas masks that fogged up every time you took a breath. When I got up to the personnel area where staff were gathering, Officer Calvin, a senior officer there, had a tear-gas gun. He said that he had gone back into the record office and opened a slide on the steel door leading from the record office to B cell house. This door was never used and was locked and padlocked. It had a view panel approximately two inches by eight inches, which was also locked with a slide bolt.

This is the slide which Mr. Calvin opened to see several detainees attempting to break open the door. He brought the tear gas gun up and fired into the unit, hitting the front end of the cells on seven ranges. Both the gas and the detainees dispersed rapidly as he closed the slide back. A few minutes later, he again checked, only to find that the detainees had blocked this entrance as they had the others; they had given up on breaking out.

One Cuban detainee was climbing the outside window of the cellblock. The only place he could go was to the top of the window on the cell bars blocking the window. However, after getting approximately six feet up the window, a fire hose from the outside fire truck struck him, pushing him back inside. By this time, many of the sinks had been busted, toilets had been broken, and the City of Atlanta fire trucks were consistently pouring water onto the main fires that could be reached from the outside. Subsequently, water stood at least six inches deep on the floor. As a detainee was struck with the water from the fire truck on the outside, he'd fall back on the floor and splash in the water, unharmed. At this, he'd get up and find himself a fire extinguisher and started returning the fire of water to the fire truck. The fire truck, standing in excess of fifty feet from the wall on the outside of the institution, suffered little to no damage as a result of his assault with water. The maximum capability of the fire extinguishers inside the institution at that time was approximately twenty feet.

As adequate staff arrived in the institution, tear gas was fired into B cell house through the inside window. This was an effort to encourage the detainees in the unit to surrender without any further difficulty. While the fires, as shown on TV by local news media, seemed to be large, vigorous fires, it was later determined that these were for the most part sheets being held by the detainees while they burned. While tear gas was being fired through the windows from the inside of the institution and into the cellblock, thirty or so staff, including myself, were being sent to the gun range—which was nothing more than a walkway around the outside walls of the building on an upper level of the building. Upon the initial arrival on the gun range, it was learned that some of the detainees had gotten onto the gun range and crossed over into A cell house, in an effort to spread the disturbance into that cellblock. While staff had been removed from A cell house as a result of the potential threat from B cell house, only two small fires were set in A unit, and no substantial damage was created from A unit. The detainees had gone to their cells and were locked down prior to the disturbance getting out of control in B cell house.

When we learned that the detainees had gotten onto the gun range itself, there was some reluctance to enter the gun range with the tear gas guns. Although there were mirrors on the only doorway entering the gun range, these mirrors had been broken. One detainee was seen on the gun range and a round of tear gas was fired near him. A second detainee ran quickly from the A unit side of the gun range back across to the B cell house side. Again, a round of tear gas was shot in his direction. When the dust from the tear gas settled, neither detainee could be seen. At this time, it was determined by Mr. Douglas, our captain, that there was a need to enter the gun range. Mr. Douglas was within this detail and directing a barrage of tear gas from the outside to coordinate the efforts by radio. It was determined that the door would be unlocked, pushed open, and two staff would step inside the gun range back to back with a tear gas gun, prepared to fire. A number of other staff were standing by with other tear gas guns as this was accomplished.

As we entered the gun range, only one detainee was seen on the gun range itself. This detainee was located about halfway down B cell house side of the gun range. One round was fired from the tear gas toward the detainee. When the dust settled from the tear gas gun and visibility returned, the detainee was not in sight. Although no one saw him, the detainee had jumped from the gun range on top of B cell house and went back down inside the B cell house unit. Several rounds of tear gas were thrown inside the unit to saturate the unit with tear gas. However, many of the detainees would take a towel, wet it, pick up the tear gas and throw it out the window.

As adequate staff was made available, the side door to the unit was opened. However, the door was blocked from the inside by mattresses, chairs, and a variety of other items. As some of the detainees got an opportunity to climb over that mound and leave the unit, they would. These were the detainees who merely desired to escape from the unit at the earliest opportunity. Some detainees would throw lockers or chains at them as they attempted to leave. Other detainees became injured or sick. The detainees never prevented anyone who was injured or sick from going to the hospital for medical attention. When one became injured, he would usually have a couple of detainees escort him to the hospital. Those who were either sick, injured, or assisting those who were injured, were never assaulted like those who were trying to escape the unit. The detainees who did not wish the disturbance to end attempted to keep all physically able bodies on board.

After entry had been gained onto the gun range by staff, a large number of staff were maintained walking patrol around it. Although we had no control over the inside of the unit, our presence provided some psychological desire to leave the unit for those who did not wish to become involved in further criminal activities or prevent potential release in the future. We moved around to the gun range and over the doorway leading to the yard and fired several rounds of tear gas, where individuals were preventing those who desired from leaving the unit. The Atlanta staff was supported by staff from FCI Talladega, Alabama, as well. Once the riot was reported, staff from Talladega were called in and dispatched to our facility. They were held at the front entrance and in reserve by the warden. Georgia State Patrol, Fulton County Sheriff's Office, Atlanta P.D. and Douglas County Sheriff's Office all sent staff and equipment to the facility. One of the agencies brought a tear-gas forger unit, which was being readied to put tear gas through the venting system into B cell house when it was determined that it would not be needed. By this time many of the detainees were tired and were giving up.

As the detainees left the unit they were shaken down, handcuffed, and taken to the recreation area initially and then from there, many were taken to the yard area for accountability and supervision. By 4:00 a.m., the number of detainees located in the unit was extremely limited. It was determined at that time that entry was going to be gained through the unit by staff, and any other detainees in there would be brought out by force, if necessary. When it became obvious to those on the inside that staff were about to enter the unit, those few detainees also gave up and came out. When staff entered the unit, we expected to find at least one detainee lying seriously injured or killed. Had that been an American uprising, it would not have been accomplished without injury. However, the Cuban culture being very different and the attitudes being extremely different, when a search was made cell by cell, inch by inch, only the remains of destruction created by the detainees were found. No detainees were located in the unit. By 5 a.m., a regained and reestablished accountability for each detainee was made. A list of every detainee by name and number located in the segregation unit and where they were located in the segregation unit was made.

All of these had to be located in the computer as to their previous cell location and a change made to a new cell location. These changes also included the hospital and other housing units as they were moved in from the yard. By 8:00 a.m., November 2, 1984, a cleanup and repair crew was in B unit making repairs. By 4:00 p.m. that day, the unit was beginning to receive detainees returning to their regular cells.

That one-night stay eventually became an extremely expensive ordeal for the U.S. Government. They claimed the cost to be over ten million dollars (two million dollars total damage to all properties and replacement of any items destroyed would have been an exagger-ation in B unit.) However, it was costly in terms of overtime units and replacement of a variety of items from other institutions as well as state and local correctional and police units.

Georgia State Patrol, the Atlanta City Police Department, the Atlanta Fire Department, and other federal correctional facilities responded to the alarm. Douglas County Sheriff's office loaned the Atlanta Federal Penitentiary a good deal of equipment, including disposable handcuffs and tear gas. Other federal facilities and agencies which responded brought items such as handcuffs and other items with them. After the disturbance was completely over, none of the other facilities could find the right amount of handcuffs or leg irons. Subsequently, with limited accountability at the beginning, the institution replaced claims with new items. (This is extremely interesting, in view of the fact that the next riot to occur inside of the Atlanta facility would result in his depar-ture in a downgrade.)

One Saturday morning, November 3, 1984, (the date the riot was actually scheduled to take place) I went to Alabama with two INS officers of Talladega and two detainees (the two brothers) who were ringleaders in the disturbance. When arriving in Alabama, a correctional supervisor receiving the detainees was surprised that our federal facility was unable to control these detainees. He assured me that FCI, Talladega, would encounter no difficulties with these two pussycats. In our conversation, the lieutenant questioned me about the number of years I had been in the service (thirteen at that time) and my pay grade, which was a GS-8 at that time. He had implied that the type of incompetent staff available in Atlanta having that type of seniority with inability to become promoted was probably the problem. He had a much shorter time working for the bureau and was already a GS-11 supervisor. While it was noticeable that the INS agents, both friends of mine, had gotten irritated by his remarks, it did not bother me. I was fully aware that those two pussycats would burst his bubble and didn't need me to entertain that useful conversation. I have long since discovered that as long as one is comfortable with himself, he doesn't have to be intimidated by other employees.

It was not long until the two detainees were returned to the Atlanta facility and placed in our segregation unit. Talladega had been unable to maintain control over them. After returning to Atlanta on Saturday evening, November 3, 1984, I saw the AW-O near his office. He was extremely cheerful (which generally meant that he was about to screw an employee) as he com-mented, "Well, everybody is getting their overtime in, and just in time for Christmas."

"Fortunately, everyone is alive and well to enjoy the money for Christmas," I responded in my typical SAWB attitude. "We were damn lucky not to have anyone hurt. You have unit staff in offices in those units and with no communication, radios, body alarms, or anything else. If someone doesn't stop in and tell them, they have no way of knowing what's going on. If a detainee had not stopped Mr. Price, he could have easily been caught in his office when staff was forced from the unit." He went on into his office without comment.

CHAPTER 10

BUILDING A BETTER RIOT

AS A RESULT OF THE NOVEMBER 1 RIOT, THE DETAINEES were placed on lockdown status once more. Since the riot had been escalated by the sight of a news media vehicle during the riot and sporadic actions after the riot, canvas was hung over the windows on the Norton side of B cell house to prevent them seeing the street. Initially, the detainees were provided with bag meals. Very quickly, the institution purchased hot carts similar to those used in a hospital to serve hot meals from cell to cell. Beginning November 26, 1984, one hot meal a day was being provided to the detainees. This required the food service department to go into a twenty-four hour operation.

On November 21, 1984, the Labor Management Relations meeting was canceled AW(O) Hosea Ramos and Union Representative Earl Lawson met in the office of the AW(O) for discussion of Union and Management's concerns.

Associate Warden Ramos consulted with Mr. Lawson on plans which are underway to normalize operations at USP-Atlanta.

Warden Blackmon has requested $1 Million and 58 additional positions under Cuban Project 58G. These 58 requested positions are broken down to six (6) Food Service, three (3) Medical, and forty-nine (49) Custody. USP-Atlanta was given seven (7) additional Correctional Officer positions with funding after January 1, 1985. We will begin to recruit for those positions immediately. On November 21, 1984, an additional ten (10) positions were provided. Distribution of those positions will be determined by the Executive Staff.

Preliminary figures show that approximately $418,625 had been spent, thus far, during the Cuban demonstration. The Bureau has $500,000 in reserve. At the current spending rate, the remainder of this emergency reserve will be depleted.

Steps will be taken to minimize physical staff contact with the detainee population. They are:

- The Cuban population will remain in lockdown status.

- Modifications to A and B cell houses.
    - All doors have been fortified.
    - Showers will be secured with expanded metal and doors will have Folger Adams locks.

- Establish a Cuban detainee work cadre.

- An instrument has been developed to assist in identifying, based on risk factors, those Cuban detainees who are able to work, those who are borderline and those who are bad risks. It is management's intent to identify approximately 424 inmates/detainees combined who would work in all critical areas within our institution. A large portion, approximately 226, would be designated to work in Unicor, and thus save our industrial operation.

- Five additional CMS employees will be on TDY from other institutions beginning Monday, November 26, through December 7 to complete installation of boilerplate on the inside of the exterior walls in E cell house. E cell house will then be converted into the Cuban work cadre unit. Cuban AD/DS will be moved to D and C cell houses. Cuff and food slots, security screening, shower doors, and doors for each range are planned to be installed. Funds have not yet been authorized.

Each department is, and will continue, experiencing overtime with no relief anticipated in the near future. Beginning Monday, November 26, we will begin feeding A and B cell houses one hot meal per day, which will meet the minimum policy requirements and increase Food Service operations by approximately five hours per cell house. We will go into a twenty-four-hour Food Service operation, which also will mean an increase of overtime hours. Custody overtime will also increase in order for officers to supervise feeding and provide escort, shower the units and provide recreation for one range per cell house each day one hour per week. Recreation pens will be constructed so that recreation can be accomplished. Every attempt is being made to minimize contact between detainees and staff and preserve staff safety. All of this will necessitate more staff time, funds, and a great lot of communication, coordination and understanding.

On Thanksgiving Day, B cell house will be provided turkey and dressing, pie or cake, and fruit salad in six oz., four oz., and two oz. Styrofoam cups.

Union's Concerns

Insufficient communication equipment for staff: a speaker system to receive all radio transmissions installed within each unit staff office and a body alarm for unit staff working in the unit is needed for unit staff to call or respond to calls for assistance.

Insufficient quantity of emergency equipment such as gas masks, radios, hand-cuffs, flashlights, etc.

Poor quality of emergency equipment for staff; the gas masks currently supplied to the staff for use in an emergency are a hazard to same.

Management's Response

Purchase Orders have been provided to purchase the majority of these items through the Department of Justice (Just us) and Bureau of Prisons Project 58G. The speaker system and body alarms suggested by the AFGE will be researched.

Union 's Concern

Supervisors' denial of sick leave. Some supervisors have denied sick leave to officers who are actually sick and are not abusers of sick leave.

Management's Response

Management will follow policy and established procedures to ensure this practice does not happen in the future.

Union's Concern

The Union does not have specifics, but understand that some individuals were charged for thirty-minute meal times when, in fact, they were not given time for meals during overtime.

Management's Response

The Union was asked to get specifics on this subject and it would be corrected.

In late November 1984, we were advised that the correctional force was going to be placed on twelve-hour shifts beginning on or about December 7, 1984. As representatives of the local union, we were caught in the middle of a bad situation. Several of the staff wanted to work the overtime; after all, twenty hours a week of overtime helps the wallet. Additionally, if we became extremely verbal on the issue and then had someone get injured as a result of insufficient help, we could be blamed for causing the injury. On the other hand, this was purely against the Master Agreement, federal law, and good sense. We attempted to encourage management to use volunteer overtime from other departments to supplement the correctional force which had been done from 1980 to 1982. When they refused this, we recommended that they have no less than three, and preferably four, twelve-hour shifts—from 6:00 to 6:00, 8:00 to 8:00, and 12:00 to 12:00, instead of their proposed two shifts from 6:00 to 6:00. Our logic was that it was not rational to believe that you needed the same number of employees at 7:00 p.m. that you needed at 3:00 a.m. This would also have permitted a rotation of assignment and shifts. Management informed us that they had considered those factors and were going to keep the two shifts. Immediately, there were several complaints. Those working from 6:00 p.m. to 6:00 a.m. got home in time to see their wife go to work and kissed her on his way to work as she got home. The 6:00 a.m. to 6:00 p.m. shift could not care for any personal business. The 6:00 p.m. to 6:00 a.m. shift could not get off the night shift; there was no rotation of hours or jobs. On January 4, 1985, the following letter was sent:

January 4, 1985
To the Acting Warden
US Penitentiary, Atlanta

Members of the bargaining unit, Local 1145, are deeply concerned about the total disregard of the Master Agreement between the Federal Prison System and the American Federation of Government Employees.

We are fully aware of the powers of management to take actions which would routinely be in violation of the Master Agreement in a time of an emergency. Article 3, Section C of the Master Agreement provides for such action providing that the Employer will inform the Local Union President of the circumstances causing the emergency and its expected duration. At this time, we have been unable to secure a response to these questions.

It is our belief that staff shortage in this facility has been a routine problem since the Bureau of Prisons began acting upon a planned closure of this facility. Vacating of post has been a daily occurrence in this facility over the objections of the Local. The staff shortage did not begin on November 1, 1984 when the Cuban detainees took over 8 Cellhouse. We are of the opinion that "indefinite" is not a sufficient expected duration of the declaration of emergency. We are of the opinion that we are now in a state of confusion more than a state of emergency. As a result of this belief, we would like a reply to the following questions:

- What is the nature of the emergency?

- What is the expected duration of the emergency?

- Why were non-custodial staff not permitted to assist the custodial staff in supplying staff to preclude the emergency?

- Why are non-custodial staff now being required to work custodial post to continue routine operations during a declared emergency?

- Why are staff being required to work overtime to complete training during the state of emergency?

- Why are staff not being provided with items of personal safety, such as radios, while being required to work under emergency conditions?

- Why has staffing not been supplemented by the region or bureau?

If the emergency conditions consist to the extent of making the Master Agreement null and void, staff working under these conditions deserve to know the logic of management. Your immediate attention to this mutual problem of great concern is greatly appreciated. Members of the Unit and all staff in this facility stand ready to support the goal and accomplish the needs of the institution. However, the only thing that has made a drastic change over recent weeks has been the working hours and conditions of these staff.

Respectfully,
President, AFGE Local 1145

On January 25, we received the following response:

January 25, 1985

To the President, AFGE Local 1145
U.S. Penitentiary, Atlanta

I am in receipt of your letter of January 4, 1985, in which you raise several questions regarding our present emergency situation at this facility.

In your letter, you inquire about the nature of the emergency. As you are well aware, we have had two major disturbances involving the Cuban detainees on October 14, 1984 and November 1, 1984. The final disturbance occurring on November 1, 1984 and increase of violence against staff has resulted in our present continued lock-down status with limited movement in the Institution for both "A" and "B" cell house detainees.

The existing lockdown status requires that the detainees be fed, showered, worked, and recreated in small groups resulting in the need for more Correctional officers to perform these functions. In order to preserve life, security, and the orderly operation of the Institution, management will continue to require that the detainees be moved, showered, fed, work, and recreated in small groups.

USP, Atlanta is, in fact, in a state of emergency and has been for some time. The duration of the emergency is difficult to define; however, it will last as long as the problem exists and conditions continue to pose a threat to the life and safety of our staff as well as the security and orderly operation of our institution. There are many factors which have an impact on our circumstances including the release plans for the Cubans, procedural changes in handling the Cubans based upon conformance of policy, further constraints from the court, and further disturbances by the Cuban detainees, as well as our ability to bring new staff on board. The impact of these external factors cannot be accurately predicted. Efforts are being initiated to increase our recruiting efforts as well as request additional positions from the Central Office. Recently, our Personnel Office staff made contacts with radio stations in Atlanta, placed an advertisement in the Atlanta Constitution and have written to in excess of 200 potential applicants on the federal register who have listed other institutions as their first choices. We have informed these applicants that USP, Atlanta has immediate vacancies which we are recruiting to fill. At the present time, custody has 238.7 allocated positions and 228 personnel on board with 320 positions at a minimum which require manning. Effective January 1, 1985, seventeen additional positions were provided to USP, Atlanta to further augment our staff. Therefore, the bureau is aware of our emergency and is taking a definitive step in augmenting our needs. Additionally, we have required thirty-seven more positions for Correctional Services from the Central Office, but this request is part of a supplemental appropriation request to Congress. As of this time, we do not know the chances of passage of our request. However, even with the approval and filling of these positions, with no additional requirements on our staff, we will be approximately forty-six (46) positions short of the three hundred and twenty (320) positions needed to fill our present roster.

In your letter you inquired about the reason that non-custodial staff have not been permitted to assist the Custodial staff in supplying staff to preclude the emergency. The emergency conditions I have described in our present lock-down situation would not be precluded solely by the use of non-custodial staff. It would only provide us with some additional resources to assist us in working under the emergency conditions. Our decision not to employ non-custodial staff on an overtime basis as has been explained previously was based upon two factors:

- First, we believed that Article 18, Section 0, in our Master Agreement prohibited us from placing employees from other departments on an overtime roster for other departments. I did not want to make a decision on establishing an exception to the Contract without receiving a copy of a specific arbitration case about this issue. It took several weeks to receive a copy of the decision. After reviewing it with my staff, I believed that the use of non-custodial staff on an overtime roster for another department would be an exception to the contract language of our Master Agreement. Additionally, management believed that, if at all possible, the work assignments of a department should normally be completed by employees of that department. Management at this Institution determined that a better means to handle the overtime situation was for correctional staff to work twelve (12) hour shifts with two days off rather than have correctional and /or non-correctional staff work sixteen hours a day with no days off. After reviewing our present situation, management does not believe that our correctional staff can fill the existing required positions on the roster even while working twelve-hour shifts. Our alternatives are limited. We can increase the Correctional Officer shift to fourteen or sixteen hours a day or reduce the number of days off. A better solution at this time which we have implemented on Friday, January 25, 1985, is to allow employees from other departments to work overtime. Exceptions would be females, who are excluded from employment on the Custodial force.

• At this time, the volume of volunteers from other departments who will request to work overtime is an unknown quantity. Management will have to monitor the number of volunteers to determine what other alternatives may have to be considered if volunteers from other departments do not meet our required staffing needs. Realizing that the prospects of receiving eighty-three additional allocated positions is remote, other options in addition to voluntary overtime from other departments, must be pursued. Toward that endeavor, we are researching the feasibility of returning to eight-hour shifts while continuing several assignments on a twelve-hour shift basis to augment the 320 position difference. Our intent, if feasible, will be to have custodial personnel rotate on a quarterly basis, from eight-hour shifts to twelve-hour assignments.

• A decision was made by Management to continue with our Annual Training Program. We believe that this training is essential for the continued development of our staff, not only at this Institution, but for advancement possibilities at other Institutions. It was management's decision that non-correctional staff would work custodial posts to allow Correctional employees an opportunity to attend training. This practice is common in the Bureau of Prisons and was upheld in an April 1983, arbitration decision at FPC, Allenwood.

• In regard to your concern about staff not being provided with items of personal safety, such as radios, while being required to work under the emergency conditions, management does not agree. Management is sensitive to any concern regarding the personal safety of our employees. Our action in this Institution in the state of emergency is proof of that. However, we must never cease to forget that our positions are covered under the provisions of hazardous duty retirement requiring exposure at many times to potentially dangerous situations. Management will continue to provide the necessary personal safety items to perform correctional officer duties. Additionally, we will continue to monitor utilization of existing equipment to determine its most effective usage. At the present time our custodial force is reviewing our procedures for the issuing of all radios and body alarms.

- Finally, you inquired about supplemental staff being provided by the Regional Office or Bureau. Management believes that it is to our advantage, if at all possible, to use our staff to handle this emergency. Our staff is familiar with the Cuban detainee population and understands their behavior far better than employees who have had no contact with them. By no means has Management ruled out the use of personnel from other Institutions. Although we do not believe this additional source of staff alone will meet our critical needs, we are presently requesting their utilization to augment our staff during this emergency.

I know you share my concern regarding staff welfare during this emergency. It is far better for us, both Management and labor to work together than to be divided on issues. We will continue to work with you so we can face these difficult problems together, as a team.

Sincerely,
Warden, USP, Atlanta

On January 23, 1985, the LMR Committee met. Prior to that date, I had written up a grievance concerning the twelve-hour shifts and a variety of other matters. The executive staff had reviewed and approved the contents of the grievance; it was signed and ready to be delivered at 1:00 p.m. when the LMR met. During the meeting we asked about every item on the grievance and heard management's expression of, "It's going to be my way because I am the boss." Not being true to our nature, we did not argue those points. As we left the meeting at 3:15 p.m., the AW-C remarked, "This sure has been a long LMR meeting, but it was probably the most productive that we have had. We covered a lot of items and resolved a lot of issues." At 3:20 p.m. the grievance was on the warden's desk. On February 21, 1985 the grievance was answered. We requested arbitration, but the twelve-hour shift ended before going to arbitration.

On February 7, 1985, we questioned the response of the January 25, 1985 letter. We advised the warden that if these issues were not addressed and resolved to a mutual satisfaction, we would take the issue to members of Congress. As a result of this statement, the warden filed a formal grievance against our local. In April 1985, I recommended that we withdraw from the LMR as a result of management's misrepresentation of their intent and continual failure to bargain in good faith. Initially, the rest of the executive staff for our local union joked about my getting radical again. On July 16, 1985, I informed the warden that we would seek information in writing but would not attend further LMR meetings. The local union continued to work for safer working conditions to no avail. By the end of 1985 we were even requesting Congress to assist in getting our paycheck on time.

During 1985, the detainees remained on lockdown status, except for a few on the work cadre to maintain sanitation of the facility. In October 1985, a detainee who was handcuffed attempted to head-butt a staff, attempted to kick another, and spat on one. During the investigation, he claimed that the officer giving him a pot shake was "feeling his ass." A supervisor investigating the report agreed that the officer should not be taking such action and withdrew the incident report. Between May 1985, and October 1985, alone, there were seventy assaults on staff reported. For the same period, other institutions averaged about three assaults each. We asked assistance from the warden on some means of release of the stress but were informed, "I believe the described individual's reactions to stress are in the small minority and are inappropriate responses to stress." It was not until 1987 that a gym was built for the staff to work out as a means of releasing tension.

During the period of lock down, the detainees claimed, "The next time we are going to burn down the factory." The lockdown was another frustration for the detainees.

During the lockdown, our local union invited Congressman Robert Kastenmeier to visit our facility and to allow us to take him for a tour. He did come and was taken through the facility. Each tour has a pattern: go into either A or B cell house and look at the first five cells (orderlies) and told that the rest are the same. He insisted on seeing each cell and was angry at some of the things which he found. He talked to the local union officers for about thirty minutes before he left.

After his departure, he mailed us a list of questions. I provided the following responses for the local.

May 7, 1986

Honorable Robert W. Kastenmeier
2137 B R H 003
Washington, D.C. 20515

Dear Congressman Kastenmeier,

I would like to offer my sincere apology for the long and overdue delay in responding to your letter. Unfortunately, we do not have the time or access to material to respond to the information as management did.

We will make every effort to respond to each question as fully and accurately as possible. Additionally, we will provide documentation as to the information provided. We are not attempting to undermine management or to make idle allegations. Our only desire is to have input into developing the safest possible working conditions for our staff.

If you have any questions as to the information provided or we can be of further assistance, please do not hesitate to contact me. My address is 601 McDonough Blvd., Atlanta, Georgia, 30315, telephone number area code 404-622-6241.

Respectfully,
Vincent Ficalore
President
AFGE Local 1145

QUESTION NO. 1

- Current number of inmates within the main facility and camp.

Enclosed you will find a computer printout of the count within the facility. The institution total count is 2,405. The camp count is 288. The balance of the institution count is inside the main facility, a total of 2,117.

- Number of Cuban inmates within the main facility.

All Cuban detainees are housed within the main facility. The current number is 1,819. See attached breakdown.

- Number of cells within the main facility.

To afford you understanding our facility, the following information is provided: A cell house, ranges 1 through 5 and B cell house, ranges 6 through 10 are identical. These are multiple (8 bed) cells. C cell house, ranges 11 through 15 and D cell house, ranges 16 through 20 are identical. These are single cells. Ranges 1, 6, 11, and 16 are on the ground floors.

Ranges 1 through 10 have a total of 20 cells per range. One cell on each range is a shower. Additionally, ranges 1, 3, 5, and 8 have cells converted into office space for unit staff. To assist you in relating the bodies with the cells, I will relate the number of cells with the range on the computer printout. Ranges 11 through 20 have a total of 38 cells per range with 2 cells (without cell division) being a shower. The total cell is thirty-six per range in C and D cell house. AWB is a multiple man cell. E cell house (listed on the form as AD1 and AD2) is our segregation unit. These units are Cuban housing units except for nineteen cells on ranges

15 and 20 which are being used for American holdovers and American segregation units. The hospital houses, for the most part, Cuban and psychiatric patients.

- Number of dormitories

Three (3), all housing Americans. However, Dorm 1 has twelve rooms. Each room houses six to twelve inmates. Dorm 4 has a total of thirty-five rooms, each housing two inmates. Dorm 3 is the only true, dormitory-type unit inside. It is a horseshoe type housing unit with a four-foot divider between two man (one double bunk) cubicles.

- Average number of inmates per cell on the average day during the last year within the main facility.

This number has had no meaningful change from today.

- Average square foot of living space of Cuban inmate.

A and B cell houses provide an average of 30 square feet per inmate. C and D have 50 square feet per inmate. AWB is probably near 30 square feet per inmate, although I have been unable to get actual information. Our segregation unit provides 83.5 square feet per inmate when the cell is shared by two or 167 square feet when housed alone. Most detainees desire a two-man room due to the number of hours spent in the cell.

QUESTION NO. 2

- MEDICAL: The institution hospital is (1) a medical clinic which provides for emergency treatment and routine sick call care; (2) a diagnostic clinic to determine what treatment may be needed and is equipped with x-ray and other medical equipment; (3) and a psychiatric inpatient care facility for long or short term needs. Inmates who need inpatient treatment for most medical treatments are contracted out to local hospitals outside of the institution.

- EDUCATION (in English and Spanish): If you will look at the response given by management you will observe numbers of participants only. It is tragic that the entire Bureau is more concerned with quantity of participants than quality of education. The instructor must (1) develop individual training material rather than using the best packaged instructions available, (2) maintain a high quantity of participants, and (3) have a high completion rate, to justify higher pay grades. This results in inmates receiving certificates of achievement from classes in which they have limited participation.

- LIBRARY SERVICES (in English and Spanish): In addition to the library services listed, many of the Cuban inmates receive large volumes of books from friends and families outside the facility. Prior to Cuban population, books could not be received from individuals from the community; only book stores and publishing companies. However, sentenced inmates and detainees in lockdown units do not have access to the library to check out reading material other than law books and must know specifically which law book they desire in order to provide a written request.

- PUBLICATIONS (in English and Spanish): Many of the Cuban detainees have been released to the street and have returned as a result of criminal behavior. While in the community they were successful in developing ties which send in a variety of publications. To complement the publications available in the library (which get minimal usage from the population) most magazine, newspapers and publications available within the community are ordered by inmates and detainees within the facility. These publications are readily shared by others.

- MAIL: Only restrictions which affect the community at large (i.e., mail fraud) affect the population. Items cannot be ordered which would be contraband to possess. Mail regulations which impede or delay mail is minimal.

- VISITING: The information previously available is accurate. The only other visitation is of greater concern to the staff in regard to both security and personal safety. This is group visitation or programming. When outside groups present or attend religious, programming, or recreational activities within the facility, the officers are always concerned about maximum contact between the guest and population with minimal supervision and no background upon any visitor. We are concerned about the introduction of drugs , weapons, explosives, or an assault upon a visitor.

- RECREATION: The Cuban inmates enjoy American TV and spend many hours in personal escape watching a variety of programs. Additionally , the institution has recently purchased VCR recorders to complement the VCR tape library.

- VOCATIONAL TRAINING: Most training within the institution is "on the job" training within the institutional maintenance or industries. Mechanical services training uses inmates to maintain the institution and for the most part it is self-taught or trained by other inmates while working as an apprentice. Industrial training is limited to areas which our facilities produce . In many cases, this is similar to the "making of license plates."

- CLASSIFICATION: Each inmate is classified within thirty days of his being committed to a correctional facility. This includes the Cuban inmates. The annual review of the Cuban detainee results in job and quarter changes based upon speculation rather than clearly planned and outlined goals. Addition ally, the Cuban detainees are not always certain of expectations with annual reviews rather than ninety-day reviews.

QUESTION NO. 3: *Please describe how each of these program areas are affected when the inmates are locked down.*

- The medical sick-call was held in the units which were on lockdown status. Detainees requiring additional medical treatment were escorted to the hospital after the in-unit examination by the Physician Assistant.

- Education : For the most part, suspended during lockdown.

- Library Services: Suspended during lockdown.

- Publications: Suspended during lockdown.

- Mail: No change as a result of lockdown.

- Visiting: Suspended during lockdown.

- Recreation: Limited to five hours per week outside the cell.

- Vocational, Industries, in prison jobs: Suspended during lockdown.

- Classification: No change as a result of the lockdown.

All except ranges 5 through 10 are currently open. The institution is seeking additional jobs in industry as rapidly as possible. Ranges 5, 6, and 7 are currently programmed to be removed from lockdown and returned to work as soon as the jobs are available. Ranges 8, 9, and 10 will be returned to work and removed from lockdown on a slow but steady basis as soon as the jobs are available. (This is the current speculated plan; our local has no direct input or knowledge.)

QUESTION NO. 4: *How do the current practices at Atlanta compare to relevant correctional standards, such as those of the American Correctional Association Accreditation Commission?*

The Atlanta Federal Penitentiary was built in 1901 and designed to house a specific type of individual. One which, for the most part, must be kept secure from society. The Cuban inmates were spread throughout the Bureau and in Fort Chaffee, Arkansas in 1980 and 1981. They were all sent to Atlanta when it was discovered that the institutions designed for the modern criminal could not withstand the destructive lifestyle of the Cuban detainee. Our facility has purchased stainless steel commodes, sinks, and water fountain stands which were designed to be tamper-proof for our type facility. Several of these units have been rendered unserviceable while others were badly damaged by the Cuban population. Tamper-proof lights were torn from the ceiling, water pipes and fire hose stands broken out under routine daily activities. While the needless destruction has been very expensive, the granite and steel structures still stand. Remodeling our facility at this time would result in additional needed waste of monies. While it is not the most comfortable housing facility available, it does not provide humane living conditions which comply with all laws and bureau policy. Suggestions will be provided in QUESTION NO. 9.

QUESTION NUMBER 5: Our local has no information concerning the consent order.

QUESTION NO. 6: *What percentage of the Cuban inmates would present a serious, demonstrable threat to the safety of the community if released?*

- A significant number of the Cuban detainees housed in our facility would present a serious, demonstrable threat to the safety of the community. However, this is a serious look at the problem with no thought to a possible solution. Many would be a serious threat because of their psychiatric (criminally insane) needs. Merely by the nature of our facility, we provide inadequate psychiatric care to have the detainee become functional within the community. The vast number of attempted suicides, destruction of property, and assaults on detainees by detainees is, in large part, a result of the inability to accept any delayed gratification, i.e., "If I don't get a cell change now, I will cut my wrists." A mental health facility designed to control and provide treatment for this group would probably have greater success in modifying behavior for potentially future release. The detainees who were released from our facility shortly after their arrival and between 1980 and 1983 were placed into a situation similar to the black population of Alabama in 1900. They were released into a slumping economy with no support groups, poor work habits and limited job skills. They were unfamiliar with the culture and language but had the great American dream. This, coupled with the inability to accept delayed gratification and emotional instability, left only criminal activities to survive. To be successful within the community, those who are prepared to enter the community must be released through a halfway house to develop stable employment and community ties before release.

• If these inmates were serving federal sentences for the crimes they committed in Cuba, how many would still be in prison? While this information is not available, many of the inmates have committed offenses within the community, served their sentence in the state institution and subsequently released to our facility pending deportation.

QUESTION NO. 7: *Why did the November 1984 riot occur?*

The explanation given by management is true, but other factors were involved. The annual progress review leaves the detainees uncertain of any goals within the institution and without recommendations for self-improvement for potential release. Inadequate unit staffing to complete the review of each Cuban inmate on a ninety-day basis is also inadequate to provide positive motivation toward self-improvement. Subsequently, the only motivating factor is negative. Incident reports are used to withhold privileges, but positive efforts (other than no incident reports) appear to be meaningless to the detainees. Since unit staff are unable to provide for job requirements and make themselves available for assistance to the detainee, the Cuban inmates write management staff for information. For the most part the response is for the detainee to see the unit staff.

The correctional staff have the same frustration as the Cuban population. The only motivation for the staff is negative. The desire to do a good job or provide quality work is seen as meaningless. The annual evaluation is seen as documentation of a pre-conceived notion, having nothing to do with facts. All promotions are also controlled by personnel. While some staff were allowed to remove their annual evaluation from the personnel office to make changes for a promotion board, other staff had their annual evaluation downgraded by the personnel without ever being informed of this change. This resulted in the staff member not being equally considered for the vacant positions. Actions such as this, leave correctional staff aware that loyalties to personnel and not work, will *make or break* their careers. Additionally, supervisors ride roughshod over staff, using intimidation as the only motivating tool. When an incident occurs, supervisors interrogate detainees to determine what staff have done to cause the incident. This, coupled with the frequency of assaults on staff, staff having urine and human waste thrown on them create a high level of stress and frustration. With the correctional officer, who is always present being highly frustrated and consistently stressful, and the Cuban inmate in the same condition. Confrontation is inevitable.

The Cuban inmate has an additional stress, which played a big role in the desire to gain public support. There is no scheduled pattern for their review by the INS release panel. The detainee is told by the panel that he must be free of incidents for an additional year before getting any favorable consideration for release. Eighteen months later, he has still not seen the panel again. If he receives a favorable decision concerning a release, he may be in our facility six months later with a release paper. No one will explain when or where he will be released. There is a limited number of halfway house facilities which will accept the Cuban population. We are of the opinion that the only reason we have not had an incident with serious consequence is that the Cuban inmates and the correctional staff identify with the plight of the other.

QUESTION NO. 8: *What steps can the bureau take in the short term to improve the conditions of confinement for the Cuban inmates?*

- The bureau could provide adequate qualified unit staff to assure that (1) programming of self-improvement programs is provided; (2) positive actions and programming recorded and provided to the panel; (3) improve labor-management relations, working conditions, and stress relief programs for violent and move non-destructive Cuban inmates to less secure facilities. This action would release over-crowdedness, provide a wider variety of training at a less expensive price for those, who qualify, and reward positive behavior.
- Long Term: Develop a larger variety of programs specifically for the psychiatric needs of our population.

QUESTION NO. 9: *What steps, if any, should the Congress take to respond to this situation?*

The Cuban inmates are extremely destructive. Spending money to remodel areas which will be again destroyed, at this time, is meaningless. The priority should be in modifying the behavior of the population to reduce destructiveness. Subsequently, Congress should require the Agency to (1) fill all vacancies in unit staffing to ensure a 90 day review; (2) require INS panels to review the Cuban population in a timely manner, much the same manner as the Parole Commission does American inmates and (3) require the Agency to establish half-way house facilities through contract or establishment to aid the detainees in pre-release.

Any efforts by Congress to return the Cuban population to Cuba will result in reduced cost of housing these individuals and reducing the crime rate if they are released. These individuals are criminally oriented with psychological instability. They are impulsive, seeking immediate self-gratification without regard for life or safety of themselves or others. They are a threat to the safety and security of staff within the facility and a danger to society if released. The Cubans should be returned to Cuba by whatever means feasible.

Many of the staffing difficulties can be responded to by Congress. Recently, Mr. Tom Burns, our personnel officer, made changes on twelve or more annual evaluations during a promotion board and without the employee having knowledge of this change. For the employee to fight the issue through the Union will result in an unpleasant job assignment, frequent harassment, and inability to be promoted. Currently, there is no governmental agency to review personnel practices. An independent agency to investigate and take action about such complaints would improve working conditions and assist in retaining employees.

QUESTION NO. 10: *What is the employee turnover level?*

Enclosed is current printout of staff employment from May 12, 1985 to current. Also, you will find a seniority record to assist in understanding more about the turnover rate.

QUESTION NO. 11: *What is the current average noise level within the cellblocks?*

The noise level changes with the temperature and activities. When it is cold, the detainees remain covered and quieter. On several occasions and prior to the riot, after having staff paged over the intercom and calling them on their radio, additional staff were sent to locate a staff member on the ranges. Due to the noise level, they could not hear the pages.

Does this level exceed relevant of correctional standards?

We do not have any knowledge of OSHA standards or any other testing.

What can be done to reduce the noise level?

With no humor or hostility intended, deport the Cuban population.

With efforts to resolve the aggression toward employees by management officials, a press release was authorized by the executive staff of our local. It was deemed unjustifiable when it was learned that the institution was using appropriated government funds to buy porno VCR tapes while refusing to buy radios and body alarms for staff. It had been learned that members of his staff had ordered pornographic VCR tapes from institutional funds and for institutional use. Spending more than $5,000.00 of appropriated tax funds for flowers to be put around the front of the institution and around the homes of the members of the executive staff at the institution who lived on the grounds of the institution, while not providing adequate emergency equipment for staff should have been criminal. As a result of this position, the following news release was made:

FOR IMMEDIATE RELEASE
PRESS RELEASE FOR LOCAL 1145

The Federal Employees at the Atlanta Federal Penitentiary are concerned about their careers and their lives; and, they are concerned about the inmates and the public. Working conditions at the institution have been allowed to deteriorate to the point their very lives are in jeopardy each day they report to work. Public attention has been focused on the care, welfare, and safety of the inmates with little or no attention on the problems of the employees. Eliminate the employees' problems and you eliminate almost all the problems of the inmates.

The non-supervisory employees of the Atlanta Penitentiary are represented by Local 1145 of the American Federation of Government Employees, AFL-CIO (AFGE). The employees have not gone public with their concerns because they have been trying to deal with them through supervisory channels and Congressional contacts. However, those channels have only produced Band-Aid type results in most cases. Additionally, the employees have a sincere concern for their safety and their careers for speaking out.

Today is the beginning of our speaking out. The employees cannot depend on Congress to protect them because Congress has proven to be less than effective in providing protection to Federal Employees who come forward and report waste, fraud, abuse, and negligence. The employees cannot depend on the employer because the employer is the one being reported, and it is a well-known fact that the employer will take reprisal action against them. However, the public not only has a vested interest in the institution, but their very safety could be placed in jeopardy because of the conditions that exist. The loss of any individual right by anyone in this country is a concern of us all. The public has a right to know. Therefore, we are going to make our views known to the news media on a continuing basis until the public demands change and the public lets it be known that they will not allow reprisal against its employees for keeping them informed.

On or about March 13, 1986, the warden stated publicly that the employees had not brought any of their "demands" to his attention. That statement as a callous and vicious untruth. These actions point to the very essences of the problems at the Atlanta Penitentiary—top management's insensitivity to the problems and inability to deal with them up front. It's almost as if the warden believes that if you ignore the situation long enough it will either go away or cure itself. He has contempt for anyone who interferes with this process. The employees have demonstrated their concerns for a long time. Here are some examples of them "not bringing their demands" forward.

On November 19, 1984, they asked the following subjects placed on the agenda of the November 21, 1984, Labor-Management Relations meeting: 1) insufficient communication equipment for staff; 2) insufficient quantity of emergency equipment such as gas masks, radios, handcuffs, flashlights, etc.; 3) poor quality of emergency equipment; and 4) supervisors' denial of sick leave. The employees' concerns were met with a "ho-hum" attitude and got little or no attention..

On November 21, 1984, the employees were informed of an increase in the overtime to be worked and a so-called state of emergency. On January 4, 1985, a grievance was filed on behalf of the employees concerning the emergency and staff not being provided with items of personal safety.

On January 23, 1985, a formal grievance was filed concerning the state of emergency, using non-custodial staff to perform the duties of Custodial Staff, important posts not being manned, failure to provide proper safety equipment, requiring staff to perform janitorial duties normally performed by inmates, staff required to work five consecutive twelve-hour shifts, without even a meal break, and quarterly assignments being extended for two months without any rotation, failure to use volunteer non-correctional staff as permitted, cancellation of scheduled leave and not having adequate supply of foul-weather equipment for employees required to work outside.

On January 25 and February 21, 1985, the Warden replied to the grievances and on February 7, 1985, the employees responded by requesting additional information. On February 14, 1985, the employees wrote to the Warden concerning all those matters brought to his attention since November 19, 1984, and the lack of results satisfactory to the employees.

On February 14, 1985, the employer was advised that the employees, and specifically Union Officials, would be contacting congressional people seeking relief from the conditions that existed at the institution. On February 14, 1985, the Union Officers wrote to Senator Matt Mattingly concerning the problems. Senator replied on July 25, 1985. On March 19, 1985, the Warden responded to the notification by the Union that they would be contacting their Congressional representatives and filed a grievance against the Union.

On July 16, 1985, the Warden was notified that the Union was withdrawing from the monthly Labor-Management Relations meetings. The warden replied on July 30, 1985.

On October 25, 1985, the Union notified the Warden of the employees' concern about the threat of AIDS and requested immediate action.

On October 25, 1985, the Union notified the Warden of the employees' concern about unsafe working conditions and requested a meeting of the Safety Committee.

On November 1, 1985, the Union notified the Warden about the conditions of employment and the increased level of stress, its impact on the employees and its potential impact. The Warden replied on November 27, 1985, with his usual defensive attitude rather than showing any willingness to discuss the subject or work out a solution.

On December 6, 1985, the Union wrote to Congressman Wyche Fowler about the employees not receiving their paychecks on time. The warden showed little concern that this was a serious matter to the already over-worked and stress-riddled staff.

These are not the actions of a work force that does not communicate with the employer. The employees, using their Exclusive Representative, have made numerous complaints about being treated as second-class citizens and working under unsafe conditions beyond the expectation of their profession, yet within the control of the Warden.

While management has refused to take action to correct severe security problems, employees are being held responsible for activities which they cannot possibly perform. However, at the slightest indication of wrong-doing, which in many cases, is nothing more than the inability to do the impossible, employees quickly receive disciplinary action. But, when management spends over $2,000.00 on video tapes over a period of sixteen months, it is only "poor judgement." AFGE Local 1145 is on record as deploring the actions of management officials concerning the VCR tapes purchased. The fact that tapes have been purchased for a non-existent library is deplorable, but the quality and subject matter is appalling. In view of the time span of this action, coupled with the fact that VCR players were not available until after the tape purchases were made public knowledge, constitutes wrongful use and abuse of a position of authority. While employees are denied equipment to make their jobs more safe, pornographic tapes are being purchased for detainees' personal use. When a management official discards over $1,000 worth of material in a dumpster and reorders a portion of the same material the next month, it is considered a "learning experience for a new supervisor."

AFGE negotiated in good faith for staff to be paid $125.00 annually, to buy their own uniform. Immediately after the agreement, management changed the entire uniform. Additionally, they provided official suppliers where staff were instructed to buy the uniform. The negotiated amount of $125.00 would require three years to buy the necessary clothing to start with. After AFGE fought to have Congress raise the allowance to $300.00 annually, which is required just to maintain a uniform, Mr. Carlson has used Gramm-Rudman to, again, assault staff by reducing the allowance to $175.00.

For years, our staff have been concerned about retaliation and have kept quiet. Now, the conditions are such that we can't sit quietly while our honesty and integrity are questioned as a result of management's actions. Management has recently implemented actions which will increase the workload while reducing the efficiency and security of staff solely to prevent public scrutiny. We have sent a letter to Mr. Norman Carlson, Director of the Bureau of Prisons, and are at this time appealing for his assistance. In July of 1985, our local Union refused to continue with the Labor-Management Relations Meetings since there was no effort on part of management to bargain in good faith. Instead, we were told that we would not be allowed to infringe upon Management's rights. We have appealed to members of Congress in an effort to receive our pay on time, after all efforts to secure something this simple at a local level failed. We received correspondence from Mr. Blackmon, Mr. Mckensie, and Mr. Carlson through the congressional assistance which placed blame on others but assured corrective action. Yet this pay period, thirty-nine staff members failed to get paid at the proper time.

Our staff has expressed the high-stress level on our staff. Staff are reminded that they receive two hours of stress training annually. Efforts to gain any means of release for stress has resulted in several members becoming disabled. Efforts toward the goal have met total resistance. Bargaining unit members are not even permitted to check a video tape from the institution library, if we ever get one opened. The average life expectancy of a male within the U.S. is age seventy-two. The expected life span for the average correctional officer is fifty-nine years. We are convinced that the undue stress will shorten the life of our Atlanta staff even more. Having commodes and sinks broken and thrown at your person causes stress. Having urine and feces thrown on staff causes stress. During a six-month period, seventy staff members were assaulted. Yet, Mr. Blackmon refused to afford any assistance to his staff suffering from stress. He claimed no responsibility for "inappropriate responses to stress" while denying the existence of appropriate responses.

Our staff has made every effort to communicate our deepest possible concern over the working conditions at the U.S. Penitentiary in Atlanta. We have complained about the lack of support from supervisory staff to all levels of management. When a staff becomes involved in a fight or an affray with a detainee, some supervisors make every effort to accuse staff of creating the problem. When staff are assaulted, it is because of *his* wrongdoing. When he defends himself to prevent serious personal injury, he is abusive to the population or the staff. Such a complacent attitude has led to a high level of frustration on the part of many of the detainees, resulting in additional assaults and stress on staff. In some cases, management is housing emotionally disturbed and depressed individuals in areas where no means exist for staff to obtain adequate protection but still hold the employee responsible for suicides.

Staffing in the Atlanta facility is insufficient and that deficiency will continue as long as the current attitudes toward labor exist. Abraham Lincoln said, "All that serves labor serves the Nation. All that harms is treason…If a man tells you he loves America, yet hates labor, he is a liar…There is no America without labor and to fleece one is to rob the other." Yet in 1986, we are to get a three-percent raise while employee contributions to the retirement plan is increased by two percent. This results in a one percent gain in the two-year period. In the field of corrections, the salary does not compensate for the duties.

In early 1986, the LMR once again began. We were still working with a self-serving executive body to some degree. The former captain had returned to Atlanta as an AWC. From a labor-management relations perspective, the AW that had retired could have been replaced by any of the population and would have been an improvement. In July, Mr. Blackmon retired also.

He had begun in Atlanta as a chaplain and retired from there as Warden. During his nine years as warden in Atlanta he was arrested for shoplifting a hairbrush at a local Kroger store and was found not-guilty of this charge. Rumors were that he had planned to remain until age fifty-five (mandatory retirement in the hazardous-duty field) but retired when he turned fifty as a result of the porno tape ordeal. It is truly unfortunate that a man who had spent more than twenty years in the bureau, over nine years as warden in Atlanta, to retire leaving memories only of the hairbrush trick and the porno flick.

Between May 12, 1985 and March 2, 1986, seventy-one new employees were brought on board, and another twenty-eight transferred in from other facilities. In spite of the recruitment efforts during that ten-month period, between the twelve terminated, the thirty-six resignations, and those transferred out, there was a net gain of only twenty-eight during that period. What actually transpired was little more than a paper numbers game. Between March 2, 1986 and November 23, 1987, another three were gained on the correctional force. The bureau raised the complement of officers as needed as a result of the disturbance in October and November 1, 1984. Before ever reaching that goal, they had already reduced the number allowed to a number below that already on board. At the same time, however, the Cuban population had been reduced from nearly 2,000 to 1,300. (When news of the deportation plans came on the news, some state facilities returned their Cuban population to the Atlanta facility, bringing the Cuban count to 1,394.)

After July 1986, the labor management relations normalized. Supervisors continued their harassment on the job since all the management officials were from the old regime. The new warden saw through many of their tactics and when charges were brought, he got a second investigative report. His decision was based upon what he felt was a fair decision and not a rubber stamp of a lower level management official. While we did not always agree with the warden, the executive body of the local union saw him to be fair in his every effort. He was people-oriented and genuinely concerned about people—with those qualities we could work together. Soon after his arrival, the AWO and personnel returned to their previous style of riding roughshod over the local and staff. Shortly after that, they found greener pastures and were transferred.

As the warden's positive efforts toward staff took effect, the attitude of staff became a little more positive. One department head was a continual thorn, but he no longer had the support or backing of the top officials. It may have been as a result of his Marine background, but it seemed as though he'd made up his mind on many issues and did not want to hear the facts of the case. During his tenure, twenty-five GS-8 officers were made GS-9 lieutenants. The Union maintained that as a result of the job assignments (sometimes replacing GS-6, GS-7, or GS-8 employees) they were lead officers and not management officials. Even after a National Labor Relations Board decision, he still insisted that they were lieutenants and assigned them management tasks. As a result of this, and other factors which I am not sure about, Mr. Blackmon's record became complete just after the riot. As the number of detainees being returned to work in late 1985 and early 1986 increased, the hostility seemed to diminish. Even the rumors of burning down industries diminished. This is revealed by the following facts:

	2/85–6/86	7/86–11/87
Inmates assaulted with weapons	72	43
Inmates assaulted without weapons	13	5
Staff assaulted with weapons	29	13
Staff assaulted without weapons	44	28
Homicides	**3**	**2**
Suicides	**3**	**1**

The Cuban detainees were much more understanding of their plight than American inmates. In December 1984, the announcement of the repatriation treaty was announced. At this time, the detainees were on lockdown status; those to be sent back to Cuba were pulled from the cells and locked in D cellhouse where they could be controlled one at a time. Some of those on the original treaty were ready and desired to return to Cuba. When the airlifts began, some of those scheduled to be returned were literally pulled from the bus going to the airport as a result of last-minute court action. Some of those pulled wanted to go back to Cuba. Many of the detainees were willing to spend life inside the Atlanta facility rather than returning to Cuba. While they obviously dreamed of and wanted freedom, they accepted their plight. Others either wanted to be released in the USA or returned to Cuba. Those who wanted to return to Cuba under any terms were very few.

The detainees were again going to the INS panel. Many of them were reportedly taunted and teased by the panel members. Statements like, "You can't go out on the street, you're too ugly!" were reported to have been made. While these hearings may not have been taken seriously by some management officials, the detainees took them very seriously. This was their future. Each of those housed in Atlanta were being housed "PENDING DEPORTATION!" While deportation had stopped, their understanding was that they would remain in jail until deportation was again started. The only chances left were death and that panel. What was equally frustrating to the detainees, was that they went there alone. Some of the detainees in my charge who worked on the job and supervised their units and recreation areas wanted me to go to the panel and make a statement for them. This was not permitted. They and a record from a case manager who saw them once a year were all that were present.

When the detainees went before the panel, they were told that they would get a final notice from Washington. Many would get the report that they were going to be released, but this, too, had no validity. During the riot in 1987, I saw a wife of one of the detainees on television. She informed the interviewer that, "I really hope that none of the hostages are hurt. Their lives and safety are the only things keeping my husband safe. I really feel sorry for the wives and families of the hostages; I know how they feel. But you need to understand our feelings." With this she lifted up a folder, opened it, and as she turned the pages, she said, "This is where my husband completed Basic English; this is where he received vocational training. These are certificates which he earned in there, trying to get ready to be released from that place. This is a letter from Washington. Here! You read it! It says that he is going to be released in October 1986! Why is my husband still in that place?"

During the riot we also saw Pat Swindall, a U.S. Congressman, on the news. Mr. Swindall, a member of the Congressional committee overseeing INS, informed us that in the past year more than 960 (I don 't remember exact numbers) had gone before the panel. Over 875 were to have been released; less than seventy-five had been released. That woman's husband was only one of many in the same situation.

Prior to the 1984 riot, we were dealing with detainees who had been confined initially when coming from Cuba. Some had been released for a short time, committed new crimes and returned. Those were hostile because they had committed a crime, been arrested by the state and served time for that crime and then returned to Atlanta pending deportation. Yet, they had been in our jails before and understood their situations. By 1987, we had a new source of hostility. We were not getting Cubans that had never been in jail in Cuba, been on our streets for five years or more with no difficulties. They had gotten married and had a child in this country. They may have had a good job and were working hard to fulfill the American dream, even though they had not yet become American citizens. One such detainee (who claimed, and I believed) was arrested for drunk driving in New Jersey. He served a jail sentence in New Jersey and was then brought to Atlanta, pending deportation.

In spite of all of these factors, the detainees were attempting to work through the system. I never knew why the government, big enough and strong enough to do as it pleased (and did just that) was not big enough to be honest. The detainees could have more easily lived with being told that they were never going to be released onto the American streets than they could the continual building of a fire for freedom in their hearts with promises and fanning the flame with worthless paper. Yet, the government continued the conversation of, "We are going to release you yesterday. Come to my office on the first of next month and we will talk about those plans." And on the first of next month they would be on vacation!

With the integration of the new breed of detainees into the population, by 1987 frustration and hostility were very high in the facility. The detainees did nothing to cause another lockdown, but you could see in their eyes and tell in their tone or unspoken words that their patience was running thin. While all statistical indicators were down at the time, it was obvious that the powder keg was very much present and full. As a result of this, the local union continued to press for more safety equipment and emergency equipment, both in the bureau and through Congress. Congressman John Lewis was invited to the Atlanta facility by the local Union to see for himself what was going on. However, when it appeared that we were getting a run-around by his staff and his only interest was to obtain publicity, we withdrew our invitation. After the riot began, he accomplished his goals; he got national publicity. In August 1987, Mr. Leon Franklan wrote a letter to U.S. Senator Wyche Fowler, Jr. which expressed our concern for the safety of our staff. While Mr. Franklan never got a response to the inquiry initiated to the bureau by Mr. Fowler's office, the following response was received:

August 25, 1987
Mr. Leon Franklan

Dear Mr. Franklan,

Thank you for letting me know of your concern about violence against guards in the federal prisons. I have initiated an inquiry on your behalf at the Federal Bureau of Prisons to determine the degree of danger that does exist and what steps are being taken to improve the situation, particularly in Atlanta.

Obviously, prison workers accept a certain degree of risk when they accept the job, but the provisions of their employment should also reflect the hazards they face while performing this necessary duty for society. While the General Schedule, by which all federal employees are paid, does not allow for hazardous-duty pay as such there are special provisions for extra compensation for specified assignments, such as participation in foreign prisoner exchange.

The dangers faced by all federal prison workers are taken into account in their inclusion in the Hazardous Duty Retirement Plan, which offers earlier retirement and an increased annuity. The Bureau of Prisons has also received permission from the Department of Justice (Just us) to implement an accelerated promotion plan, by which workers move on to the second grade of employment in six months instead of a year.

I certainly understand that prison guards face extraordinary pressures and hardships, and I will continue to monitor the pay and safety provisions of the Bureau of Prisons with your comments in mind.

I appreciate hearing from you. Please continue to let me know your thoughts on issues of importance to you.

Sincerely,
Wyche Fowler, Jr.
United States Senator

This letter, like the bureau's response, refers to the hazardous duty retirement plan, which people must live to enjoy. The most recent statistics available revealed that the average life expectancy of a penal worker after retirement (at age fifty-five) was two years. On November 20, 1987, the fuse was lit to the powder keg on national television. Mr. Leon Franklan, too, became a hostage.

CHAPTER 11

THE RIOT: A CHRONOLOGY OF EVENTS

FRIDAY MORNING, NOVEMBER 20, 1987 STARTED OUT AS a cool, crisp fall morning in Atlanta, where a light jacket felt nice. By 10:00 a.m., the detainees in the furniture factory were all busy cutting out and assembling desks and a doctor's credenza. The temperature outside had warmed up sufficiently to render the jacket uncomfortable. Little did anyone in Atlanta know that the snowball, which would cause an avalanche, had already been started rolling downhill from the mountain top in Washington, D.C.

At 7:50 a.m. on November 20, 1987, the State Department had informed the Department of Justice (Just us) of the resumption of the treaty to deport 2,700 detainees...one of which 201 had been flown to Cuba in 1985. From the Justice (Just us) Department, this information went to INS (Immigration and Naturalization Service) who notified the B.O.P (Bureau of Prisons) at about 10:00 a.m. of the resumption of the treaty. The director of the BOP, Mr. Quinlan, immediately notified the BOP's South Central Regional Director and the Southeast Regional Director, Gary Mckensie, in Atlanta. These directors, in turn, notified Warden Johnson in Oakdale and Warden Joseph Truman in Atlanta. This notification was given to the wardens about two hours before it was made public through a press conference by the State Department.

Much information concerning the agency and management official actions in this chapter is taken directly from "A Report to the Attorney General on the Disturbance at the Federal Detention Center, Oakdale, Louisiana, U.S. Penitentiary, Atlanta, Georgia, United States Department of Justice (Just us), Bureau of Prisons, February 1, 1988."

At approximately 10:30 a.m., Joseph Truman was informed of the planned 12:00 p.m. news release. He knew that some of the 2,500 detainees to be deported would come from Atlanta but had no idea who or how many. Sufficient time to obtain a list of names of the 2,500 detainees to be deported then locating and separating those still confined had not been given. It was suspected that many of those to be deported had been released to the street. At 11:00 a.m., the warden held a meeting with top level personnel. The top level personnel, consisting of AW's, Department Heads, and Unit Managers, were instructed to "Keep their ears to the ground," in an effort to determine the detainee reaction to the news. He called the Regional Director for INS in Atlanta, who informed him that ninety-four to one-hundred of the detainees in Atlanta would be affected.

At 9:00 a.m. Central Time (10:00 a.m. EST), the administrative staff in Oakdale, Louisiana met to discuss and develop a contingency plan. Extra staff were called in on an overtime basis immediately

At 9:30 a.m., Warden Johnson received a phone call from a reporter with the Miami Herald and was asked to give his reaction to an advance press release on the new Cuban exchange program announced by the State Department.

At 12:30 p.m., the warden, unit staff, and all bilingual staff circulated among each of the detainee work details to inform the population about the announced agreement. The statement prepared by the warden read: "The United States and Cuban governments have announced that some Marielitos will be returned to Cuba under a previous agreement. Parole reviews, halfway house and family releases at Oakdale will continue as before. Cubans at Oakdale can help their chances to gain community release through continued positive behavior and respect towards staff and other detainees. We have no details on how many, if any, Cubans at Oakdale will be deported. We will keep you advised as we receive more information."

At approximately 1:00 p.m. on Friday, November 20, 1987, the detainee furniture factory workers, had returned from the noon meal and were at work without incident. Mr. Bart, the furniture factory manager, began calling staff to his office. We were informed that the Superintendent of Industries had called for all bilingual staff to report to his office. The 12:00 p.m. news had broadcast the report about an agreement between the U.S. and Cuba to return some 2,500 Cubans to Cuba under the 1984 agreement. He informed us that he had been informed that it would only affect a handful from Atlanta, but detainees in Seg and the Hospital were shouting out of the windows that everyone was going to be deported. To prevent misinformation, the bilingual staff was going to explain that only a few, if any, would be affected by this agreement. We were to do everything possible to downplay this news release. When the bilingual staff came into the department, they went from section to section. First, packing and shipping, then assembly where I worked, and then to mill section. As the news of an agreement was explained, the group would become very loud and vocal for a short time and then they went very quiet.

The detainees then began to break up into small groups. When a small group was approached by staff, the group would break up and move elsewhere or those individuals would join other small groups. All production was discontinued for the day. When I would approach key individuals with whom I had developed a close working relationship, they would walk off or refuse to discuss the issue. I knew that we had severe problems. This information was discussed with the bilingual staff who saw for themselves and reportedly passed the information to the superintendent of industries. The Superintendent of Industries reported to the warden that work in Federal Prison Industries (UNICOR) was slower than usual, with some idleness, but most of the detainees continued work throughout the afternoon. At 11:00 p.m. Friday, November 20, 1987 in Oakdale, Louisiana, detainee reaction was mixed. A small number were vocally critical—many became extremely sullen and quiet. Some walked off their jobs and mingled in groups. This reaction prompted some concern on the part of administration, particularly in view of their (erroneous) belief that the 1984 disturbance at Atlanta was caused by the treaty. At 3:30 p.m., a window was broken in the laundry by an unidentified inmate or detainee.

At 4:00 p.m., as a precautionary measure, the evening shift posts were doubled or tripled and extra staff were placed on perimeter patrol. At 6:30 p.m., an incident occurred in the dining room when an intoxicated detainee turned over a food tray in front of a staff member, proceeded to the serving line, and threw a food tray across the steam table—striking a food service foreman in the forehead. This situation escalated with the majority of detainees throwing trays, food, dishes, etc. Two staff members sustained minor injuries. No detainees were placed in administrative detention as a result of this incident, in an attempt to avoid provoking a confrontation. At 3:45 p.m. in Atlanta, the warden held a closeout meeting with the top level personnel. The warden assessed the situation as manageable. The evening shift would continue to assess the situation and report any problems.

While the warden and top level personnel felt the situation to be manageable, many of the lower level supervisors and staff who worked closer to the detainees were more skeptical. The supervisors were advising the day-watch correctional staff that if they left their home during the weekend to leave a phone number where they could be reached. Serious trouble was expected at any time.

Correctional officers had never seen or discussed Oakdale with any staff who did know that facility. Yet, I will bet a paycheck against a Coke that most of the extra staff were without radios or body alarms to respond to or call for assistance. All shifts were given the same instructions throughout the weekend. However, the supervisors failed to report this during the later investigation...or the bureau chose not to believe this information. In a letter dated May 18, 1988, Ms. Mary F. Wieseman, Special Counsel, Office of the Special Counsel, Mr. Quinlan responded that, "No staff were put on 'riot alert' at Atlanta on Friday, November 20th; there were no signs on Friday of any impending disruption which would have prompted such an action." The balance of Friday and Saturday went without incident until later that evening when the detainees learned of the disturbance in Oakdale.

At 9:00 a.m. Saturday morning in Oakdale, Louisiana, a Cuban informant went to the lieutenant's office and informed the acting captain and S.D.O. that some detainees had weapons and were planning on going through the front entrance. Over the next hour or so additional information was received from detainees that a significant incident was going to take place at approximately 6:00 p.m. that night. Detainees were going to rush the front lobby entrance in an effort to escape. Also, a note was received indicating that the detainees were going to try to escape through the front entrance, and that they were going to "take out" the electrical room behind the hospital to disable the Control Center to aid in their escape. At 9:30 a.m. the warden, the AW, INS, and the acting captain met with three representatives of the Border Patrol Tactical Team (BORTAC) stationed in El Paso, Texas. During the meeting the acting captain suggested that there was an immediate need for the BORTAC team but the warden did not believe that the team was needed at that time. At about noon, the warden decided that since the mood of the compound appeared relatively normal and additional staff were already in place, in case an emergency should arise, he allowed the AW's and Department Heads to leave. He left shortly thereafter.

During the afternoon the acting captain continued picking up information that something was going to happen with female staff taken as hostages—rape and violence would occur. The warden was advised and considered information of this sort as not unusual; similar rumors in the past had not materialized, and he did not perceive a major disturbance as imminent. At 1:15 p.m., a plan was developed by the acting captain that involved protecting the front lobby, removing female staff, and positioning staff at key locations. The acting captain advised the warden of this plan and of his belief that a disturbance was imminent. A lockdown of this facility would have been virtually impossible as a result of the open four-man cubical design of most living quarters. Also, a lockdown was regarded as the type of action which would spark detainee rioting.

During the course of the day, extra staff were assigned to work each shift and the day shift was held over. Correctional counselors were appointed as team leaders and assigned three team members. Each team was provided with tear gas and handcuffs and assigned certain areas inside the perimeter of the institution to prevent escapes. About twenty INS staff were also brought in and assigned perimeter security responsibility.

At 3:00 p.m. the Oakdale Chief of Police and Mayor were advised that a disturbance was likely. At 3:30 p.m. the SDO (staff duty officer) advised the warden he believed that a significant event was about to occur. At 3:40 p.m., the evening shift was briefed by the acting captain as to possible problems.

Unit officers were advised that if they were in imminent danger they were to surrender their keys and radio. All females were removed from the compound except a female lieutenant, the captain's clerk, and one female officer working in the secure control center. At 6:00 p.m., a staff member notified the lieutenant's office that 200 to 300 detainees were going to attempt to scale the fence between 6:30 and 7:00 p.m. At 6:50 p.m., a group of more than 200 detainees gathered on the compound. They began screaming, brandishing clubs and other weapons and moved towards the front entrance. When the control center detected this movement, a prearranged signal was given. At this time several volleys of tear gas were fired and the detainees' planned escape was successfully averted.

Some of the detainees began to attack and set fire to buildings on the compound while a large group readied for another assault on the front entrance. The second assault occurred about five minutes later, followed by two or three more frontal assaults occurring every two to three minutes. There were also two assaults on the front entrance from one side, one of which was a coordinated effort with one of the frontal assaults. The conditions continued to deteriorate during the evening. At 8:30 p.m., the warden notified the Regional Director that the staff were being evacuated.

The reason for the detail in Oakland is that Oakland and Atlanta were very similar in the beginning. In both facilities, the red warning lights began flashing early on. Subordinates who worked daily with the detainees as their profession saw the red lights and informed "top level personnel." In both facilities, a top level official who worked with staff on a daily basis as their profession, had made up their mind and did not want to be confused with facts.

I am reminded of a story about the Texas Rangers. During the early sixties, a race riot had broken out in a small Texas town . As the story goes, the Chief realized that he would be unable to control the situation so he called for assistance from the Texas Rangers. During the early evening hours, a Texas Ranger drove into town. The Chief, already breaking out in a sweat, stated, "Boy, I sure am glad to see you! When will the rest of you be here?" The Texas Ranger responded, "What do you mean rest of us? All you have is one riot, isn't it?"

There are several important facts to know in understanding how and why the riots were allowed to occur in light of the knowledge available. Atlanta is more difficult to understand in view of the fact that:

a) All of the Cubans in Oakdale were from the Atlanta facility. In some cases, the Cuban detainees rioting in Oakdale had family members in Atlanta.

b) The capability of physical destruction was visible to the Atlanta management officials.

c) Communications were going upward to the U.S. Attorney General. Both were giving the same information until 6:50 p.m. on November 21, 1987. "The detainees are upset and asking staff for more information, but there is no indication of trouble."

d) Atlanta could have been locked down.

e) The detainees began informing staff (in both facilities) at the earliest planning stages in an effort to prevent harm to themselves.

As most of us know, the U.S. Government does not operate as most businesses. There are many sane reasons for the insanity. First, federal employees are not regulated by federal law.

The federal employee can be required to work in conditions that any other firm, to include a state facility, would be closed and fined for. Since the federal employees are not controlled by federal labor laws, management officials operate with immunity from all responsibility except offending their supervisor. Under Jimmy Carter's reorganization of the Federal Civil Service, the Office of Personnel Management established broad guidelines as to what management could do. The agency, Bureau of Prisons, had to submit a plan to OPM under which they were going to operate and receive OPM's approval to this procedure as being within its guidelines.

For a simple explanation—for the Atlanta Falcons to play ball in Atlanta, it has been decided that they would be allowed to play football in the Atlanta, Fulton County Stadium. They submitted plans and even marked a section of the stadium off as a playing field and another area for parking cars. If Mr. Jackson was a government official, he could move the game onto the freeway at game time with complete immunity from repercussions. Neither OPM nor any other agency requires the agency to comply with their guidelines.

The agency, or agent of the agency, cannot be held accountable for his actions outside of the agency. Federal law is simply that a federal employee who is working within the scope of his duties is protected by the agency. Again , to oversimplify—a ball carrier for the Falcons got the ball and ran around behind the team benches, and every player formed a wall down the sidelines while he ran out between them and the bleachers. Rankin Jackson only needed to say that carrying the ball was within the scope of his duties and getting the ball to the end zone was his job and the score would count and the officials have no additional input. Then, for the ball carrier to get injured or the team to lose is unlikely, especially if you require the other team to comply with standard rules. The federal government is amoral; it is neither good or bad, moral or immoral, but within its boundaries, it is all-powerful.

The Justice (Just us) Department operates out of intimidation. Like the IRS, they have unlimited resources and tools available to do serious damage to your lifestyle with total immunity. The truly unfortunate thing is that most Americans believe that, whether true or not, that if you have nothing to hide, you should cooperate with the agents. The Justice (Just us) Department is staffed with trained professionals; if they bring a charge, you must be guilty, because where there is smoke, there is fire. The Justice (Just us) Department is people of integrity.

If you don't use drugs, why object to a drug test? If you don't haul drugs, why object to your car being searched? If you don't sell drugs, why object to your house being searched? Who is doing the testing? Who is searching?

The past practice of the U.S. Government was that an employee for the Air Traffic Controllers signed a statement which, among other things, stated that it was being signed under duress. It said that many of the Air Traffic Controllers and by name were using drugs on a regular basis on the job. Those individuals were tested and found to be negative, even in spite of the fact that some drugs can be traced in the system for thirty days. They were still forced to attend drug abuse classes and have this in their records. Had they worked in private industry they could have recourse; this recourse causes private industry to have persons of integrity in "top level personnel" positions. The Justice (Just us) Department is now operating under skills gained from organized crime.

If I were to be caught with a gallon can of cocaine, they could show me ten pictures of individuals that I may or may not have ever seen before and explain that they know that I bought the cocaine from one and was taking it to the other nine...so make it easy on myself. I can testify and be set free while innocent people end up behind bars. If I was charged by the FBI, most of my closest friends would say, "He sure had me fooled. I never would have thought that he would be dealing in drugs."

In the Atlanta Federal Pen, we housed a man who had been charged with distributing drugs all over the world and was planning to escape from our facility. While I am sure that the inmate was guilty—after all, the FBI went to Columbia to get him—the Assistant U.S. Attorney used another convict as their star witness. The man had a history of lying from the first time he'd spoken, "da-da" as an infant. When the court becomes as corrupt as the crooks, there is no place for the innocent to hang their hat.

The Bureau of Prisons operates under the power of intimidation. As an officer, if an inmate really got me upset, I could get him more time to spend in jail without his going to court. The Bureau of Prisons gives what is called, "good time." Some is earned by work; other is given by law. That which is given can be taken. If he gets under my skin, I write negative reports and that time is taken away, giving him a later release date. On the other hand, if he helps me, a positive report may help his chances of parole. An American inmate can be intimidated through everything to a visit with his mother if he is not cooperative with the system.

The biggest single reason for the riots to be allowed to take place is money. As a result of riots, the Bureau of Prisons will gain many new positions, programs, institutions and money. The government operates much like a kingdom system. The one with the largest kingdom is the most important king. As a result of this, each agency pushes to gain new programs and new positions. After the 1984 riot, the U.S. Penitentiary in Atlanta had an open checkbook called 58-G. This account was established to replace those items destroyed by the Cuban population or build new control structures for the population. It came out of the INS budget but was spent by the institution with the only accountability being something needed uniquely for the Cuban population. Mr. Blackmon was upset because a car phone could not be installed in the warden's institutional car for him from the 58-G fund.

In the Executive Summary, it was noted that physical limitations would have made lockdown difficult in Atlanta. Two cellblocks were under complete renovation and no detainees could be housed in them. (As a result of this renovation the Cuban population had been reduced from nearly 2,100 to 1,394.) One cellblock consisted of eight-man cells, which are highly undesirable in lockdown situations; the cell doors in another block were so dilapidated that they might have been breached. The eight-man cells were used for lockdown during parts of 1984 and 1985. The cell house with the problems with the doors was P Block, which had been designed as an honor dorm and converted for usage into a segregation unit. More than ten percent of the detainees lived in an open dorm; to get into an open dorm in Atlanta, the detainee was screened to be sure of no difficulties being encountered. Those would have been the least likely to be deported or cause a problem.

The report continues with the fact that had inmates rioted and set fires while under lockdown conditions, a wide range of management and life-safety problems could have resulted. Despite the fact that the warden called in his local Executive Staff at 6:00 a.m. on Sunday, November 22, and advised them to go out and monitor the situation in the institution by speaking with the detainees. The information he received was that the inmates were calm and that traditional indicators of prison unrest were absent. In actuality, line staff had overheard detainees' conversations about hostage-taking, received warnings from informants, and noticed other indications of potential unrest. They reported this intelligence to their supervisors, but much of it was never transmitted to the warden. Most of the "top staff" believed until mid-morning on Monday that the institution was not in jeopardy. The events in Oakdale and Atlanta suggested the need for improvements in BOP policy and procedures. The study teams that prepared "A Report to the Attorney General," proposed 107 recommendations for improvements.

The recommendations will result in new programs, more staff, more equipment, and much more money poured into the kingdom. The most frightening of the group is those areas which deal with the news media. The scope of the recommendations is to stop all communications except for the government (negotiators) information through a Public Information Officer. This implies some form of integrity exists within the Department of Justice (Just us), which I do not hold as true. Chapter 13 will cover activities of the hostages during the ordeal and will provide a basis for my concern.

At 5:30 a.m. Monday, November 23, 1987, the lieutenant on duty reported that he called an associate warden to obtain approval to open cells for breakfast. (The fact is that the shift supervisor advised the AWC of the reports made by line staff and requested to keep the detainees on lockdown but was refused.) Several correctional officers had prepared reports during the previous evening and early morning hours which suggested that serious problems could be expected during the day. Several staff reported seeing the documents in the lieutenant's office. The lieutenant reported that he was reluctant to open the institution for breakfast because of the information he was receiving. He stated he called the AWC for approval. The AWC came to the institution at about 5:40 a.m. The lieutenant stated he'd discussed the information with the AW and was told there would be "normal operations." He opened the institution for breakfast at approximately 5:45 a.m. The AW denied any knowledge of receiving this call as well as being asked about opening for breakfast. At 7:30 a.m., the AWC asked for and obtained approval from the warden to hold over the morning watch staff for two hours to be available for any emergency.

Approximately 10:30 a.m., the riot began. From then until 12:00 p.m. there was, for the most part, mass confusion both inside and out of the facility. The additional staff which had been either held over or brought in were being rescued or were attempting to maintain the areas not already taken over by the Cubans.

For all purposes, the Cubans controlled all the institution except the main building and segregation. There was some delusion as to who had control of the hospital as a result of the detainees within the hospital deciding to allow the medical staff to continue providing medical treatment freely and the officers to hold the key.

At no time in segregation did the inmates get into hand's reach of the staff. The towers were immediately able to hold the detainees away from the building on the outside. However, the doors were so dilapidated that the detainees who desired were able to break out. That issue had been argued and fought by the local union from the onset, of converting an honor's unit into a segregation unit. While management argued that the unit was adequately safe for employees to work on a daily basis, it became a justification not to lockdown before the disturbance. The staff from the segregation unit were taken out by the FBI only minutes before they would have become hostages by the Cubans. The Cubans had managed to get to the southeast corner and break into the unit through the cover of the warehouse, coupled with staff's fear of shooting while hostages were held.

The detainees in the hospital were instructing staff not to open the door for anyone until after they were checked at the door by the doctor and determined to be in need of treatment. Even then, the door would not be opened until all other detainees were away from the area. Those detainees inside of the hospital were aware that they did not need to display a weapon or attempt to intimidate staff. Staff could not leave the hospital or take any action beyond their job. The detainees assigned to the hospital were also concerned about some of the population getting in and breaking into the drug room and some "crazies" would end up getting everyone killed. For the most part of the afternoon the towers were attempting to locate and identify hostages. At about 1:00 p.m. the Special Agent in Charge of the Atlanta office of the FBI began to set up a command post in the warden's office.

Along with the keys, the Cuban Detainees took the radios and body alarms from all staff. They began to communicate with each other as well as with the administration over the radios. When any action was taken by anyone outside, which led the detainees to believe that the Government was going to make an assault or retake the facility by force, they would grab a hostage (preferably a supervisor), place a couple of shanks under his neck, put a radio in front of them, and instruct the hostage, "Tell the people if that don't stop, I am going to kill you and all of the hostages!" The hostages were glad to comply. Additionally, one Hispanic supervisor, Lt. Ricardo, began communicating early on and began negotiations with the detainees. One of the detainees who claimed authority to negotiate for the detainees was allowed out of the dining room to talk with the lieutenant. Later, the lieutenant was joined by the FBI negotiators who took

149

over the negotiations. The FBI was also given the responsibility of developing a tactical plan to retake the facility by force and would have coordinated efforts with the U.S. Marshalls, other SWAT teams, and their own personnel should those plans be implemented.

At 5:30 p.m., a decision was made by the Regional Director for the Bureau of Prisons, the FBI, and the warden to rescue the sixteen staff members from E cell house. The Cuban segregation unit had been protected from the population as a result of two towers being located near the entrance to that building. Although hostages had been brought to tower 10 and threats made that the hostage would be killed if they could not go into seg, the detainees backed down from those demands when the tower still refused to allow them to enter. About 2:00 p.m., I had been taken to segregation from the Chaplain's area and used as shield in their efforts. The fire department dropped scale ladders over the wall and the FBI SWAT team scaled the wall to provide cover for the sixteen employees.

A plan to rescue the hospital staff was developed, considered locally and in Washington, but rejected due to location of the hospital. The likely risk of engagement with detainees and the inability to protect the other hostages while attempting the rescue of the staff in the hospital made it too risky. In fact, all information being received suggested that the detainees were permitting the hospital to continue to be fully functional, i.e., providing necessary medical care and treatment of both staff and inmates inside the institution. Rather than risk certain harm to the seventy-nine hostages in the chapel and American dorm, the rescue of the hospital was not undertaken. Also, by this time, television news cameras were in a position to observe and show live any tactical rescue operation that may have been attempted.

CHAPTER 12

TWELVE DAYS OF HELL: OUTSIDE

WHILE MUCH PUBLICITY WAS MADE OF THE MORE THAN one-hundred hostages taken in Atlanta, those employees who were not physically captive of the situation were also held hostage. The Warden and many of the executive staff remained at the facility most of the time during the siege. The Atlanta staff and some T.D.Y. staff were assigned to work twelve-hour days. During their twelve hours off, many of them spent free time at the institution attempting to reassure the hostages' families. They also had difficulty getting rest when going home. The captain was in training and out of town when the riot started. He was returned to the facility on Tuesday. Few employees were sent T.D.Y. to Atlanta as a result of the Oakdale situation.

On Tuesday morning between 1:00 and 2:00 a.m., the safety manager and his assistant escaped from the safety office they had locked themselves into. The detainees who worked for them assisted them in getting to the East Gate. At about 7:30 a.m., the captain established perimeter security procedures while the FBI, U.S. Marshals, INS, and other law enforcement agency staff assumed other responsibilities relating to the crisis.

The balance of this chapter is reliant upon "A Report to the Attorney General" beginning with Atlanta-23. All information is attributed to and drawn from that publication.

12:02 P.M. Tuesday, November 24, 1987

An extremely dangerous, high-security inmate released by the detainees from a secure housing unit, who had previously appeared relatively passive, was now observed organizing a group of at least ten Cuban detainees and reportedly was making plans to "Take over!"

1:25 P.M. Tuesday, November 24, 1987

One of the hostages in the American dorm sent a radio message that the hostages are all doing well (approximately thirty there) and that the detainees will consider releasing hostages if representatives of the media were permitted inside to speak with them.

2:00 P.M. Tuesday, November 24, 1987

The Warden held a press conference with news media and described changing detainee leadership and demands as well as the rationale for not locking down the institution on Monday morning.

Associate Attorney General Trott's press conference was televised live on Cable News Network (or CNN) during which Bureau of Prisons' Director Quinlan stated that the safety of the hostages is paramount and his "patience is endless." At Atlanta, the hostages (reported after their release) noticed a marked improvement in the treatment they were receiving. Most attribute this to the director's statement that "no intrusive efforts" would be made as long as the hostages are not hurt. Above all, the detainees feared an armed assault on the institution and became most agitated and threatened to kill the hostages when the helicopters flew over or other incidents occurred which suggested an armed attack by Government forces was imminent.

Although there is no cable television for detainees at the Penitentiary, a local television station does re-broadcast "Headline News," a production of CNN.

2:45 P.M. Tuesday, November 24, 1987

An unidentified detainee was heard over Bureau of Prisons radio threatening to kill the hostages if the Bureau of Prisons, FBI, etc. rushed the institution. Also heard are orders to throw hostages out the windows if helicopters showed up again.

The detainees continued to release hostages rather liberally at first. During the first few hours of the takeover, several staff were let go. At 1:30 Tuesday, an officer was released and at 4:30 a teacher suffering from chest pains was released. Beginning Tuesday, Cuban detainees and American inmates were also surrendering when the opportunity presented itself. There was little to no effort put to keeping the American inmates inside, but the Cuban leadership wanted the detainees to remain united.

By the end of the siege on December 4, 1987, over 290 of the 1,394 Cuban detainees and 177 of the 197 Americans were released from inside the facility. Tuesday evening contact was established with a local attorney who had previously represented the detainees in litigation, and who had offered his services. He met with detainee representatives and discussed their concerns. At Central Office, Cuban-American exiles were contacted to discuss a possible role for them in the negotiation process.

A hostage released on 11-29-87 reported that the only time he felt the hostages were in danger was on 11-24-87, when Cuban leaders entered the second floor of the chapel with acetylene bottles, threatening to blow up the whole place, killing hostages and detainees alike.

10:20 P.M. to 10:30 P.M. Tuesday, November 24, 1987
Regional Director Williams called the Director's Office to discuss with the Director whether or not to attempt rescue of hospital staff. Once again, a rescue attempt was rejected because the safety of all the hostages was paramount. He also reported that several inmates have "escaped" or been released from E Cell house (a high security unit for the Cubans) and were walking around the compound.

11:55 P.M. Tuesday, November 24, 1987
Five staff members were released by the detainees. The hostages were examined and found to be in good physical condition, quickly debriefed and returned to their families.

11:59 P.M. Tuesday, November 24, 1987
Late evening discussions in Washington, D.C., led to appointments of special teams to handle hostage family issues. Warden Doug Larson (assigned to Atlanta) and Charles Turnbo (assigned to Oakdale) were assigned to coordinate these efforts. Warden Larson left for Atlanta with instructions to do whatever was necessary for the hostage families, some of whom had remained on the grounds of the institution since the beginning. Negotiations during the day were sporadic with leadership of the detainees being described as "fragmented."

12:25 A.M. Wednesday, November 25, 1987
Regional Director Williams called the director to advise that five hostages were released, and that he believed the hospital had been taken over by detainees within the last half hour.

12:33 A.M. Wednesday, November 25, 1987
A staff psychologist, held hostage, was released from the hospital through the rear corridor due to a medical problem. He was briefly hospitalized and then released. Thirty-three Cuban

detainees and twenty-five American inmates surrendered through the East Gate and were processed into A Cell house for transportation to other Bureau of Prisons facilities.

At 1:15 A.M. Wednesday, November 25, 1987

News media personnel were permitted to enter the main corridor and briefly meet with detainee negotiators. The news media was provided with taped messages and video tapes of the hostages, reportedly. At 3:30 A.M. Wednesday, three recently-released hostages asked to speak to the news media. They talked positively about their treatment while held. It was extremely important to the leaders inside to have the American people know that no physical harm was coming to the hostages. The safety of the hostages was dependent upon their own safety, was their desired message.

7:25 P.M. Wednesday, November 25, 1987

Regional Director Williams called the Central Office to again discuss the option of tactical assault of hospital. The decision not to attempt a rescue hinged on the estimation that to do so would further endanger the hostages. An inmate at Atlanta forced a physician's assistant and medical officer in charge (OIC) to open hospital door to treat an inmate—the inmate then took the hospital keys from the OIC. Within two hours, the keys were returned to staff by another detainee.

9:20 P.M. Wednesday, November 25, 1987

A loud banging noise on the B cell house door to the main corridor was initially interpreted as being gun fire. Investigation and verification by tactical forces confirmed no gunshots were fired in either the Cell house or main corridor. All assault forces were directed to "stand down."

9:35 P.M. Wednesday, November 25, 1987

Armored personnel carriers arrived and staged at the institution pistol range. Military hostage rescue team arrived to assist with planning and advise on rescue efforts. During the day, many unconfirmed news media reports were aired, making negotiations problematic and more difficult. As a result, a Department of Justice (Just us) Public Information Officer (PIO) was sent to Atlanta to assist the local PIO. It was decided that Warden Truman would give periodic press briefings to deal with some of the unconfirmed news reports. Also, the captains from other Bureau institutions who had been detailed to Atlanta from training at FLETCH, Glynco, Georgia on Monday were returned to their respective institutions. Additional Correctional Officers were sent from FCI, Butner, Norton Carolina, and FCI, Tallahassee, Florida.

On Thursday, November 26, 1987 (Thanksgiving Day)

Reports were received from inside that the commissary had been broken into.

6:55 A.M. Thursday, November 26, 1987

Staff observed numerous staff hostages moving from area to area. No restraints were visible on the hostages, which contrasted with earlier sightings. Hostages were reported to be "well."

11:00 A.M. Thursday, November 26, 1987

The director's Thanksgiving message was delivered to hostage families. Regional Director Mckensie met with the three Cuban-exile advisors.

4:08 P.M. Thursday, November 26, 1987

After establishing the boundaries of their potential involvement and gaining the confidence of Atlanta Bureau of Prisons and FBI Command Center staff, the three Cuban-exile advisors were escorted into the institution to assist negotiations.

6:00 P.M. to 9:30 P.M. Thursday, November 26, 1987

Negotiations appeared to take a favorable turn as government negotiators believed an agreement was reached with the detainees to release fifty of the staff hostages in return for a full press conference with live TV coverage for the detainee leaders. However, the detainee negotiators returned with only three hostages, saying this was the best they could do. The government negotiators objected that the agreement was for fifty hostages and not three, and therefore the government would not agree to a full news conference. However, when the government negotiator attempted to continue the discussion about a deal for reduced news coverage, the detainee negotiator bolted from the negotiations and took the three hostages with him.

11:45 A.M. Friday, November 27, 1987

The Mayor of Miami, Florida and a group of elected Florida officials, former Cuban political prisoners, and religious leaders, arrived at USP, Atlanta and were escorted to the Regional Office Conference Room for a discussion of their potential involvement in the situation.

1:45 P.M. Friday, November 27, 1987

An FBI Special Agent from Philadelphia briefed the Miami Mayor and his group on the progress and status of the negotiations. An agreement was reached to have the mayor and another representative meet with the Cuban exiles who were assisting with the negotiations, and the meeting took place.

This incident was later reported by the news media as an example of racial discrimination affecting the negotiations. The three staff hostages brought to the door of the dining room leading into the main corridor where the negotiations were being conducted were black. It was mis-reported that the government negotiators refused the hostages solely because of their race and not because of the refusal of the detainees to continue to live up to their earlier agreement. The government negotiators tried to get the three released, but the detainees refused to continue to negotiate.

10:20 P.M. Friday, November 27, 1987

A Cuban detainee presented a set of seven demands to the government negotiators. There were serious questions raised by the government negotiators and command staff as to whether or not the demands represented the views of the majority of the Cuban detainees.

6:40 P.M. Saturday, November 28, 1987

Detainees were heard on the radios threatening to kill three hostages unless water was turned back on within twenty-four hours.

7:30 P.M. Saturday, November 28, 1987

A small fire was observed in E Cell house. The fire did not last long and appeared to have been suppressed by detainees.

8:59 P.M. Saturday, November 28, 1987

Staff in Tower 10 reported that another fire was breaking out on the second floor of E Cell house.

9:00 P.M. Saturday, November 28, 1987

Cuban Detainee leaders "broadcast" message over Bureau of Prisons radios to outside radio personnel.

10:04 P.M. Saturday, November 28, 1987

Now, it appeared that the fire in the UNICOR building was actually a fire in the Education building which is attached to the UNICOR building.

10:15 P.M. Saturday, November 28, 1987

Staff in the towers reported hearing what sounded like gunshots on the compound. They quickly determined, however, that the source of the sounds were aerosol cans exploding in the education building fire.

10:58 P.M. Saturday, November 28, 1987

Four Cuban detainees were observed on the roof of the hospital waving flags and shouting toward the groups of people lining McDonough Boulevard, the street in front of the institution.

11:00 P.M. Saturday, November 28, 1987

The three Cuban-American exile advisors used a public address system to speak directly to the reluctant faction of approximately 200 radical detainees, encouraging them to release 50 hostages as a show of faith.

12:10 A.M. Sunday, November 29, 1987

Cuban detainees announced they are ready to release three hostages as soon as the telephone between detainees and the government negotiators is repaired.

12:45 A.M. Sunday, November 29, 1987

Four hostages are released by detainees—apparently one hostage from each faction of detainee leadership. Each hostage reported that they and their fellow hostages had been well treated, well cared for, and protected from other detainees who might pose a risk of harm to them.

7:00 A.M. Sunday, November 29, 1987

A video tape of a hostage who was released at 12:45 a.m. was played on local television in Atlanta. The video tape had been released by the Bureau of Prisons in lieu of the hostage making direct contact with the news media and being questioned. The released hostage had wanted to make a statement, but not directly, so this arrangement was worked out with the agreement of all parties.

11:30 A.M. Sunday, November 29, 1987

The government negotiators began to see some development in detainee leadership, as face-to-face negotiations were initiated. The three Cuban-American advisors continued to function as resource persons for the government negotiating team. Mail received at the institution for the detainees since Monday was given to the detainees as a sign of good faith on the part of the government.

2:28 P.M. Sunday, November 29, 1987

Partial water pressure was restored inside the institution after the negotiators explained that it had been turned off previously to increase water pressure for fire-fighting. The detainees were advised that water would be diverted for fire-fighting once again, if additional fires were set.

3:34 P.M. Sunday, November 29, 1987

Staff at Atlanta received word that all hostages had been released safely from FDC, Oakdale.

4:11 P.M. Sunday, November 29, 1987

Cuban detainees announced a call for a meeting to draft a letter to be sent to the government.

6:30 P.M. Sunday, November 29, 1987

Face-to-face negotiations renewed between three Cuban exile advisors, FBI negotiators, and three Cuban detainee representatives.

8:15 A.M. Monday, November 30, 1987

Detainees were overheard on the radio, referencing an explosive charge being in place and ready to explode. At about the same time, the captain, along with FBI, recognized the voice of the high-security American prisoner, working in the tunnel to the Duck Mill (textile factory), where detainees were working with what was believed to be a core drill.

11:40 A.M. Monday, November 30, 1987

There continued to be significant activity in the tunnel, and an FBI SWAT Team was dispatched, along with five Bureau of Prisons staff, to secure the outside exits of this area.

5:15 P.M. Monday, November 30, 1987

A U.S. Attorney arrived at the institution.

5:30 P.M. Monday, November 30, 1987

The three Cuban-American exile advisors, with the knowledge of the government negotiators, met with the media and advised that their efforts had proven to be unsuccessful. The advisors stated that they would be willing to return if needed.

Throughout the siege, the detainees continued to test the boundaries of the staff-controlled areas of the penitentiary. Earlier on this day, several detainees encountered a party of law enforcement staff in the auditorium, which is directly above the dining room and which was still under staff control. The detainees saw the officials; departed and immediately returned with two or three hostages, including a lieutenant being held hostage in the American dormitory; and demanded the staff abandon the area or they would kill the hostages. The detainees were forced to back down from their demand and the hostages were not hurt.

9:20 P.M. Monday, November 30, 1987

Cuban detainees turned the high-security American inmate over to the U.S. Marshall SWAT Team posted at the door leading to the West Yard from the rear of the main corridor. Reports indicated that he had been sedated by Cubans and was then shackled with handcuffs and leg irons. The detainees reported they had to remove this inmate or risk he might "kill a hostage."

3:55 A.M. Tuesday, December 1, 1987

A fluoroscopic examination of one of the surrendering detainees revealed the presence of a handcuff key hidden in his rectum. A digital search was authorized by the Warden. The detainee gave up the key without the medical staff having to perform the search of his rectum.

2:27 P.M. Tuesday, December 1, 1987

Cuban detainees were observed passing out sheets of paper. They brought a copy to staff in Tower 3. It was a copy of the Oakdale agreement.

2:45 P.M. Tuesday, December 1, 1987

While burning material around forklifts, two detainees' clothing caught fire. One detainee was burned; he surrendered and was taken to an outside hospital for treatment.

9:00 P.M. Tuesday, December 1, 1987

Detainees gathered on the hospital roof and sang "Happy Birthday" to a leader of the "Coalition to Support Cuban Detainees." On the radio, the detainees announced an intention to release one hostage.

9:15 P.M. Tuesday, December 1, 1987

A local attorney who had previously represented detainees in litigation against the government was allowed to speak again to the detainees and explain the language of the proposed agreement to settle the Atlanta siege to the detainees' representatives. He did not participate in the negotiations themselves.

9:48 P.M. Tuesday, December 1, 1987

A Correctional Officer held hostage was released by detainees in return for a meeting with the attorney.

10:30 P.M. Tuesday, December 1, 1987

Detainees continued to use the roof of the hospital to communicate with the public and the media, primarily through the use of a homemade public address system.

9:00 A.M. to 4:00 P.M. Wednesday, December 2, 1987

Discussions between detainee representatives and government negotiators continued with the assistance of the cooperating local attorney. The detainees, however, continued to hold out for a "No deportation to Cuba" agreement, which of course, was unacceptable. The posture of the negotiations became more negative and negotiations broke off.

10:30 P.M. Wednesday, December 2, 1987

The Catholic Chaplain, who had been held hostage since November 23rd and was still in detainee hands, presented a petition at the rear corridor. It was signed by forty-three hostages, and requested that no assault be undertaken because the helicopters flying overhead have the detainees "extremely upset."

The chaplains held hostage were granted somewhat more freedom of movement than the other hostages.

2:09 P.M. Thursday, December 3, 1987

Government negotiators reported that Cuban detainees were still demanding there be no deportations to Cuba. Regional Director Mckensie reported to the director that the detainee negotiators have returned to negotiations ready to sign the seven-point agreement which does not include "a no-deportation agreement."

Regional Director Mckensie reported to the director that the detainees took a vote with the majority in favor of the agreement. The count was 750 detainees in favor of signing the agreement and 150 against signing.

9:14 P.M. Thursday, December 3, 1987

The local attorney returned to the institution and was escorted to the negotiation site.

9:24 P.M. Thursday, December 3, 1987

The Regional Director Mckensie reports to the Director that the attorney was meeting with detainee negotiators at that very moment, telling him he and the Bishop would be the only witnesses to the signing.

9:45 P.M. Thursday, December 3, 1987

Bishop Roman arrived via helicopter at the institution and was escorted to the Regional Office for discussions with Mr. Mckensie, and then to the institution.

11:47 P.M. Thursday, December 3, 1987

Cuban detainees insisted that the Attorney General, rather than the Regional Director, sign the agreement.

12:04 A.M. Friday, December 4, 1987

Stephen Trott, Associate Attorney General, spoke with a detainee negotiator on the telephone to assure him that Regional Director Gary Mckensie had authority to sign the agreement for the government.

12:06 A.M. Friday, December 4, 1987

The detainees' request to add an additional witness to the signing of the agreement was approved, and he was permitted into the negotiations.

12:25 A.M. Friday, December 4, 1987

Media teams were escorted into the institution to record the signing of the agreement and release of hostages.

12:28 A.M. Friday, December 4, 1987

Cuban detainees climbed onto the hospital roof and announced there would be a meeting of all detainees in the chapel area immediately.

12:49 A.M. Friday, December 4, 1987

Certain outside observers were permitted into the institution at the detainees' request as witnesses to the agreement.

12:54 A.M. Friday, December 4, 1987

Staff in Tower 10 reported they observed a large group of Cuban detainees carrying knives and moving toward the AWB building and chapel. It was not known at this time whether or not this group was going to attempt to harm the hostages or prevent their release.

1:00 A.M. Friday, December 4, 1987

The agreement was signed by Regional Director Mckensie and detainee representatives and witnessed by Bishop Roman and the others. Live TV coverage of signing of agreement at Atlanta was broadcast by CNN.

1:09 A.M. Friday, December 4, 1987

Staff in Tower 10 reported seeing hostages being brought out of the hospital and being moved toward the dining room.

1:12 A.M. Friday, December 4, 1987

The first hostages were released and began filing out of the institution.

1:33 A.M. Friday, December 4, 1987

An accurate count of all hostages was confirmed; all 89 remaining staff had been released unharmed.

1:45 A.M. Friday, December 4, 1987

Bishop Roman exited the institution and departed for Miami.

8:30 A.M. to 12:00 Noon Friday, December 4, 1987

Regional Director Mckensie agreed, after discussing this issue with the Director, that staff would not begin processing detainees out of the institution until 12:00 Noon on Friday.

12:00 Noon Friday, December 4, 1987

Processing of detainees through the East Gate began and continued for over twenty-four hours. Temporary dressing rooms and search facilities were constructed in the East Gate sally port and two portable fluoroscopes were brought in to facilitate the processing. Detainees were removed from the compound through the East Gate one at a time with their property. They were searched, their property was boxed for shipment and restraints were applied and checked before they were placed on buses for transportation out of the facility. The process was conducted entirely by Bureau of Prisons' staff and video tapes were made of all the processing.

8:48 A.M. Saturday, December 5, 1987

The last two Cuban detainees surrendered at the East Gate and were processed out of the institution. No force of any kind was necessary to locate, move, or process any detainees or inmates. Bureau of Prisons and FBI teams entered the compound and searched and secured the facility. No hidden inmates were discovered, no dead or injured inmates had been left behind.

CHAPTER 13

THE RIOT BEGAN: AN INSIDE LOOK

PREVIOUS CHAPTERS WERE A CHRONOLOGICAL REPORTING
of activities of management officials during the riot. They had a set of times which looked very impressive and organized. The reality of life is that much of the documentation was "as well as I can remember," information which deletes items which don't make the bureau look good. There were no minute-by-minute records being kept. Should there have been, and why? The entries, between 8:00 a.m. and 9:00 a.m. more honestly sometimes mean after 7:30 a.m. (work call) and before 10:30 a.m., the approximate time of the riot.

Immediately upon release and before we were reunited with our families, a bureau official during the short debriefing told us that Mr. Quinlan, the director of the bureau, had frozen all vacancies throughout the bureau after the disturbance in Oakdale and Atlanta began. Those positions were being held for staff from those two facilities, with the hostages having first priority as to the vacancies. As a result of this, the hostages as well as many of the Atlanta staff were transferred all over the nation. Subsequently, I have no authorization from most of the staff to use their names. Many of the individuals will identify themselves but will find another name being used. There is no effort to mislead or confuse anyone; the facts are all accurate; it is just that I do not want to offend any hostage by writing their name into something that they want to forget.

Friday, November 20, 1987 was a cool, fall morning in Atlanta, Georgia. The light jacket felt good as I went through the yard and into industries. Although I had no specific plans for the weekend, it was Friday. I enjoyed my job very much as a foreman in the prison furniture factory . It had been nearly eleven months since I had been promoted from the correctional force to industries. After getting away from the harassment from some supervisors who were totally incompetent, and a job that I had begun to hate reporting for, every day, I was truly happy in my work.

When I got unhappy about something that was involved in my work, all that I had to do was to look toward the East Gate; that was the last job I had on the correctional force. The tower 10 officer, a post that in reality did not exist since the tower remained closed (only eight of the eleven towers were operational much of the time), was assigned as the escort officer. Mr. Barley, a young, energetic, black officer, was working with me in the East Gate when not escorting a vehicle inside the institution. He and I had mutual respect for each other and worked well together. For the quarter change, which was December 23, 1986, Mr. Barley and I talked about the change. I told him that I would stay on the East Gate through the winter if he wanted to stay there with me. If he did not want to stay out, I too, would get inside, out of the cold. He agreed to stay on the job as long as it was with me; after we requested to be on the job another quarter and it was posted, I was promoted out of the job. Mr. Barley and I had worked cell houses and segregation together in the past and I had found him to be a proven friend. When he was at my back with a knife, I knew that I was well protected. One evening on the gate I had closed the gate at 3:15 instead of 3:30, which I had been doing. Lt. Nonitz had called Mr. Barley and asked for a memo concerning the closing that evening; I immediately started getting phone calls. The tower 5 officer who was responsible for opening and closing the outside gate electronically while protecting me, Mr. Nilson, and another control room officer all called to find out what was going on and to see what they may need to say. I told them all that I closed the gate at 3:15 p.m. and left the institution at 3:23 p.m. I only remembered because I had a doctor's appointment at 3:30 p.m., which I missed. Monday about 10:15 a.m., Lt. Nonitz came to the gate.

"Ah, Mr. Lawson, you know normally I try to handle things going on my shift. But Friday, something came up that has got blown up so big, that I can't handle it myself. Uh, you know, Mr. Lawson, we all may leave early from time to time; this never really is a problem as long as you have your work done and have been relieved. The problem comes up when you leave early and then you are needed but can't be found. Now I have read your post orders. and found that you don't get off until 3:30. Now I called down here at 3:10 and the phone rang and rang and no one answered. I called tower five and had the same results. I had to get Mr. Nilson and another officer to come down to open the gates to let two contract workers out that you had left locked in.

"Well, Lieutenant, there has been no one to touch that clock," I said, pointing to the clock in the office, which hung over the phone. "You can call the lieutenant's office and see if there is more than five minutes difference in the clocks, but I walked by the clock at 3:15 on my way out. The only reason that I am certain of the time is that I had a doctor's appointment that I needed to make, but there were people in the gate and I couldn't get it closed earlier."

"Well, the five minutes or so is not that important. Your post orders call for you to be on duty until 3:30," he said in his low, quiet, and confident voice as he stood with his hands stuck down in his belt over his back pockets. Lt. Nonitz was a black lieutenant who dressed very well, looked sharp, stood upright, and when he kept his mouth closed, left a positive impression.

"I am glad that you read the post orders," I responded in an angry tone. "You could have looked at your duty roster to see what time I got off, but you read my post orders. You know that this damn gate closes at 3:00 p.m. I have stayed out here until 3:30 all quarter, just to help some of them bastards…that has been done for the last time. Tonight, I will close the gate at 3:00 p.m."

Each post has a set of orders which are explicit on everything that must be done. They must be signed by staff every quarter and are kept in the lieutenant's office.

He responded quickly, "I know for vehicle traffic, but you work until 3:30 p.m." This made me even more angry, "Fuck a bunch of vehicle traffic, Lieutenant! No vehicles come in after 2:00 p.m., to make sure they are out by 3:00. Starting today, that is going to take place, too. You and I both know that I have turned papers into your office at 4:00. From 3:00 to 3:30, I am supposed to be bringing those papers to you, but you apparently missed that when you read my post orders!"

"Now take it easy, Lawson. I'm going to take care of this," he quickly responded. "I don't need you to take care of me; I will take care of myself. All I need from you is for you to do your own damn job."

I expressed in my still-angry manner, "You can tell your friend working the outside detail, that anyone not out of my gate at 3:00 p.m. may as well be ready to walk around unless you want to have someone come down and let them out."

"Now Lawson, we have those contract workers in here and they don't get out until after 3:00 o'clock. How can we get them out if you close up at 3:00?" he asked.

"Change your post orders! You write the damn things and I go by them. If you want the gate open until five, just change the post orders; that is your responsibility!" I yelled at him. He immediately left and called back an hour or so later. After his effort to screw me, he ended up paying Mr. Barley, Mr. Nance, and me an hour overtime each day. Every time that I got upset with the job in industries, all I had to do was look out in any direction and I could remember such an event.

The lead foreman, Mr. Mann, was highly respected by all staff. He was a highly talented individual who knew woodworking completely. He was aware of the job to be done and was successful in motivating employees to want to do the work and do it right. He knew enough about the material the equipment, and people, that you could not bullshit him. The factory manager, Mr. Bart, had come up through the correctional officer ranks. He was an officer in Atlanta when I got there in '73 and was respected then. He was a typical manager who believed that any decision made by management was right because management had the staff and production at heart. He never asked staff to do anything that he would not do—but did not believe that the staff of today worked up to their potential in production. He was, in his opinion, a fair-minded individual and was certain that all other management officials were as well. He was always complaining of the need for greater production and closer supervision of inmates to ensure more productivity. On one occasion, he personally wrote an incident report to get a detainee locked in segregation.

Mr. Bart had left the correctional force to go into Quality Assurance. In our furniture factory, the Q.A. specialist was an intelligent, bilingual who was aggressive, energetic, and probably headed for a warden's position. Braxton was liked by almost everyone but found himself run thin. He was pulled from the furniture factory frequently and used as an interpreter on a regular basis, even when in the unit as a result of his skills. Another employee who was still a trainee had just been reassigned from assembly to packing. Milner had been a locksmith in the institution but had been in the furniture factory about nine months. He worked extremely hard but was too willing to do something for one of the other foremen. As a result, he was used by others from time to time and Mr. Bart was not sure of his productivity.

I was assigned to assembly 1. The raw material was brought in and went through the mill, where it was cut, shaped, and put into form. It then came to me, and I had the different parts put into a desk or whatever. The AW attempted to apply pressure on me for my union activities, since I was a trainee in industries. From there, it would go to assembly 2 and have the drawers put on and finished. Assembly 2 was supervised by a quiet, mild mannered, black foreman who took everything so seriously. B.T. took everything so seriously that other staff would pass rumors to him just to see him get so upset. The mill area had over a million dollars in modern equipment and completed detail work that must be within 1/32 of an inch perfect. Anything beyond created a crack of 1/16 of an inch in the assembly of the product, and Q.A. would not accept it. That foreman, Mr. Ray, was a senior employee in federal prison industries. He had taught me much about the job, but even more in supervising and motivating a detail.

Incident reports are usually written by supervisors, even if a result of an order.

When I went into the furniture factory, it consisted mostly of an upholstery factory. The upholstery section had been dissolved and the furniture production increased. On November 20, 1987, a new line of upholstery production was planned for Atlanta. Mr. Mills hated working in the sawdust and furniture was exited. He was now going to return to upholstery. That area alone was expected to produce products valued in access of $100,000.00 each month. The furniture factory was slowly becoming a larger kingdom.

On Friday, November 20, 1987, the detainees were sent to lunch. They returned and started to work normally. It was not long until I was called to the office. Mr. Bart wanted to see me. When I arrived there, he told me that a news release had been made concerning the deportation of the Cubans. The State Department had made the release without giving the Bureau time to prepare. Now, Cubans housed in the hospital and segregation were yelling out the windows, claiming that all of the Cubans were going to be sent back to Cuba. The superintendent of industries had called for all the bilingual staff to come up. "In a few minutes they are going to come down and let our people know that this is not true; if it is any at all, it will only be a handful out of Atlanta to go back to Cuba. They are going to break them down into sections, so just watch and let me know what's going on. Now, tell Lonny to come in."

It was just a short time until Mr. Braxton came in. He started in packing and moved up the line calling the groups together. In each case as he spoke, the population got louder and louder…and then silent. It was almost like a drum roll for the coming event. Some of the staff, myself included, thought the event would come before the day was over. The detainees that I had become friends with, who, over time, I'd learned to respect and could depend on, would walk away when I would approach. Everywhere over the department were small groups of five or six detainees; if approached by staff they would all walk and either join other groups or meet together somewhere else. No work was done in the unit the rest of the day. I sure was glad when the day was over and I carried my jacket out into the warm afternoon sun.

On Monday, like most of the other staff, I was surprised that the day started with business as usual. When I went into the front lobby I could see that the institution was open. While I had less trust and respect for management than most employees as a result of my union activism, I felt sure that some form of control was in place before they'd opened up. I would have suspected that those being deported had been identified, separated, and locked down. I knew that telling the detainees that were in the Atlanta Federal Penitentiary pending deportation that the U.S. State Department had signed an agreement to deport 2,700 Cubans, but they were not affected, went over like setting up a bar in the Southern Baptist Convention—nobody was buying!

Mr. Ray had asked Mr. Bart if he should cancel his leave, scheduled for the week of November 23 through 27 before leaving on the 20th. Mr. Bart insisted that he take his vacation. Mr. Mills had a doctor's appointment but said that he would report to work after the appointment, sometime during the afternoon. After the disturbance was over, Mr. Ray was as disturbed as any of the hostages. For the most part, we were a cohesive crew. Like in a marriage, we may be bastards, but we were our bastards.

From November 23 until December 4, 1987, Mr. Ray sat on a tower watching the Cubans walk around, knowing that his friends were inside and could die at any time. There was nothing he could do but sit there for twelve hours a day. I am certain that many of the Atlanta staff felt the same way.

I went on back to the furniture factory, put my lunch box—which contained a love note from my wife (that I never had a chance to read) into my locker. I hung up my jacket and put a pot of coffee on, waiting for starting time. The detainees began to come to work. They checked off and went to their work area and again started milling around in small groups. Many of them wore their heavy coats and had brought extra clothes, in spite of the fact that a light jacket was adequate. Many of them were wearing or carrying their tennis shoes. Steel-toed shoes were required for inmates on any work site. One inmate, Cruze, said that he had gone by the business office to have every penny in his account, over $3,000.00, sent to his sponsor in California. Mr. Milner and I told him that he should go up at noon and have it put in a savings account in a local bank until he got out. He agreed that this was a good idea and was wondering if he could have that done at once. Finally, 10:00 a.m. came and the American inmates went out to eat. I noticed that all the Americans left and for the first time, none of the Cubans attempted to leave early. Even those who had a special diet card and were scheduled to eat early did not.

It was not until much later that I learned what had transpired since Friday. Every institution in the bureau except Oakdale and Atlanta who had a Cuban had been given orders to lock them down and to transfer them to a maximum security facility. While Milan, Michigan had two Cuban detainees locked down, Atlanta was open. As early as Friday evening, detainees were still gathering in small groups. Saturday, the situation did not change; a few detainees talked to staff about their killing an American staff to get a federal sentence in the U.S.A. before returning to Cuba. Emotions were high and fear of being returned to Cuba was once again paramount on the minds of most, if not all, of the Cubans. They had begun reviewing their options; for most of them a return to Cuba was the least desirable of all options. Whatever was necessary to prevent this action would be done.

On Sunday, November 22, 1987, they had a standard fifty-eight correctional officers plus an extra eleven in, working on an overtime basis to provide additional coverage throughout the institution. (For the professional mind games, a more-than-ten-percent increase in staff was a show of force.) Another fourteen staff were also called in and held in reserve outside the institution. During the evening shift the standard fifty-one correctional staff was augmented by an additional eleven officers until midnight and another nine until 9:45 p.m. On Monday, seventy-nine correctional officers were on duty with thirty-five more from the morning watch held over. At 9:15 a.m., an additional thirty staff were called in on overtime to form disturbance control squads as the U.S. Government flexed its muscles.

On Sunday, the correctional staff was directly and indirectly being informed (being told or overhearing) of plans to take some form of action which included the taking of hostages in support of "their brothers in Oakdale." Additional snitch notes were passed to the lieutenant on Sunday indicating that on Monday a riot was going to take place around lunch when the officials were inside to be kidnapped.

On Monday, the midnight to 8:00 a.m. shift had been informed even more about the impending takeover. All of this information had been shared with the AWC at 5:30 a.m. He refused to accept it. He ordered that the institution be opened. At 7:30 a.m. work-call was given. Moments after work-call, Dr. Belchenski, the institution's dentist had been told by his detail that he always displayed care and concern for the detainees; he should tell everyone that he was sick and go home. He was told that at 10:30 a.m. that day; the institution was going to be taken over and staff taken as hostages. He called the warden's office and left that message. At 8:00 a.m. he was informed by the warden's secretary that the warden had been advised. At 7:40 a.m., Mr. Braxton was called to the front office (warden's office) and instructed by Mr. Smalls, the superintendent of industries, to go into industries, from department to department and encourage the detainees to work without an effort to enhance their potential chance for release. After discovering that his efforts were futile, he returned to the warden's office to relay this information back. After leaving

THE RIOT BEGAN: AN INSIDE LOOK

the warden's office this time, he met Mr. Smalls on his way toward the front, he passed his secretary Lue Ann who had gotten a call from personnell and instructed to come to the front immediately. He instructed her that he would take care of it, just stay there and continue her work. Mr. Smalls also passed told Mr. Braxton, telling him "Go on back down to the broom department and try to get them started to work; I will be right back there."

At 8:15 a.m. that morning was the last time Mr. Braxton saw the superintendent. Ms. LoAnn was the last female to be removed from the back. Her husband was still on the job in the back. {She was told by a Cuban detainee to get out before a riot started and was escorted to the rear corridor by the detainee}

At 8:45 a.m., a detainee in A cellblock told the counselor, Mr. Bard, that there was a problem in the back of the unit. When Mr. Bard got back there, a detainee stepped out of a broom storage area and handed him a note and ran off. The note was written in Spanish, so Mr. Bard took it to a bilingual counselor to have it read. It explained that a riot was going to take place at 10:30 a.m. and that hostages would be taken. The note also stated that the factory (industries building) was going to be burned to the ground. Mr. Bard took the note to the AWO (Associate Warden Operations) at about 9:00 a.m. and told him of the contents. The AW informed Mr. Bard that he would handle it from there. At about 9:30 a.m. the hospital OIC called the warden and told him to call the governor and get the National Guard in to support the staff. (Actually, a call to Ft. McPherson would have produced a quicker response.)

The Chief Medical Officer had been informed to remove all females out of the institution. One female psychologist had been called and told to come to personnel. She felt that it was in regard to a proposal for disciplinary action on her husband who was also a psychologist. She went down toward her husband's office when she met the Chief Medical Officer, who informed her not to worry about the matter, she could wait until after lunch to go to personnel. She then returned to work. Shortly afterward, (after the Chief Medical took the other female staff out), a detainee confronted the female psychologist and asked her why she was still there. He told her that she had to leave; there was going to be a riot. She then went down got her husband and they both went out the front. Dr. D.O.D. had been ordered to go to Unicor to hold sick call; he returned when there were no detainees reporting for sick call and after being informed that he should not be in Unicor (prison industries) by some of the inmates and detainees. By 9:00 a.m., the entire hospital staff knew that the riot was going to take place at 10:30 a.m. When the OIC called the warden to suggest assistance, he understood the gravity of the problem. He was ordered to go to the captain's office and the AW told to relieve him. He was never relieved and remained as a hostage for the eleven days. The magnitude of destruction had already been displayed in Oakdale, but management operated on hope rather than facts available.

At about 9:15 a.m., the AWC made the decision to call in thirty or forty off-duty staff to be available as disturbance squads. They began to arrive in about fifteen minutes but were not immediately dressed out into riot gear. They were sent to the training building to wait until they were needed. When they were issued helmets and batons, they started back to respond to the calls. With the use of the batons, they were able to keep the detainees away from the rear corridor doors and to maintain control of A cell house and C cell house. The Cubans attempted to enter the rear corridor from both the east and west sides by using their shanks to protect the detainee who had the keys, but since he could not open it quickly and the staff inside the bars had clubs, they were repelled. Later, even though the staff had the means to keep control of C cell house, an AW ordered it evacuated and closed off. The detainees then broke in through the side door which went directly into the East Yard. The detainees used that unit as sleeping quarters during the takeover.

At 10:00 a.m., Officer Wilson was at the compactor when a detainee took his keys from the clip on his belt and took off running toward the industries building. Officer Davidson, standing nearby, took off in pursuit. When the detainee went into the industries building, Davidson got as far as the door before stopping abruptly. He returned to the East Gate quickly and explained, "There is a bunch of them inside! They all have clubs and machetes!" The trainee on the tower had been ordered to shoot toward the detainee with the keys, but he did not respond. Officer Davidson was sent to assist in that tower. Later, he did the shooting from tower 3. Yet, industries staff had no idea what was going on. Radios were not issued to factory staff and even if they were, in most of the factories the noise level was too high to hear a radio. We were dependent upon "top level personnel."

At about 10:15, three of the extra officers from the midnight shift were in the front ground floor of the industries building. Neither Officer Tyler, Kellar, or Cobb had a radio; they had been assigned to patrol the industries building with no communications, in spite of the fact that management officials had been informed of the plan to burn the buildings by the detainees. An unusual noise was heard on the second floor. Mr. Tyler, a black officer who had served actively in the Marines, informed the other two that he would investigate. Shortly afterward, Mr. Kellar and Mr. Cobb heard Tyler running toward them and down the stairs. As he neared, he shouted, "Run! Run! They are after me!" As he was going by, they looked to see several detainees running toward them waving knives, machetes, and clubs. They too, ran. Mr. Kellar tripped and fell. Before he had a chance to get on his feet, a Cuban swung at his back with a knife, cutting his coat. Before the detainee could take another slice or stab Mr. Kellar, Mr. Tyler struck the detainee with a metal pipe he had been carrying. Mr. Tyler realized that Mr. Kellar had fallen, had stopped and come back to his assistance. He helped Mr. Kellar to his feet and both ran to the safety of the East Gate. While this was taking place, the factory foremen were still attempting to get production and the superintendent of industries was still in his meeting with the Warden and outside the front gates. He had removed all of the staff from his office but one—and ran from industries at about 10:00 a.m. The one, a female, was approached soon after being left alone and informed that if she did not get out quickly, she would be taken hostage, then raped, and abused. The inmate walked with her to the rear quarter where she was safe. Her supervisor never told her, the one, what was going on as he made his way to the front of the institution.

At about 10:30 a.m., B.J. walked quickly toward the window, which overlooked the recreation yard and back wall. "What's going on?" I asked. " I don't know. I just heard some shots from one of the back towers!" He went on over and peered out. "What's happening?" asked Mr. Bart, who had been coming back toward me. I just shrugged my shoulders as I started toward B.J. with Mr. Bart following only a few feet behind me. I later learned that a detainee had attempted to have one of the yard officers, who he thought was a nice guy, to go on up and out the East Gate. The officer, very near a tower, was shown a shank that the inmate had and told that he should go out of the East Gate, go to the camp for lunch. He was told that a riot was about to take place. As they were talking, the tower officer saw the knife. Feeling that the officer was in danger, he shot the detainee.

That is when the riot began. Within seconds, phone calls were being received from all over the institution on the emergency number and announced over the PA.

As I got about ten feet from the window, I heard the noise of a scuffle just behind me. I turned to see Mr. Bart on the floor and being kicked! Several detainees were around us. As I reached for the one kicking him. I pulled the detainee back only slightly, while telling them all, "Break it up! Okay! That's enough!" By then, a detainee got me by the belt and started pulling me back as another detainee got the detainee doing the kicking and pushed him back away from Mr. Bart. As I looked back, I saw a young detainee who had no idea how strong he was. He was on my detail; he and I had always gotten along really well. As he pulled me back, I was reminded of the Flintstones and "Bam Bam." Brito kept telling me "Take it easy! Be cool! We don 't want to hurt you; just be cool!" By this time, other detainees held each of my arms. "Where are your keys?" one asked. "Where do you want to go? I will open the doors for you," I responded. "Just take it easy and give us the keys! Be cool! We don 't want to hurt anyone; we just want the keys!" Brito again said.

I looked all around to see the rest of the staff being contained much as I was. Mr. Bart had been picked up, dusted off, and was being held much as I was. I reached my hand into my right front pocket, pulled out my key ring and handed it to Brito. Each of the detainees were also looking around to check on other staff. They then started taking us back to the upholstery shop. While those few detainees (four or five per staff) held us, the rest of the detainees were running in different directions—but each looked like they knew where they were going and what they were to do when they got there. Even in the commotion, they seemed organized. Each staff member—Mr. Bart, Mr. Mann, Mr. Braxton, Mr. Milner, B.J., and I—were all taken back to the hot room, a metal grill-type room, which was located in the upholstery section of the furniture factory. As we entered the upholstery shop, we saw that someone had already piled cardboard against an outer wall and started a fire. This was quickly extinguished.

Each of us had our hands tied and were placed in the large, steel-wired cage. As the door was locked with a padlock, we all began looking to see what could be used to pry our way out. There was nothing but an aluminum ladder there. We started talking quietly among ourselves about how we would get out if we were left there. Six or eight detainees kept standing outside the door assuring us just to be cool; they did not want to hurt us. As the smoke began to thicken from the furniture factory section, and even though each of us appeared calm and self-assured, I am certain that none of us thought that we were going to leave that room alive.

At the same time that this had been transpiring, emergency calls were still being placed from every section of industries by phone. The control room continued bellowing out calls over the radio, directing staff to respond to different areas. As the staff reached Unicor, they were taken hostage by a large number of well-armed detainees and escorted to the Unicor conference room. The Dorm 3-4 officer came out in time to see a large number of detainees knock over and destroy the metal detector area. Mr. Franklin returned to Dorm 3, locking himself in. He ran up the stairs, entered his office and again, locked himself in. He called control and advised them that they should start locking down rear corridor and every other area possible. There were 200 to 300 detainees taking staff as they came out and moving toward the front. At this time control ordered, over the radio, that the rear corridor be locked down.

Around 11:00 to 11:30 a.m., smoke was beginning to fill the upholstery shop. It had started coming slowly from the furniture factory, but now had increased in volume and thickness when several detainees came running out. "Come on! Let's get out of here!" one shouted. With that, the detainee standing by the door to the cage and holding the keys started fumbling for a key to open the lock. "Let me see; it is that one right there!" Mr. Bart told him as he pointed to the right key. 'This one?" the detainee asked as he held the keys up by one key. "Yeah, try that one!" Mr. Bart said. The detainee took off the lock and pitched it back onto the floor. As we started out of the cage, one detainee got each of our arms and at least one was behind each of us. For the most part, one held us under our upper arm, another held our hands (tied behind us), a fourth one following. Each detainee had a weapon of some sort. Most had a club of some sort (steel pipe) but a few had a handmade knife (shank). They did not attempt to drag or hurt us; we both knew who was in charge and the fact that the fire was behind us so we moved right along.

When we got out of the cage, we went into the stairwell by the cage. I expected us to go down for some reason but we went up instead. I believe that the reason that I was reluctant to go up was that there was only one floor made of wood between us and the fire that we were being led from. Then, too, we did not need to go over the fire; we went out of the stairwell and across an area just above the upholstery shop. We crossed only about fifty yards of the canvas shop before we were in the section with concrete floors. Smoke was slowly seeping through the wood floors and, after getting onto the concrete floor, I realized that the broom factory—which was separated only by a wood wall—was also burning. This area, the parachute shop, was rapidly being filled with smoke. As we reached the Norton side and the stairwell, I again expected us to be going down; but again, we went up. The Unicor (Federal Prison's Industries) business office was four to six steps up from the factory's top floor. We were led up the stairs and into the industries' conference room. Once entering the conference room, I found that we were probably close to the last group to be brought in there. (As it turned out, no one else did come in.) I could see the foremen from the other shops, the acting captain, and several supervisors. A larger segment of the fifty or so staff there were correctional officers. Most of them had their hands tied together or handcuffs on. There seemed to be some confusion as to what the detainees wanted; some wanted our hands tied in front and some tightly behind us. This was soon resolved by either handcuffing two staff together or tying the hands in front of us and passing water out to all of us. My hands had been tied in back when I first came up. When I asked that he (a detainee) reach in my pocket and get my nitroglycerin spray out for me, he tied them in front and very loosely. The rope fell off, so I wrapped it around and pulled a single knot in it to prevent getting caught in the middle of conflicting attitudes about where and how the hands would be tied. The detainees passed out cups of water and asked all the staff if they wanted a cigarette. I had not smoked a cigarette since the first day of Lent. After smoking three packs a day for years, I was convinced that I would not take one or I would be right back to three packs a day—if I made it through the day.

CHAPTER 14

THE RIOT: AN INSIDE VIEW

WE (FROM THE FURNITURE FACTORY) HAD BEEN IN THE conference room for what seemed to be an eternity. Actually, we had been there about thirty minutes when the detainees became very upset. One of them pushed a radio in front of Lt. Howard's (the acting captain's) face and ordered him, "Tell the officer no more shooting! They keep shooting, you die! All of you!" Lt. Howard did as he was told. Another detainee repeated the same thing with Lt. Higgins. As Lt. Higgins sat back down, he asked me, "Do you think that they are going to take us out of here?" We are going someplace soon...the smoke is getting worse and won't be getting better," I responded. Again, another detainee grabbed Lt. Howard and made the same demand and threat.

This time Lt. Howard was a little more composed. "This is Howard to Control! Control! Control—tell all towers to stop shooting! There are forty-six...no, forty-seven of us staff in the industry conference room! If the towers keep shooting, we are all going to be killed." The Cubans counted to be sure that he was correct in his assessment of the potential damage. This time Lt. Rodriquez, who was obviously on the outside, responded. As soon as his voice was heard on the radio, Charlie, a Cuban detainee who was one of the powers, began to shout over the radio, "Rodriquez! Rodriquez! This is Charlie!" From there he continued his conversation in Spanish. One Cuban took another staff over to the window; he busted the glass out with his stick and then pushed the staff's head out. "Now shoot! Go ahead and shoot," he shouted as he put his head out the window. "What's wrong with you mother-fuckers! Why you no shoot now?" he again shouted as he pulled the staff's head back in. I could not help snickering to myself as I was thinking, he really is a brave bastard. He cannot even see a tower from there.

It was only moments until the detainees started taking us from the building in small groups. I was about three quarters of the group back. I don't know what their rationale was, but they did not take us out in any order. They pointed out the individuals and left the room in groups of five. As I got up, I was the last of a group. We started down the hall and turned the corner toward the stairwell. Those in front of me were getting down and crawling through the door and down those four to six stairs. I could see that the windows had been broken out, but now it was obvious that hostages were being moved, at least from the inside. No staff would shoot in a building full of hostages after being told to stop. I started to get down like those before me, but did not worry about being shot, when one of the detainees with me pushed his shank under my chin and said, "No, you no get down! You walk!"

He kept the knife pressed tightly against my chin. As I walked the six feet to the stairs past the windows, I did not even attempt to look out. I went on across the flat and down the stairs. I remember thinking to myself as he crawled along, "How did I end up being so lucky as to get you with me?" As I started across the next flat and past the door leading back into the factory, I heard something hit the wall behind me and bounce around as I heard the crack of a carbine.

"You likee that? You likee somebody shoot at you?" the detainee shouted, pushing the knife a little harder into my chin, giving me a good look at the roof. "No! I don't care for this bullshit at all," I responded, talking about the shooting and the knife. I really believe that his push was from muscles tightening up out of fear; whatever the reason, I never saw where I was walking, but kept my head back. My muscles were tightening from fear. As we got to the bottom of the stairs, several detainees got as close as possible to each staff. All had some type of weapon; some had shanks and others had clubs. With each hostage, at least one detainee held a shank at their neck. Mine was still under my chin. Walking from the industries to AWB was the most vulnerable area for the detainees. This was the area in which the tower had just shot three detainees, killing one. I was not aware of the detainee's death at that time. All that was on my mind was that knife under my chin. This shooting is what precipitated the detainees coming in and threatening the staff if the shooting continued. The round in the stairwell was one of the last shots that I heard; yet it had struck the concrete wall just a few feet away and caused the knife to be held firmly under my chin.

When the detainee had been shot, the one that had been shot in the head died immediately; the other two that had been shot in the leg were less serious. The next hostage to be brought out was taken back. Mr. Lathen was a broom foreman who had been in industries about a year from the correctional force; he was also a Vietnam Veteran. The detainees took a rope, tied it around his neck and started to hang him. Other detainees came running up and stopped the action. They said that the detainees would accept the loss of one brother in the takeover. If the other two died (and the spokesperson for the Cubans preventing the hanging did not know the injuries of the other two) they would accept the loss of the three as a result of the takeover. His probable reasoning: They understand that we have control of the institution and we will kill the hostages one for one until we all die.

The detainees removed the rope and took him across with much more caution.

During this action Charlie and other detainees had the acting captain talk over the radio. After the supervisors had informed staff not to shoot, Officer Franklin was taken out with several weapons against his body and used as a shield to get through the fences and to the hospital with the three downed detainees. Efforts to gain entry into the hospital by threatening to kill Mr. Franklin failed. The detainees were told by Officer Patton, the hospital OIC and the Cubans working in the hospital to leave those injured and leave the hospital, and they would be brought in. Santiago, the lieutenant (Cuban in charge of the unit) working in the hospital told the other Cubans that Castro respected the hospitals; they would not lower themselves below Castro. The doctors would work to care for sick detainees or staff and the hospital would not be breached. This, with some extended conditions, did not change throughout the takeover. They even carried ladders up and went to the roof from the outside even though there was a stairwell to it just inside.

After getting me out of sight and the direct line of fire of the tower, the detainee pulled back slightly on the knife from my chin. When we came from industries, they took us into the chaplain's area. They opened the door and took us into the worship area, which was located in the back, for only a couple of minutes. Then, they busted the door open into the smaller classroom area located in the center of the unit that had glass walls. Again, we were in there (at least part of us) for only a short time when they again decided to break us down into smaller groups. From there, they started putting the hostages in the rooms along the outside wall. When they pulled me out, I followed Mr. Best and Mr. Mann. I thought that I was going into their room when another detainee motioned that I be brought on. Both of the detainees were leading me by my arms and I assumed that I was going to the next room. As one started to open the door, again they were told to bring me on toward the front. He opened the door leading me out of the chaplain's area and I was joined by at least six detainees. One told me that they were not going to hurt me, but they did not want any more shooting.

As we got closer to being in a direct line of fire the detainees got closer to me. By the time we got in view of the tower, the one who had done the talking was walking in front of me and holding a shank back and against my chest. There was another shank on each side of my neck, and under each of my arms and one in my back. After we turned to go behind the food service building going toward seg, the detainee with the shank in the small of my back was about a half step ahead of the others as he looked back watching tower three. The others were all watching Officer Nilson on tower 10. I finally got the attention of the one behind me and he backed off.

I was later told that another detainee was following with a shank held above my head and pointed down but I never knew of his presence. When we arrived at tower 10, Officer Nilson was standing in the tower's open window with a carbine (rumors from the detainees was that Officer Nilson was the one that had shot the detainees) and they were nearly as frightened as I. We got near the base of the tower and they began talking to Mr. Nilson in Spanish. (I speak and understood limited Spanish under calm conditions.) I never knew what they were saying but I knew what they wanted; they were wanting to go into seg. Mr. Nilson, as well as I can remember, never opened his mouth. I wondered then, if our roles had been changed, what would I have done? Even now, I have no answer. He had been ordered not to allow entry to be gained into seg. Had I been on the tower and Mr. Nilson down there and the Cubans had gone on toward seg, what would I do? On the ground, I knew what I would do—I would bleed!

The Cuban detainees expressed a desire to open up seg, let that population out, and to house all of the hostages in seg. This sounded good on the surface. The problem is that once they got us in seg, the detainees could be isolated with us. The Cubans were not going to put us all in one place where they could be separated from the population. That building could be separated off as it was being at this time; the population could have been reduced to only a few and very quickly. The detainees only desired to free all Cubans. When the tower denied access, they backed down and took me back in the same manner that I was brought over. By this time my chest felt as though it was about to explode.

Once in the kitchen, I joined many of the food service staff, Mr. Franklin, Mr. Green, the case management coordinator, and several other unit staff. Some of the detainees were inside an office area with us. All were armed but were assuring us that they did not want to hurt us. Again, they handcuffed or tied everyone. When they realized that I was ill, they left my hands untied. They offered us water, brought us cereal and milk, and gave anyone who wanted them a pack of cigarettes. (Every time they were offered on Monday and Tuesday, it was harder not to light up a smoke since I had quit less than a year earlier.) They then began to escort the hostages to the bathroom. For each of us, we were escorted with a shank in each of our ribs or at our neck. I was told that it was for my protection, but I was told this by the Cuban with a shank in my ribs!

About 3:00 p.m., some of the detainees who had worked for me who realized that I was having chest pain attempted to get me out. They took me from the kitchen to the dining hall to let me out in the rear corridor. However, between the time the riot had started and that time several of the staff had been released. Some for health reasons and some because the Cubans nearby at the time of the takeover liked them and they were close to an exit. One detainee forced his way through several other Cubans with a hostage to turn him loose, even with the other detainees objecting.

When I went into the dining hall, a large group (200 or more) of detainees were gathered near the door. The two Cubans escorting me took me past a small room with other hostages and made the stand. The detainees realized that the only value in my life was to prevent their dying on the way and one stopped with me while the other detainee approached the crowd. The one with me started forward slowly but after getting to the middle of the dining hall, the one who had gone ahead returned to tell me that we should go back and wait awhile.

At about 4:30 or 5:00 p.m. on Monday, my chest was still throbbing and the nitroglycerin spray would help only a short time. Subsequently, I was taken to the institution hospital. When getting to the hospital, the detainees who took me over told the OIC, Mr. Patton, that I had heart problems and needed to come in. He told them just to leave me and get away from the hospital and I would be admitted and checked. They insisted on taking me in and remaining with me.

The orderly from the hospital then said that he would get the doctor to check me at the door. A minute later, he returned with the doctor.

After a brief exam at the door and through the bars, D.O.D. informed them that I needed to be brought in for a better exam and treatment. When they said that I could not come in without their being with me, D.O.D. said, "Well, take him on back if you must" as he turned and walked away. They took me just outside and told me not to worry. "We are going to get you in." They went back inside to plead my case (and their admittance into the hospital.) After three or four minutes they came out and walked off, leaving me standing there alone. As they walked out, one motioned for me to go on in. As they walked down the range I went into the hospital and was admitted. I was examined, admitted, and spent the remainder of the takeover as a hospital patient.

Throughout the day on Monday, each area had its chief. Each Cuban leader was vowing more power. A few of the detainees seeking power ended up with nothing as a result of their continual movement from area to area, seeking to increase their power rather than remaining in one area to develop a leadership role. Some of the detainees had a leadership role from their years of confinement and their having developed a following. One detainee who had a following of 200 or more homosexuals had an aggressive disposition. He had been locked in the hospital, but his followers threatened to break the doors down if he was not released. The medical staff turned him out. It was this faction and their followers that possessed the greatest threat to the hostages. While the leader had never become aggressive or assaultive toward staff, he functioned solely on what was in his best interest. He did not have to become aggressive. He could cause it to happen and then come in to rescue staff.

The leader on Monday ended up being a black Cuban who had one arm cut off at the elbow. On Tuesday, he started telling the lieutenants (Cubans in charge of a given area) that he had prayed about the situation and God had told him to kill all of the hostages. Tuesday night, all of the hostages would be killed. Mr. Braxton overheard this conversation since he was able to understand the conversation which had been spoken in Spanish. He explained to the lieutenant in charge of the chaplain's area that killing any hostage was suicide. "Should any of the hostages be killed, SWAT will come in shooting. You don't have to kill all of us; when they come in they are going to shoot anything that moves! They don't know either one of us and don't care! Maybe you lieutenants need to get together and have a prayer…see if God really wants everyone, including you, to die!"

I am uncertain as to the prayer, but after a conversation among themselves, it was decided that a new leader was needed. The medical staff talked a detainee—by the name of Santiago—to take that role. Santiago, a tall, slender detainee who had a college degree, was intelligent and enjoyed respect from many of the population, was reluctant to take that role. After some persuasion about the need for a level head to be in charge and being reminded that his life, too, hung in the balance, he accepted the role. He was informed about any inmate or detainee with the psychological makeup which would be beneficial in motivating and directing them. Had it not been for his ability and intelligence we would have probably been killed. He was on the compound when another Cuban detainee came out with the American flag. The detainee with the flag had between 200 and 300 followers, all going to burn the American flag in front of tower 10 where the FBI was with a VCR camera.

When Santiago realized that they planned to burn the American flag, he walked up to the detainee with the flag and pulled it from his hand. There was some irritation to say the least among those few detainees preparing to set the flag on fire. The crowd that had come for a flag burning was also tense with the new development. Realizing the magnitude of the tension, Santiago took the Stars and Stripes around his neck and, with something, drew it together around the front of his neck. The flag covered his back, but never touched the crowd. He then took a torch from one of the detainees who had planned to burn the flag. Turning toward the tower, he lifted the torch high and proudly shouted, "Liberty, Liberty!" The irritation was turned into jubilant cries as the frustration of the moment was vented through hopeful cries from an angry mob, "Liberty, Liberty, give us liberty!"

When I went into the hospital on Monday, a detainee by the name of Sanchez was the lieutenant. While Officer Patton had the keys and was giving orders, Sanchez was standing behind him with suggestions. Any hostage would be permitted in; only those detainees who were injured would be allowed in; no detainees would be allowed to accompany them. After an examination by Dr. D.O.D., I was taken to F Ward, the psychiatric ward. Beds were set up in the open area for the hospital hostages. When I went in, Officer Schultz had the keys. The mental patients were still locked down and one was throwing urine and feces out through his food slot. All movement was decided by Sanchez downstairs. The medical staff and officers who had been in the hospital had freedom of movement within the hospital. Sanchez decided early on to keep the hospital running as normally as possible.

Late Monday night or early Tuesday morning, Mr. Patton asked Michael, a black officer who had been assigned to a number 2 post in the hospital to relieve Mr. Schulze because of his blood pressure getting so high that it was near stroke level. Officer Michael told Mr. Patton, "Get fucked! I got off duty at 4:00 o'clock. I am not doing nothing." For the most part of Tuesday and Wednesday, Mr. Michael and Mr. Tysor, the ATS ward officer, remained out of sight. When Michael refused, I took the keys and they were rotated between myself and Teach.

At about 5:30 to 5:45 p.m. on Wednesday evening, Mr. Evans, the hospital administrator, told me that a decision had been made to rescue the hospital staff. Earlier in the day, we had watched as the detainees had broken into seg and let those locked in seg out. We learned from the TV that staff had been rescued from Seg on Monday night and knew that we, too, could be rescued with very little difficulty. Directly behind the hospital was the wall. The area between the hospital and the wall was isolated, fenced in, and not accessible to the population by view. No one had a desire to go back there, since one end was directly under the tower that had prevented their initial entry into seg and the other end protected by SWAT in B cell house. From the hospital window, we talked to staff in the tower, sending precious words to our families. In fact, that is how my medication got sent to the rear corridor to me. A Cuban detainee brought it from the rear corridor to the hospital for me.

We all knew that a ladder could be dropped over the back wall, open either of the two fire escape doors and we could go out very quickly! The unknown factor to that attempt would be the safety of the other seventy-nine hostages. At the time, Mr. Evans was quietly passing the word around that we were to be in E ward of the hospital when the evening (6:00 p.m.) news came on or shortly thereafter. On Wednesday, November 25, 1987, I watched as staff began to pass through F ward and on to A ward. I had the keys to F ward and was letting those from downstairs come through. As the detainees were deeply tuned in to the reports of the riot on the TV, I slowly left the unit, locking the steel door behind me; I was the last at about 6:15 to 6:20 to go into A ward and again, locked the door behind me. There were two steel-grill doors between us and the detainees, except for the medical patients who were watching us. Damn, I felt guilty as I was waiting to escape and knowing that they were just as frightened as I…but could do nothing about their plight.

We were all beginning to worry; it had already been a long time but Mr. Evans was still in the solarium talking out the window to the FBI on the tower. Finally, about 6:45 he came in and told us, "Okay, come on; they are coming over the wall to get us!" As we stood there by the window with the steel screen on the inside (and could not find a key to remove) and bars on the outside, we took turns pressing our face against the screen only to see an outline of the wall and our own reflection. At about 7:05 p.m., someone downstairs called over the hospital intercom asking for a P.A. At about 7:10 p.m. it was a more pleading call for a doctor. The detainees had realized that no hostage was available to them and we had the keys. At about 7:20 p.m. someone looked at their watch, gave the time, and commented, "I want to know the time when I die!" There was one door between us and the detainees within the hospital.

We all realized that if the fire escape door was opened, then before we could get over the wall detainees would be holding onto our feet. If the tower staff could determine who was staff and who was not, one shot onto the compound would result in the other seventy-nine hostages dying within less than one minute. Mr. Evans opened the door and we all walked out and through the detainees who made no effort to put a finger on us. Mr. Evans went back to the solarium to see what had happened.

He was informed that a decision had been made in Washington not to attempt the escape. Just before leaving the window, I motioned to the tower in the detainee sign language, "You have got us all killed! Why?" Instead, when we went out, it was business as usual. The steel door from F Ward had been bent so badly that we were unable to close it again, but we still had the keys. At about 9:00 p.m. Wednesday night, the lieutenant in charge of the hospital came and informed us that the detainees outside of the unit felt that we had too much freedom. They were going to take the keys to prevent problems.

When Brito took me by the belt and two others had my arms, I did not hesitate in giving them the key. I did not even think about being killed; my only thought was to give them what they wanted and get out of there. My chest began to throb and felt like a hand squeezing my left breast—from the inside. Even then I did not think of my dying. After getting our keys they started leading us back to the upholstery factory. As we went through the door separating the furniture and upholstery (all part of the furniture factory), a stack of cardboard thrown against one wall was burning; then, I realized the possibility of death. One of the detainees ran over and put out the fire. But as they tied our hands and put us in the steel cage, I knew what was going to happen to the building. I suspected that our plight was the same as the structure, except maybe shorter term.

They took all the keys but the ones from the P.A. to the medical supplies. The keys to the drugs were controlled by the medical staff. All medical staff were still having free movement within the hospital. A couple of the P.A.s were being escorted in and out of the hospital to the other areas to see the hostages when they claimed illness. Other staff and I, who were patients, were limited in movement. The medical staff wanted to keep as many patients as possible—hostages and detainees—to assure the hospital was given what it needed and to keep it operating. The medical staff was just as concerned about our (the patients) movements as the detainees. After the keys were taken from me, I laid down on the floor and went soundly to sleep. I had been mentally and physically exhausted. When I woke up, I found that the correctional officers had been taken out of the hospital and across the compound with the rest of the non-medical hostages. Officer Schultz, as a result of his nearly having a stroke, had been left as a patient.

Early Thanksgiving morning, the Cubans started escorting hostages from their holding area to visit staff in other areas. In the hospital, we were not permitted to leave. Several of the other hostages came over, and some were even taken down to talk to the tower officer, giving messages for their families. Thursday, they started asking us what we wanted from the commissary. Later in the day, they brought a big bag of commissary items for each of the hostages. They had listed the items, soap, toothbrush, tooth paste, two cartons of cigarettes, deodorant, snacks, cokes, and so forth, on a commissary list. Each of us had to check the list and sign for what we received. Mr. Franklin informed me later that they had broken into the commissary but required that each detainee make his shopping list and sign for anything that they got. The detainees had formed their own police force and IDC system. When a detainee would break line at the commissary, the police would arrest him, the disciplinary committee would try him, and he would be locked down in the hospital.

Thursday evening, Santiago came into the hospital extremely upset. He called all the hostages from the hospital to F Ward to talk to us. As we all got there, he said, "1 want to tell you what is going on." He then pulled his rosary from under his shirt and gave the sign of the cross. Tears were coming from his eyes and it was obvious that he was fighting to keep from breaking out crying. "1 swear to you on Mother Mary and all that is sacred to me, I no lie to you. We go for the negotiations to get you all out and this thing over with. The FBI, they say to me, 'we no talk to you. You no good Cubans make problem for everybody. You going to cause Miami to be burned down. You no give us fifty hostages to show you bargain in good faith, we no talk to you.' I no can release fifty hostages. I try to turn loose fifty hostages they kill me. They crazy? They think we take the institution and give it all back with nothing? I don't know what to do! I can do nothing. I want to end the problem, but now I can do nothing!"

"Take it easy," responded one of the dentists. "Negotiations is not demanding; it is asking for more than you can possibly receive and settling for less. They ask for fifty, they will be happy for ten. You ask for freedom for everybody and settle for no reprisal for anyone…that is negotiations. "

"Yeah," Santiago responded with new life in his voice and face. With that the others joined in to aid in explaining the process. Shortly afterward, he left in much higher spirits. We later learned that the detainee council had met and he had attempted to have ten hostages released, but the council agreed to only three. They took the three out to the release point, but the staff would not take them out. They went back to get a fourth. They asked a factory foreman that had once been a supervisor, but he insisted that they release a food steward who was older and in poor health. They took him to the door, but even four was not good enough.

The reason for the fourth was the first three were black. The Cubans reasoned that since staff had taken others, it must be because these are all black. They added a white staff. When this did not work, they took them all back. They attempted to create racial friction among staff. The Cubans were very angry at the government's refusal to accept their sign of good faith. In one area, the hostages were being threatened by an angry group of Cubans when B.J. said, "Hold it! Now just hold it! Let's join hands and say the Lord's prayer." All of the hostages joined hands and bowed their heads. As the prayer began, staff could feel others getting hold of their hands and joining the prayer. When the prayer ended, the Cubans, too, had joined in prayer.

On Friday morning, I was told that I was going to be released sometime that day by Mr. Evans. The medical staff still maintained influence with the Cubans and especially with Santiago. "You were supposed to have been released last night, but I don't know what happened. They took some hostages up last night, but the staff wouldn't let them go. As soon as I find out what happened, I will let you know, but you will definitely be going today." Dr. Dore, a psychologist, then responded, "We know that you are a Union Representative, which gives you a reason to talk to the press about our safety. We have told the Cubans that you can and will hold a press conference and explain what is going on in here. You know these people are organized and do have leadership. They try to bargain with those three Cuban exiles and keep hearing the news say that the problem is that no one will talk to them and we are all going to get killed. We need someone who knows what is going on and is not afraid to talk to the press. We have told them that you would be the best man for the job. Will you do it?"

"Absolutely!" I said. "I am not sure that I am the best man for the job, but I have no problem in talking with the press. You're right, if we don't get some information beyond these negotiators, we are all dead!"

Friday went by very slowly with nothing happening. Santiago came by Friday afternoon and attempted to gain support for the racial issue, since he was then attempting to use it to get new negotiators. Some of the American inmates had talked him into adding a demand for several local black civil rights workers on the negotiating team. I had the Teach ask him, "Why don't you have the Cuban exiles talk for the detainees? They know your culture, your problems, and at least one of them has been in prison."

"Those dogs have no interest in us! They had no interest in the Cuban people in Cuba, just themselves! Now they have come to America and got even more rich! We have tried to get them to help us for seven years but where have they been? Now they come because they want to get more money from our blood! No! They no talkee for me! Never!"

I then responded, "Just as you will not allow the government to pick someone to talk for you, they are not going to allow you to pick who you are going to talk to and representing them. If it is important enough for you to die for, you may as well start killing us now, because you are not going to get it. If you are not willing to die for that, you might consider trading that demand for having the press, John Lewis, or at least someone that you can trust at the signing of the agreement to ensure that what you agree to and sign is understood by someone other than the government. In the meantime, you need to forget the messenger and go on with the message." He listened very intently to what I was saying. I would really like to have and would strongly encourage all future negotiations to be recorded on VCR so that good or bad points could be detected later.

On Saturday morning, November 28, 1987, I was listening to the news. The news commentator was reporting that the government was refusing to give any information. The only source of information was from other reporters. If nothing broke by next Wednesday or Thursday all of these news crews would be leaving us. Keeping all this equipment here is expensive and there is just nothing here to report. I did hear over our monitor for the institution radios which are controlled inside by the Cubans, the negotiators asking for someone, anyone of the Cubans to come up and talk to them. They were almost pleading to get someone to negotiate with. They still maintain, apparently from that, there is no one in control inside and there is just nothing going on. This sent cold chills down my back. Friday, with hopes of being released, I had calmed down some. Now, I realized that we were being set up by people with no vested interest in the place. The exiles would come out winners no matter what happened. They could keep the press out and without news and they would all leave. In two more weeks, the press would be calling every day to see what, if anything, had happened. While they were there they were being used by the negotiators to set the scene for an attack. For seven years, the U.S. Attorney General had insisted that the detainees were the most dangerous population ever to be housed in an American jail. Now, with the military, FBI and assorted other agencies there, who have been trained to kill, and enough firepower, they were ready to prove that point. I am still convinced that groundwork for an assault on the institution had been laid.

Saturday evening, Santiago's secretary (a Cuban detainee who stayed with Santiago, ran errands for him) came into the hospital. I stopped him and told him that I was sure that he had seen the same news (all of the Cuban leadership attempted to listen to the press) but immediate action must take place. I recommended that he should send the Teach out. Teach, a contract worker, was highly respected by all the detainees, even the more violent ones since he taught classes to the segregation population. As I expressed my fears, he just stood there staring intently at me. I told him that a list of the demands should be carried out to the press as well as an explanation of what was going on. Teach could do it since he was not a Bureau employee, and the detainees would have less problems with him leaving. "I don't give a damn if you have to put him on a stretcher and cover him with a sheet, you have to get someone out!" I explained.

After I finished, he just stared at me with no response for about ten seconds. He then turned and ran off. I had no idea what he had in mind. I went to my bed and lay down, still attempting to get my chest to quit hurting, if only for a short time. I was still lying there when I began to hear what sounded like a riot. Again, I wondered if I would be stabbed to death or shot. Slowly, I got up and walked around the corner to see the hostages watching TV and the Cubans listening to the radio. The detainees were intent as to what was being said. I asked someone about the noise. "Oh, they have put a speaker up on the roof," he responded. One of the Cubans told me that they had fired a transmitter with one of the walkie talkies and were broadcasting over the local Cuban radio station. This was the breaking point of the ordeal. Minutes later, ABC news announced a list of demands had been given to the government and that leadership was now developing.

Saturday night after the broadcast, four hostages were released. One was to talk to the warden about what was going on inside and the threat the Cuban exiles were presenting. Additionally, the water had to be turned back on as a sign of good faith on the part of the government. The rest of Saturday night, Sunday, and most of Monday, the detainees were happy. Saturday night some of the detainees got all the mattresses together in seg (E cell house) and poured gas (or some flammable liquid) over it and set it on fire. This burned every mattress, but the concrete and steel never burned. The Cubans kept commenting on their disbelief of the amount of flammable liquids in the institution. I know that during the fires, I kept hearing explosions.

By Monday evening, the detainees again began to have a mood swing. Tuesday, Wednesday, and Thursday, it was cold out and the masses appeared to want it to end and didn't know how to accomplish it. I was really afraid that the frustration which had started in the riot would again set in. It seemed that at any moment our lives depended on less than the toss of a coin. Wednesday evening, my chest was really hurting. It felt much like a hand squeezing and twisting my left breast from the inside. Finally, I called Dr. D.O.D. to come up. He and a P.A. brought up oxygen and gave me a shot of morphine. I attempted to hold back my tears, but I couldn't; it hurt too bad. After the shot, the Doctor told me, "Don't worry, we are going to get you out of here." Then they left. As the shot began to take effect, my chest began to feel a little better and I could once again get my breath more easily, although the oxygen tank ran out. I realized that the only way that he could get me out was if I died. I became extremely angry. Here I was in a prison hospital in Atlanta, Georgia and could die of a heart attack and no one, including the Cubans, could do a thing.

I made up my mind—Sunday at the latest, I was leaving. The Cubans can cut; the government can shoot; or I will burn the hospital down myself…but, I am leaving. Thursday evening, we were told that an agreement had almost been reached; we would go home maybe Saturday, Sunday at the latest. The rumors began to flow about maybe Thursday night. We were assured that it would be Friday at the earliest. Someone announced, "Hey, they are signing the agreement!" We all got to see the news. The late show had been broken into to present the special news.

As we were watching the news, someone knocked on the door. The detainee who had been throwing urine and feces had the keys (and had been working the unit most of the time since the keys were taken) and opened the door. In walked the leader, who was leading the 200 or so that did not want us to go. Waving a two-foot machete, he and a crowd of his followers walked in the door. I knew then that the paper was going to be signed in blood. As the shouting continued, someone finally said in English, "Line up in single file, you're all leaving! It is over!" The Cuban and his followers had formed an aisle with machetes on both sides for us to walk out. Cubans in the background were cheering us as we left.

When entering the rear corridor, flood lights were in our eyes. All we could see was the table and negotiators, detainees, and government. We then walked around a curtain to face an aisle similar to what the Cubans had formed. This time it was American soldiers with weapons pointed inside the institution. We were walking, facing gun barrels. As I walked out the door, it was full of bodies and cameras from the door to the street. I remember hearing myself pray, "God, just help me live through the release."

CHAPTER 15

AN AFTERVIEW

THE MORNING AFTER THE RELEASE, I RETURNED TO THE institution. The shock of this visit was as traumatic as the takeover. When I saw the corridor with fire hoses and standing water, it was more than my mind wanted to accept. I saw Warden Truman and inquired as to his health. He looked like warmed over death and it was obvious that he had suffered as much as the hostages. My wife and I then went around and on top of the outside warehouse at the insistence of a friend who was working at the time. when he showed us industries and told us about the tanks parked behind the back wall which were going to be used to rescue, it was obvious to me that God had completed another miracle by getting us out alive. By then, all I wanted was as to be as far away from that place as possible and as quickly as possible.

As a result of the takeover, I wrote the following document and gave a copy to the warden, the Director of the Bureau of Prisons, the Attorney General, and the President of the United States. I also gave a copy to the FBI.

I believe the year was 1979 when the U.S. Congress passed a bill in the budget to close the United States Penitentiary. At that time the American inmates started being transferred out as did many of the staff. As the population dropped, so did the staff. The industries were being removed from Atlanta to other facilities within the bureau. Education and vocational classes were being discontinued and many staff who did not want to pull up roots and move were beginning to seek other employment in the community of other federal agencies. Efforts by many employees individually as well as the local union, were being made to have Congress reconsider their decision.

In 1980, the Cubans began to arrive on the shores of Miami. At first, the two had nothing in common, even though from early on many of the immigrants were being locked up in other facilities as it was being discovered that Castro had opened up his jails and mental institutions for deportation to our shores. (According to some of the detainees who later arrived in Atlanta, some were informed to get on a boat or be shot there.) It was not until the detainees burned Ft. Chaffee, Ark., and massive destruction at other facilities, that the decision was made that Atlanta remain open and Cubans housed there.

As the detainees began to arrive in the Atlanta facility, a token effort was made to teach a few of the employee a little Spanish. No effort was made to resolve the most serious problem, and that being the cultural difference. The institution employed interpreters so that employees and detainees could talk, but in retrospect, this did not add to the understanding. In many cases, employees would run in between two detainees who were shouting and waving their arms to be informed that they were only holding a simple and agreeable conversation. Staff started a separation list of detainees who reported others for having weapons or such things (which would have resulted in an American inmate killing another) only to find that this was an acceptable practice among the detainees.

The biggest cultural difference was the rapid emotional change and response by the Hispanic population. While the American population may have been motivated by emotions, the act was logical (predictable) and thought out. In most cases, the American inmate knew the consequences before making a decision to act. The detainee would often become assaultive strictly out of emotions and without consideration of consequence. With limited knowledge of their culture, staff would find themselves in a fight from the middle of a calm conversation. They would not even know why the detainee would suddenly get up and start swinging.

The detainees did not understand our system of corrections. They did not understand how they could strike a staff member and get a pink piece of paper, cut another detainee, throw urine or feces on staff, or go into an out of bounds area and get a pink piece of paper. Placing them in segregation too, was no difference to any other housing unit initially. It was not until late 1981 or 1982, when the detainees when up for the review for release that the pink piece of paper held any relevance to them. Prior to this, many committed acts just to get a pink piece of paper in a race to see who could get the most.

Initially, the hearings appeared to be fair and rational to the detainees. The detainees expected those who had caused problems to remain locked up for a longer period of time and those who did not cause problems could understand that it may take a while for them to get out to the street. A few got released, and it appeared as though the American dream was possible. As time passed and some of the detainees who were consistently in trouble were released while others worked hard and stayed out of trouble got a notice to return to the panel in two years. The detainees sensed a lack of fairness. This was the first step toward November 1, 1984.

The detainees had a need and desire to believe the U.S. Government. They truly wanted to do whatever they had to do to get the opportunity to go out on the street. I am convinced that if we told them that if they could walk around the institution on their hands without falling we would release them to the street, we could have them all walking on their hands. Instead, there was no effort to place requirements or develop skills for an eventual release. The entire conversation was deportation.

Had the U.S. Government started deportation (with or without the consent of Castro) the American people and the detainee population could have understood and supported the idea. Instead, we were developing a policy of holding the detainees until deportation. At the same time, we were undergoing a change in population from those who had rioted at Ft. Chaffee to some that had been out on the street for two or three years and had been arrested on a variety of charges, both felony and misdemeanor. The detainees (especially those on minor crimes) had served their time when and where they were charged and could not understand their being brought to Atlanta. Many of them had never been in jail in Cuba and could not understand our laws. The instructions, "Remain until deported," with no deportation, was in reality, "Life imprisonment with no parole."

At the same time the tension was building in the detainee population, staff too, were getting more dissatisfied. Labor Management relations were limited to non-existent and the employees were burned out. The correctional force worked for over a year putting in as many hours as the employee could withstand. Some of the officers worked sixteen hours a day and up to seven days a week as a result of the implementation of the plans to close the facility and transferring of staff. Yet, the annual evaluation of the employee reflected neither the hours, jobs assigned, or type of work performed by the employee since the evaluation played a major role in promotions. Morale was very low, tension was high, and upper management was allowing low level supervisors with limited abilities, at best, to make many key decisions.

On November 1, 1984, a combination of these factors touched off a disturbance in B Cell house. The detainees had no desire to hurt staff but wanted the public to know of their situation. They started in the back of the cell house, forcing staff toward the door. One employee who had been out of the unit and was not aware of the problems developing, entered the cell house and started toward his office in the back of the unit when he was met by a large number of detainees. Rather than allow him to get back into the mob, one picked up a bucket and threw it at him. They did not hit him, but let him know that he was going the wrong way. While it would have been just as easy to block the door and keep the staff in at the time with a ratio of 150 detainees to 1 employee, the detainees pushed the employees out of the unit and allowed the door to be closed and locked. While the government claimed them to be non-existent, they wanted the world to know that they were alive and alone.

This situation allowed management to clamp down on the detainees even more, placing them on lockdown. Additionally, while many of the staff worked thirty-two hours straight, sometimes more, during the riot, the only award was given to a supervisor. The staff was placed on twelve-hour shifts and in such a manner that it angered almost everyone. Again, during the twelve-hour shifts and difficulties suffered by staff, most got only "fully successful" evaluations. At the same time, labor management relations were discontinued and congressional assistance was requested on behalf of both the detainees and staff. This request was for the most part ignored until the warden got caught up in the porno flick scam. As a result of this, Mr. Blackmon retired at age fifty instead of age fifty-five as had been rumored as his earlier plans.

When Mr. Truman came in as warden, the situation with staff began to improve. Some of the former administration had been transferred, labor management relations were becoming normalized, morale was still low as a result of some of the supervisors who were still around from the prior administration. A majority of the employees within that or any correctional facility are on the correctional force. Subsequently, problems within that department have greatest impact in the institution. The department head and many of the supervisors had limited to zero compassion, consideration or concern for the needs of the employees. In spite of these factors, employee morale continued to slowly rise.

The detainees were unhappy with the system of release, but Oakdale led them to believe that efforts were being made to release them. When Oakdale opened, the rumor was that the detainees were going to Oakdale for six months or so and then on to the street. Even though many of them had received a written notice from Immigrations in Washington that they were to have been released months earlier, they were willing to work their way through the system to get out. They were unhappy that they could not take a representative or witness on their behalf to a hearing where they were required to prove that they were alive, but they were tolerant.

Some of the detainees who were sent to Oakdale began to return with stories that no one was getting released from Oakdale either. Additionally, we were getting more detainees who had never been in jail in Cuba, had been in the streets (and had become Americanized in thinking) and had married and had children in this country. While being told that they were going to be deported, it was just not happening. Castro had said *no*. On November 20, 1987, this changed. It was on the noonday news that Cubans would be deported once again as a result of a signed agreement.

I worked in the furniture factory within the federal prison industries. Our detainees had returned from work before the newscast and had no knowledge of this. The staff was called into the department head's office and told that some type of news release had been made and that the detainees from the hospital and segregation were shouting that all detainees were going back to Cuba. A decision had been made by the factory superintendent to call all of the detainees together, area by area, and relay the accurate news to them. Some detainees, only a handful from Atlanta, would be deported.

When this was done within our department, the detainees became very loud at the news; then it became very quiet. Small groups began to form all over the department. When I would approach some of the detainees that I really go along with, they would break up and walk off. The meeting was held about 1:00 p.m. in our department and I honestly did not think that we would be alive to see 3:45 p.m. No one went to work, and we just stood back and prayed. Fortunately, that quiet mood did not change and nothing set them off.

After Oakdale started their riot, the correctional officers were placed on alert in the Atlanta facility. During briefing before the shift began, some of the officers were informed that during the weekend they were not to leave their home without notifying the institution as to a phone number where they could be contacted in case of emergency. Apparently, at least some of the staff believed that the facility would also riot. In spite of all of this, the decision was made not to lockdown the population. It was rumored that a meeting was held between the warden and several of his subordinate management officials to discuss the need to lockdown. The rumor continued that only one of the subordinate officials called for a lockdown. The warden took his advice from staff, some of which should have known what to expect, and kept the institution open.

On Monday morning, November 23, 1987, the inmates came to work at 7:30 am as scheduled. They initially got their tools from the tool room just as any other day. Beyond that point, nothing was the same in the furniture factory. No one went to their job assignment and started to work. Instead, they just walked around. When I confronted several of my key detainees asking if they were going to work, have a work stoppage, or what was going on, they would not look me in the eye. I could not get an answer from even my best workers or the people that I got along best with. About 9:30 a.m., a few of my detainees started to work. Even with this, there was an uneasy feeling as a result of the tension in the air. Nothing that you could put your finger on, but it just wasn't right.

At about 10:25 a.m., the American inmates were let out for lunch as usual. Usually, twenty or so detainees attempt to go out at that time also. This day, only the Americans were going out, and not all of them went out. Those who did were glad to be leaving the area, although this is not unusual at lunch time. Although I gave it little thought other than the fact that no detainee attempted to go out, in retrospect, the people and attitudes should have told me something; it did not. I then went back to the tool room to see how the tools were getting back in since very little work had been done, and again, all work had stopped. They were getting the tools put up when I discovered that two screwdrivers were missing.

I checked to see who had the screwdrivers out and went out to get them. That detainee (and I have no idea who it was at this time) denied getting the tools. He went back to the tool room with me and informed the tool room clerk (a detainee) that he had given the tool to someone else and put the wrong chit up. At this time, I went in to inform the factory manager, Mr. Beasley, that they were missing. As we came out of his office (Just in front of the tool room) I was informed that they had been located. I then went back to my work area to check on the progress of the day before lunch. As I was checking over the area, Mr. Beasley called to me and I started walking toward him. I saw several detainees and another foreman,

Bobby Williams, run over and look out the window. Mr. Beasley asked what was going on and I shrugged my shoulders and started toward the windows.

All of a sudden and before I got to the windows which had been only a few feet away, several of the detainees grabbed Mr. Beasley, knocked him down and started kicking him. He had been just a few feet away, and I grabbed one of the detainees by the shoulder and shouted, "Hey, knock it off!" By this time a detainee by the name of Brito who worked for me got me by the belt and in the back and started pulling me back. Another detainee who I did not see and could not identify put a long, handmade knife (machete) up by my cheek. Brito started telling me just to cool it; he didn't want me to get hurt.

Brito was young and very strong. As he pulled me back to a steel support beam, I remember thinking that he alone could start banging me around like "BAM BAM" in the Flintstones. By this time, other detainees had stepped in and gotten Mr. Beasley to his feet. As I looked around, each of the detainees had a knife, club, metal bar, or a weapon of some sort. Each of the foremen were in the same condition as I was. A detainee by the name of Metamoris came running up to Mr. Beasley from the Mill area where he was assigned. He started pointing his finger into Mr. Beasley's face and began shouting about *now we will see what you are running*, but other detainees stepped in front of him and sent him on away from Mr. Beasley. As they pulled me back with my back against the support beam, Brito again told me just to keep calm, they did not want to hurt me. The knife was moved from my face and by this time, five or six detainees were around me.

Each of the detainees kept telling me to be cool and asked for the keys. I told them that I would be glad to open the door for them, but again, I was told just to keep cool and to give them the keys. By this time, it was obvious that they were going to get all of the keys within the department no matter what we wanted. I told them that they were in my right front pocket. They took my keys and my wallet. They then started moving me to the east end of the department. At the east end of the department was a separate room which was going to be set up as the upholstery area. This room was separated by a wall with a drive through door. when we went into that area, a fire had been set, but some of the detainees ran over to put it out. We were taken into a secured room (an area partitioned off with quarter-inch steel mesh) which had been used to store furniture material such as locks, mirrors, etc. Our hands were tied behind us and the door was padlocked. During the entire time that we were in that room two or three detainees, at least, were standing around the door and kept attempting to calm us down. Inside this room was Mr. Beasley, Mr. Manear, Mr. Perez, Bobby Williams, Lanny Miller, and me. While the detainees standing outside the door were attempting to calm us down, smoke began to come from the furniture department area. Ted Manear asked me what I thought they were going to do and I told him that I had no idea. Frankly, he and I both had the same idea; we were going to burn with the building there. I was looking to see if there was anything that could be used to bust out with but found nothing visible.

As the smoke thickened, coming from the other area, detainees began to come out and go through the door into the stairway. Several still stayed with us to be sure that we didn't try to escape too early as far as I was concerned. Finally, some came out and said that everyone was out and they opened the door. Each of us had two or three get us and take us out and up the stairs. When we went into the canvas shop, the top floor of the industries building, it was already filled with smoke. We then went through the towels department, also filled with smoke, and on into the industries conference room. Inside there, there was already fifty or so staff hostages .

Someone, (a detainee) busted out the windows and took a staff member over to the window to protect him while he looked out. Then they had Lt. Howington (acting captain) call over a radio to tell the towers to stop the shooting. Both he and Lt. Hogan used the radio which was controlled by the detainees at that time, to ask the towers to quit shooting. They were at knife point by some hysterical detainee and happy to oblige. Lt. Hogan asked me if I thought that they were going to keep us there and I told him that we would not be there long. The smoke was already filling the room. Soon, they began to take us down out of the building one or two at a time at first, but it got to be a continuous line as the smoke thickened. Each of us were well escorted. As I got near the doorway at the top of the stairs, I saw all the people in front of me crawling by the window. I did not know why, but as I got there I started to stoop down when the detainee put a knife under my chin and informed me to stand up and walk. As I got down the first flight, five stairs or so, I heard something hitting the wall above and behind me. The detainee asked me how I liked being shot at and I assured him that I was not excited.

He still had not removed the blade from my chin and, for the remainder of the trip, I looked mostly upward. As we got to the bottom of the stairs he was joined by several others who put the point of their blades against me and kept me as much as possible between themselves and the tower. They too kept telling me that they did not want to hurt me, but it was so hard to believe that it was my best interest they had with a blade being pointed at me. We went directly to the chaplain's area from there. We ended up for a short time in the prayer room located in the center with windows all around. They then decided that they wanted to break us up, so they started putting everyone in different rooms. I was taken to where I thought was going to a room on the south side of the unit. Instead, I was told to come on with some of the detainees. There had been some discussion about taking us all to the segregation unit; I was told that I was going to segregation. As I went down the stairs, I had at least six knives touching me. One under each side of my neck, one under each arm, and at least two in my back. As we started walking, one of those with the blade in my back got about a half step in front of everyone else. It was difficult to keep his pace with the blades under my neck. Finally, I got his attention and he slowed down.

They took me to the top of the hill near seg and under the tower. Phillip March was working on the tower and just stood there looking down at us and holding the carbine. They did most of the talking; I do not believe that he ever responded. As I stood there I wondered what I would do if I was up there. I never came up with an answer and hated for him that he was in that situation. We then turned around and went to the dining hall. There we were offered water, food, milk, cigarettes, and opportunities to go to the bathroom with guards.

By then, I was taking a shot of Nitrolingual for my chest pain about every ten minutes and it was not helping. At about 2:30 p.m., some of the detainees who worked in the furniture factory and knew that I had heart problems attempted to have me released. When we left the kitchen and went into the dining room area, another group of detainees had gathered. After a discussion between those escorting me and those in the dining room, they took me back to the kitchen. On the way back, I was told that no more staff were going to be released.

After sitting in the kitchen for another hour or so, they took me to the institution hospital. Just before that, I had borrowed a coat from Mr. Greer, the case management coordinator. I took it with me because I expected to be back shortly. That was not the case and I saw Mr. Greer leaving on a cold night in his short-sleeved shirt. I tried to have a PA take it back on one of their trips over to the kitchen area but was assured that a box of coats had been broken out and that it was not needed by Mr. Greer and that I should keep it. I had worn a coat in, but it was in a locker in the building which had burned early Monday.

When I arrived at the hospital, Dr. Davis was at the door and talked to me. He then informed the detainees that I needed to be brought in to be seen, but that they were going to need to leave. After a discussion, the detainees told Dr. Davis that if they could not come in and stay with me, I was not coming in and started out with me. As we stepped outside, they told me that I was going in, no matter what, just wait there a few minutes. They went back in and argued with Dr. Davis, Mr. Prattor, and one of the Cuban orderlies. Finally, they walked out and walked off telling me to go inside. I was taken back, given an EKG and sent upstairs. I knew that it was not a heart attack, but angina pain. During the time that I was a hostage, and for that matter, even since that time, it has only been short periods of time that I have been able to get rid of the pain in my chest.

Officer Prattor had the keys to the hospital door and Dr. Davis was checking all patients at the door. The Cuban orderlies were actually making the decision as to who would or would not come in. They were armed, but their weapons were not displayed as those outside of the hospital. They did not want the open population coming into the hospital, which would have required that they also display weapons to protect the hostages and themselves. The medical staff had freedom of movement to fulfill medical needs. The hostages who were patients were restricted in movement and required to have a guard to go to the restroom. These guards did not display a weapon, but when a friendly pat was given the weapon was under their shirt.

When I got upstairs in F ward, a hospital ward which was used by staff to keep the mental patients, Officer Stultz was working. He had apparently been the F ward officer at the time of the takeover. This was a very unusual situation for everyone; the orderlies (Cuban detainees) were aware that they were now in charge and did not feel comfortable with that role. They were most happy for us to keep the keys and let people move with their consent. They did not want any detainee in there that did not work there or was not a patient. They were content with giving all staff as much freedom as possible and still showing the outside that they ran the hospital. They were actually afraid that someone would come in and get into the drugs and they would all be killed.

When I first got up into F ward, I just rested. After awhile (sometime late into Monday evening or night), I realized that Mr. Stultz was exhausted and physically in just as bad, if not worse, condition than I was. I began to relieve him. He passed out and fell onto a cart of food, spraining his back. His blood pressure was something like 180 over 140. He was having severe chest pain, and they put him in bed by Thursday. After that, they would not let him get up, being afraid that they would remove him from the hospital. The detainees in the hospital knew his condition and they were afraid that he would be removed from the hospital and die, causing everyone to die. Also, in the hospital as a patient was a young officer by the name of Mr. Spencer, who had been employed by the Bureau of Prisons four weeks prior to the takeover. Thursday they finally took the keys from us (late Wednesday night) and sent Mr. Prattor, Mr. Thrasher, and Officer Mitchell to the chaplain's area. These staff were not medical so they were sent over with the rest of the hostages. This was the big takeover that the news told about.

Actually, the takeover of the hospital was not a takeover, but a murder plot by the FBI, as far as many of the hostages in the hospital were concerned. Mr. Levens, the hospital administrator, was a hostage and was doing a log of the administrative directing while Dr. Davis identified himself as the Chief Medical Officer (senior medical official) and all care of patients was going as usual. While the medical staff did not have a blade under their throat, the blade was within reach at any moment and the medical staff or patients had only the freedom that the individual there at the time chose to give us. We did have the advantage of being able to talk to the staff on the tower and get phone calls out to our family up through the first Wednesday after our captivity. On that date, November 25, the FBI came up with their plan to remove us from the hospital just as they had removed the staff from segregation on Monday night. We all felt sure that this plan would work as far as the staff from the hospital was concerned, but each of us was concerned about the consequences to the remainder of the hostages. At the same time, we were not sure of our future for more than the next thirty seconds at any given time. For example, when I went up to F ward on Monday, a patient was throwing urine and feces out of his cell. On Friday, he had the keys and the only other detainees in the unit were the formal patients, or whoever came to the door.

At about 6:30 p.m., we were told to start moving toward B ward. The plan was that someone from the outside was going to climb over the wall, bring the keys for the emergency entrance, which were never brought in except during an emergency. They were going to open the fire door—which only opened from the outside. We were going to go out the door and over the wall in the same manner that the man from the outside had entered. The hospital, located on the west end of the institution and only fifty feet or so from the wall, was protected by a tower. The wall itself was protected from the view of the detainees by the hospital. The area outside of the hospital where we would have crossed is a dead area and during normal situations, was used only a couple of hours a week for recreation for hospital patients. This area was too close to the towers for the detainees to be around. We could have gotten out without detection.

About 6:40 p.m., we were all there and the rest of the building was locked. We had the keys with us and were waiting on the officer to open the door. We had been told by the FBI agent on the tower that the officer was coming over the wall. We waited and waited for the door to open. We each tried to push our face up to the window to see if we could see the ladder on the wall. We could not. About 7:05 p.m., the orderly called from the front door downstairs and asked for a doctor to come to the door. Then a second call. A few minutes later, it was more like a pleading call. apparently, he had discovered that no medical staff were on the first floor, no door was open, and he had no keys. I am sure that every one of the twenty-six of us felt some guilt at that moment about our plans to leave, but we were motivated by our fear of staying and from a passive position could make the most rational decision. We continued to wait.

By 7:15 p.m., we called to the FBI and advised them that the detainees were getting much too close to us. They were getting through the locked doors and would be in with us shortly; was the man coming over the wall? There was no response. Finally, about 7:20 p.m., we realized that we were not going to be rescued. We decided to go on back and face the mob. To us, we felt that we had made our bed, now we could go back and die in it.

The FBI then informed us that the rescue attempt had been canceled in Washington at the last minute. The idea that the decision was made not to take us out did not bother us; it was the timing that got to us. Why did they wait to let us know that it was canceled until the Cubans had broken a couple of doors and were working on the only door between them and us? We were forced to abort the effort. We were saved only because the detainees in the hospital never wanted to let the masses know of our attempt to escape or they would have lost control of the hospital. The rest of the population throughout that the institution was being invaded. The FBI wanted to come in, but until some of us were hurt by the detainees, could not justify such action. I am still convinced that the plan was to cause justification to come in.

Thursday, Thanksgiving Day, was a quiet day. The detainees brought things such as cigarettes and Cokes from the commissary to us. They appeared to be tiring out a little. Santiago, who the medical staff had convinced to take over as the leader of the detainees, was angry because he had met with the three Cubans that the government had sent in to negotiate. They were demanding that he release fifty hostages or they were not going to talk to him. He had given them a list of demands on Wednesday, but they would not discuss the demands without his releasing fifty hostages. We had talked him into releasing ten, but the masses had only agreed to release three. Santiago wanted to release the older employees and those in poor health. Some of the others from the council, which they had formed, were not in agreement with this. Within their group it was decided that since the first group to be released were all white, the three should be black. The detainees are for most part not racially motivated but wanted to show every sense of fairness. Again, they wanted to show the world through the press that they were not the animals that the U.S. Government had labeled them.

I was an official of the local union (secretary-treasurer) and a member of the executive committee. He was being requested to make a statement on behalf of the local union and members of the bargaining unit. Such a release of information would be as a direct result of the adverse impact facing the bargaining unit, and as such would be protected and even required under Title 5, USC. In effect, he was the official spokesperson for the local union within the facility, and the local union would defend him should the institution have an objection to either his making a statement or any of its content. He still was not happy about it (having knowledge of the institution's ability to become vindictive) but he also knew the consequence of not getting a message out of the institution while the opportunity was available.

As a result of this broadcast, four hostages were released. Santiago made the decision to release three of the hostages that night and the English-speaking secretary to Santiago pushed a fourth one in the group out. One of the four was told to explain to the FBI—or whoever was running the show, that their continual playing games with the highly-emotional detainees was going to directly result in the death of all the hostages. The newscast denying communication with the detainees, the turning off of the water, the refusal to accept hostages, and other such actions was going to cause the detainees to select a leader other than

Santiago. Such action would reduce the likelihood of any additional hostages leaving the facility on foot. It was my opinion that had we not been able to get a hostage out that night who could and would talk to those in charge, we would all be killed.

The attitude of the detainees was much more positive over Sunday and Monday. They too, were tired of the ordeal and wanted it to end from all indications. They began to move the hostages around, taking them by the towers so they could have the officers call their families and take pictures for their families. None of us from the hospital were taken out but several of the hostages were brought by to visit with us. I was so tired of lying around but did not feel like doing much more. By Tuesday, the mood was again cooling off like the weather.

By Wednesday, the visitation had stopped and the detainees were again becoming restless. They were ready for it to end, but about seven American inmates had made this their case. They had gotten law books from the education department and were advising the detainees as to what they should add, which was only causing confusion and aggravation. The detainees (with advice from the American inmates) had insisted that Congressman Lewis, Rev. Lowery, a representative of the ACLU, the Cuban Bishop from Miami, and three others were to be brought in to the negotiations. Through Mr. Lebon, I asked Santiago if he would allow those three Cubans that the government had brought in to negotiate for the detainees since they were familiar with the culture, with the situation within jails and all. He got furious at that idea. I then told him that just as he would not let the government select his negotiator, neither would the government allow him to select theirs. What was most important was the message, not the messenger. While it would be a good idea for them to demand some of those persons and the press at the signing of an agreement to insure its validity, the government would select who was going to talk for them.

On Wednesday night, I had severe chest pain and problems breathing. Doctor Davis gave me a short of morphine and put me on oxygen for a short time and said that he was going to attempt to get me out. I got so angry as I laid there in a hospital and in a metro area like Atlanta, and could have died of a heart attack and there would have been nothing that anyone could have done. I made up my mind then that this was not going on beyond the weekend. I remembered the Indian Chief in the movie *Little Big Man* as he sat on his horse and said, "THIS IS A GOOD DAY TO DIE." The hostages were caught in the middle between our friends and our enemies. Our friends, a group of FBI agents, US Marshalls, and the Delta Force, all wanted to get some action. They wanted to come in shooting. Our enemies, about 1200 Cubans, who had only about 150 who wanted to cut my head off. About 1050 of my enemies had made themselves responsible for keeping those two elements apart and keeping me alive. I was at the point that I did not care which side acted first. I was going to start my own fire inside and fight my way outside, no matter who won.

This paragraph following the one just above may sound hypocritical, but I would not have put off until the next weekend had it not been true. God was present and with us at all times inside those walls. As I prayed many times, "God forgive me for believing my lying eyes instead of your proven love for us." Many of us had group prayers as well as our individual prayer time on a regular basis. Not only the hostages, but many of the detainees were in regular prayer also. Each of us thanked God for remaining in charge of the facility and when you realize the number and types of elements involved for that period of time and no serious injuries after the first half hour, GOD WAS IN CHARGE.

The hostages were not the only individuals who saw themselves as victims of actions which could have been prevented. One inmate (actually several signed it) wrote the following letter to President Reagan:

THE FOLLOWING IS A LETTER FROM THE SEVENTEEN AMERICAN CADRE WHO FACED DEATH DURING THE RIOT AT U.S.P. ATLANTA, CONCERNING THEIR ACTIONS FROM NOVEMBER 23rd TO DECEMBER 5th, 1987

This letter is addressed to you from the seventeen American Cadre whom were accused of being participants in the riot at U.S.P. Atlanta, sixteen who are being held in Maximum Security at Seagoville, Texas, in the Special Housing Unit. It is our hope, that with hearing our story, and having the opportunity to review and evaluate the facts concerning our actions during the riot from November 23rd to December 5th, 1987, you will consider the possibility of granting us a full and unconditional pardon.

We are imperfect human beings, but nonetheless, human beings with feelings, compassion, love for our fellow man. We are serving our time, paying our debt to society, and doing our best while incarcerated to prepare for our return to society as law-abiding, productive citizens in this great nation.

When the riot began, some of us were encouraged to stay by staff members such as Chaplain Russell Mayberry, Chief Psychologist Dr. Carl Gates, and Unicor Factory Manager Mr. Tom Campbell. We would like to point out that we all are in the custody of the Attorney General and were designated to the U.S.P. at Atlanta as a working Cadre. At no time during the riot were we instructed to leave the institution by any governmental authority. Upon release of the hostages, we asked the officer in charge, Lt. Flores, and Captain Craddock, what we were supposed to do. We were instructed to remain in the prison until all the detainees were processed out. At approximately 5:00 a.m. on December 5, we were notified via the public address system, to report to the East Gate immediately, which we all promptly did.

During the course of the siege we were under tremendous stress and were clearly a minority among some 1,300 Cubans, most of whom brandished weapons. We lived in extremely unsanitary conditions, had no water or heat in our dorm with freezing temperatures. Our meals were irregular, and we had no clean clothing. Toilet facilities consisted of portable units on the construction site. Cubans ran through the dorms twenty-four hours a day pounding on doors and screaming, making sleep almost impossible. We endured these hardships because we put the well-being of the hostages ahead of our own needs and safety.

We believe this is the first time in history there has been a group of men working inside a hostage situation for the safety and welfare of the hostages, acting as a positive mediating counterforce, who stressed the safety and good care of the hostages to the Cubans. We were a calming influence overall. We could be likened to the Peace Corps. We were not trying to be heroes. We felt in our hearts their need, and we felt it was our duty to take our obligation as a working Cadre one step further. We decided to stay and do whatever we could to help our brothers by seeing this to a safe and peaceful end for all concerned. To construe that we stayed in that stressful environment under the aforementioned conditions, for any reason other than helping the hostages would be totally asinine. We, the American Cadre, feel that our goals were met and our prayers answered with the safe release of all the hostages on December 4, 1987.

The following is a summary of our involvement as well as a recap of some key incidents that we played a major role in.

* Some of us visited the hostages daily, giving our support and encouraging them to have patience and faith. It was obvious from day one that our presence alone was a positive and spiritual uplift for them. We made sure they had proper medical attention and whatever medications that were necessary. (One American Cadre whose job was X-ray technician in the hospital, remained there twenty-four hours a day, helping and assisting the medical staff. He realized the stress they were under and took on many extra duties, enabling and encouraging the staff held there to rest as much as possible.) We were also able to provide them with amenities, such as clean socks and underwear. We kept them abreast of the situation as best we could. We asked the Cubans to remain calm

and flexible and most importantly, <u>do not hurt the hostages</u>. We told them if they hurt the hostages they would lose the battle and any chance for freedom in America. It seemed that those of us that remained behind gained a certain respect from the detainees and they listened to our pleas with regard to the comfort and safety of the hostages.

- On the evening of the third day, November 25, the Cubans were still struggling for power and leadership. The leader of one of the factions struggling for control decided to make a show of authority by tying and handcuffing hostages in the chapel. Upon seeing this we were very disturbed. Many of the hostages, being bound together, were lying on their stomachs on the chapel floor. We immediately left the chapel and found as many Cubans as we could who we knew would help us convince the leader and his guards that this was not the right thing to do. After several meetings, and two hours later the hostages were released from their bonds. Every time a government helicopter left the ground, hostages would be tied to the tank full of explosive gas. They were informed that if anyone came in, none of the hostages would live.

- On Thanksgiving Day, November 26, Federal negotiators asked the Cubans to release fifty hostages. When this request was announced to the Cuban population, it triggered great unrest among them because they thought it was a ridiculous request. We talked to as many of the Cubans as we could and told them that releasing the hostages on Thanksgiving Day was a good idea. With it being evident that they would not release fifty hostages, we tried to ask for ten as a gesture of good faith. This idea was taken before their committee, and after several hours of debating, a decision to release three black hostages was made. That brought the total number of hostages released to eight. Four whites and four blacks. They decided on releasing the three black officers after we urged them to show no prejudice in their release of hostages. Much to our dismay, the hostages were rejected, and not released, by the government authorities at the main corridor.

- On the evening of November 28, a group of young militants decided to try and take over the main corridor, using hostages as a shield. When we became aware of their intentions, we found the older, more responsible Cuban leaders and insisted that was a mistake. We were able to convince them that this move would bring about disaster. After a heated confrontation in front of the chapel, this situation was defused.

- On the evening of December 2, at approximately 9:00 p.m., a certain American Cadre was in the chapel area visiting the hostages. As the helicopters hovered overhead, a young Cuban rebel came into the room where all of the hostages were held and shouted, "You Americans are going to die!" He then ordered all the Cubans out of the room and sat what appeared to be a small bomb in the center of the room. The American Cadre remained with the hostages, who had all moved to one area. The young Cuban kept shouting, "Everyone is going to die!" he looked around the room and noticed an American inmate standing with the hostages and screamed, "What are you doing here?" The inmate said nothing. He screamed again and raised his weapon toward the American. The inmate did not move. The young rebel ordered his men to take the inmate out. He was handcuffed at knife point and led from the chapel. By this time the Cubans had led the inmate to the front of the chapel. The helicopters had pulled away. It was then that the Cubans that believed an invasion had begun, realized it was a scare tactic and a false alarm. By that American being there and diverting their attention from the hostages long enough to avoid disaster, a blood bath, and execution of the hostages. This incident clearly illustrates the magnitude of the short-fused powder keg we were sitting on because the strain of the last ten days had begun to wear on the Cubans. Our point in this is that we were in just as much danger as the hostages. It also stresses the importance of us being there to help the hostages.

- On December 3, approximately seven hours before the agreement was signed, the proposal was read to the masses and ballots were passed out by the leaders. There was much dissension among the Cubans when they realized that there was no guarantee that they would not be deported. We walked the compound and talked to as many of the protesters who would listen to us, encouraging them that it was a good agreement and to vote *yes*. Many asked our opinion of the agreement and our reply was that it was positive for them. We believe out of respect of our opinion, many Cubans were persuaded to vote *yes,* who otherwise would have voted against the agreement. Several of the American inmates that stayed were bilingual and played a major role in this mission. Again, our presence was instrumental in bringing this ordeal to a peaceful end.

- Even after the hostages were released, we continued to be a stabilizing force. There were some Cubans that did not vote for the agreement and were very hostile. They wanted to burn the hospital, the chapel and the dormitories. We were able to convince them that these acts would be considered major misconduct and they would be prosecuted and ruin any chances they had for freedom. Another point that should be made here is that before the hostages were released, Chaplain Russell Mabry indicated he felt that we all should leave with the hostages. His concern was that the Cubans that did not agree with the settlement might decide to take us hostage to further negotiate with the government. We decided to stay and wait for orders from the authorities, even though our lives may have been in greater danger. In doing so, we were able to stop any further destruction.

Besides the aforementioned incidents, our actions were continuous throughout the siege. Incidents such as negative news broadcasts, the cutting off of the water supply by the government officials, the buzzing of helicopters, and the turning away of three black officers, set off outbursts and threats of violence and harm to the hostages. These happenings made our tasks even harder and more frustrating. Many of the hostages were our supervisors or men we interfaced with daily over the years in Atlanta. It was out of respect, devotion, and loyalty to these men that we received the additional motivation to overcome these deterrents. Those men knew why we were there, appreciated our presence, and knew we were not leaving until they did.

As God is our witness, the following staff members can also attest to the reason we stayed there and to the validity of our testimony.

Mr. Tom Campbell, Unicor Factory Manager	Mr. Bruce Long, Unicor Business Manager
Mr. Mahanny Echevellia, Head Teacher	Mr. Russell Mabry, Chaplain
Mr. Roy Dowling, Chaplain	Mr. Kenny Martin, Unicor Foreman General
Mr. Gary Stevens, Unicor Foreman Glove	Mr. J. W. Clark, Unicor Foreman
Mr. Bruce Green, Unicor Foreman Mailbag Repair	Mr. Perry Weimer, Unicor Accounting Supervisor
Mr. Elliton McKnight, Asst. Food Administrator	Mr. Wendell Beasley, Factory Manager Furniture
Mr. Carl Gates, Chief Psychologist	Mr. Paul Timons, Dentist
Mr. Buddy Levens, Hospital Administrator	Mr. Sam Lee, Unicor Asst. Business Manager
Lt. Howlington, Acting Chief Correctional Officer	Lt. Hoga, Correctional Lieutenant
Mr. Marvin Morrison, Unicor Foreman Tarp	Mr. Bobby Williams, Unicor Foreman Furniture
Mr. Al Villoch, Accounting Supervisor	

These were just a few of the hostages who, upon leaving, shook our hands and hugged our necks, thanking us for all we did. Seeing those people walking out of that prison alive and smiling, while heading to their waiting families made all our risks and efforts worthwhile, and gave us a feeling of accomplishment.

Upon leaving the prison in Atlanta, none of us expected a brass band to be playing and banners to be waving, but we certainly didn't expect what was to follow. We were chained and shackled and shipped to Seagoville, Texas, where we are being held in maximum security, assumed to be participants in the riot. We are locked down in solitary confinement in 7' x 10' cells for twenty-four hours a day. We get no sunshine or fresh air. We get three showers a week and are handcuffed to go to and from the showers and handcuffed to go inside recreation. There is no TV, radio, newspapers, or magazines, and have been allowed only one phone call a week.

Some of us who have had visits, which are limited to two hours, are handcuffed and chained during those visits with our families. We have been basically isolated from our families and the outside world. For what reason? Doesn't the governing law of our nation specify innocent until proven guilty? Is this the way our government shows gratitude to those who have gone above and beyond the realm of responsibility?

We would like to think we set a good example to those inmates (and other inmates) by acting unselfishly as we did. But if those actions are not recognized and rewarded, what will the attitude be of those inmates in the future who are confronted with similar situations where staff members' lives are in danger? We are not traitors, but with the way we are being treated, it makes one wonder.

We took no part in planning the taking of hostages, nor the destruction of government property. That was the Cubans' revolution, not ours. What other motivation could we have had to help the hostages? For that matter, what other motive? Just because we are incarcerated doesn't mean we are incapable of moral and just acts. We are Americans, and we love our country. We stand proud with what we have accomplished.

Why should it be so hard to believe that a handful of American inmates could have been at least partially responsible for the safe and peaceful end to the longest prison riot in American history? It's time to give credit where credit is due.

We experienced the same emotional stress, the same tension, and the same danger and frustration as the hostages. Although the crisis is over for them, it continues for us. While the hostages spend Christmas with their families, we spent ours in a 7'x10' cell…alone!

Most of us are Level 1 (in and out custody) security status incarcerated for non-violent crimes. But we are being treated like murderers! We should never have been designated to U.S.P. at Atlanta in the first place since Cubans were unsentenced detainees.

We are upset at the way we are being treated, feel we have been wronged and pushed to the side while other people take the credit.

We are aware of provisions within the Bureau of Prisons that would enable us to be granted a full and unconditional pardon for the positive influence we exhibited during the riot, and for risking our lives for the staff members at Atlanta. We are aware of individuals who have been granted pardons for saving one life, while we helped to save over one hundred lives.

We are asking that after you have had the opportunity to review the merits of this petition, you will grant our request of full and unconditional pardons.

We pray that your immediate attention will be given to this matter.

We, the American Cadre, solemnly promise that all the facts stated in this petition are accurate and true.

We, the American Cadre, humbly submit this in the name of God and our country.

Sincerely,
The American Cadre

In an effort to bring attention to the plight of the American inmates, the following article was written by an inmate and sent to several magazines, trying to have it published.

THE FORGOTTEN AMERICANS OF THE ATLANTA RIOT

We, the "forgotten Americans" at Atlanta Penitentiary, feel the time has now come to disclose the true facts pertaining to the Cuban riot which occurred on November 23, 1987. What is written in the following text is based on eye-witness accounts which might otherwise go unshared for fear of reprisal within the Federal Bureau of Prisons and US Parole omission. The travesty stands with unanswered questions and we remain with hopes that the media will print this story so that people across the country will have a chance to see how the prison officials and the Justice (Just us) Department have needlessly squandered a sizeable amount of the taxpayers' money while maintaining a policy of total disregard for the rehabilitative concerns and efforts of its inmate population. We hope the facts contained herein will awaken the public to what really happened here as witnesses and experienced by the eyes, ears, and hearts of those perhaps closest to the action.

Friday, November 20, 1987, Cubans and other Unicor factory employees of the Atlanta Penitentiary were gathered at approximately 1:15 p.m. and read the announcement made by Attorney General Edwin Meese, that 2500 Cubans would be returned to Cuba. This announcement concluded that the State Department had agreed with Fidel Castro to return the "undesirable" Cubans who had migrated to the United States during the Mariel boat lift. In return, the U.S. agreed to allow 27,000 Cubans which could not be fed and housed in Cuba, to enter the U.S. The Cuban detainees at Atlanta USP sensed their eventual fate upon returning to Cuba. The tension was so thick you could cut it with a knife. The detainees immediately began protesting by quitting work and gathering in groups to discuss their course of action. American inmates who worked at Unicor were told by their foreman to return to the American dorm, as they feared what the Cubans might do. We, the American inmates, had no doubts about what was going to happen. As you may know this was not the first uprising by the Cubans at Atlanta. In 1984, due to Administrative foot-dragging in not providing detention hearings for many of the Cubans, who were being held without any criminal charges, and rumors of actual deportation where Castro shot the first twenty Cubans who came off the airplane, the detainees set their mattresses on fire. During that disturbance, however, the administration had enough sense and foresight to keep the detainees locked in their cells and as a result there was only smoke damage as their limited mobility kept their emotions in check.

After the announcement of November 20, 1987, Cubans who were friends with Americans told us what was going to happen the following Monday. They were getting their weapons ready and there was going to be big trouble. We immediately began apprising corrections officials of the developing crisis as we had no desire to be caught in a potentially dangerous and volatile situation. Many Cubans who, likewise did not wish to be involved, were also telling anyone who would listen, but the answer was always the same, "We're ready for their asses." Mariel Monday was fast approaching and as history has shown us, they weren't ready. Or were they?

The Cubans at Oakdale, Louisiana, due to them being at a less-security conscious facility, were able to riot earlier than in Atlanta. They began on November 21, 1987, yet the warnings were not heeded in Atlanta where they held fourteen-hundred of the most violent Cuban inmates. Correctional officials in Atlanta knew as early as Saturday, November 21, 1987, the exact time Monday that the riot would occur. Prison guards and members of their families have said on public television that they made repeated reports both verbally and via written memorandums to the officials, such as the associate wardens of the impending riot. Inmates and staff asked to see Warden Truman and were assured that the warden had control and would make the appropriate decisions. We have since learned that the warden was a member of a sixteen-member panel who reached the decision that, after Oakdale, it was not prudent to lockdown the Cubans at Atlanta until Oakdale was resolved. In retrospect, this can hardly be considered a prudent decision and, considering the intelligence and data available at the time from both staff and inmates in Atlanta USP, as the Sixteen Wise Men. On Monday, November 23, 1987, and right on schedule at 10:30 a.m., the riot broke loose and the administration was not ready. Or were they? All women employees had already been evacuated from the prison, no outside contractors were on the premises, none of the higher officials and visitors who are always present in the dining hall were there, and the SWAT teams could be seen already gathered outside of the prison walls. Do you think they were exercising caution?

Inside the walls it was war, pure and simple. One hundred and sixty Americans who were not involved, among fourteen-hundred knife and sword wielding, screaming, and rioting Cubans. Guards were trampling over American inmates to escape to safety, locking doors behind them, leaving us to fend for ourselves. There were several cases where the American inmates actually made it possible for a staff member to escape but then were denied the same safety by having the door slammed in their faces. Although there were one-hundred extra guards on duty Monday, they too, fled to safety at the first signs of the disturbance. The guards who manned the towers began indiscriminately shooting. The back of a Cuban's head was completely blown off and his eyes were laying on his cheeks. Bullets were ricocheting off the ground and building walls. Hostages were being taken with knives at their throats, while handcuffed. A guard was being repeatedly stabbed as he tried desperately to help a fellow police officer who was being badly beaten. There were explosions from the burning buildings and people trapped inside and on roofs were screaming for help. Cubans were herding groups of hostages to different locations while automatic-rifle fire continued. This was only the beginning. Since there was no clear cut leadership among the Cubans, they grouped in roving bands of forty to fifty per group. The controlled over a hundred "two-way radios" they had taken from the staff that were being held hostage. They were constantly screaming back and forth over the radios, running from one location to another waving knives and swords and shouting, "Death to Americans," and "We die," "We no go back to Cuba," in broken English. The American inmates were to live a nightmare throughout the rest of the day and long night. During this time, the smoke was so intense it turned the day to dark. Breathing was nearly impossible and visibility was nearly zero as the Cubans were shoving and bumping into everyone with their knives and swords. Chaos prevailed in a situation where we were not sure if we were being stabbed, burned, shot or just experiencing a very bad nightmare. As night fell, we made every effort to keep our backs to the walls.

Most of the Americans had been assembled in the American dorm along with a large group of correctional staff hostages. We found out that the Cubans had decided to burn the laundry, which is located in the basement just below where we were being held. Several American inmates went down to the basement and found some Cubans who could speak English and attempted to reason with them. They begged and pleaded with them, saying we had done them no harm and asking them to not burn us alive. Our American emissaries stood back in horror as our fates hung on the outcome of this macho power struggle. The other American inmates had already begun tying sheets together and throwing them out the windows in hopes that they might get out and not be burned alive. Thank God that cooler heads prevailed and the Cubans decided not to burn the laundry and us at the same time. Our troubles were still not over by any stretch of the imagination.

A short time after the incident at the laundry, the Cubans who were still locked in "E" block, (which was the segregation unit), were released. These were the really violent types that the prison officials deemed too dangerous to ever be unlocked or to mix with the rest of the inmate population. They were out of control and wanted to kill everyone. They came storming through our dorms screaming, "Kill, kill," with almost demonic vengeance. They were intoxicated by their new-found freedom and the smoke from the fires burning the buildings of their oppressors. The electrical-adrenaline ambiance created by the riot only furthered their frenzy and they did not differentiate between American inmates and institution staff. The non-segregated Cubans, who were greater in number had to stab and cut some of them in order to keep them under control. This power struggle continued on through the night. The Americans didn't know if they would live or die from one moment to the next. Common sense, and what we were witnessing, told us we were all expendable, both to the Cubans and to the United States Bureau of Prisons. If the Cubans didn't kill us, it was certainly feasible that the first SWAT teams, elite Military, FBI, GBI, Prison SWAT teams, Local Law Enforcement, etc., could and would, if given the opportunity. We were certain that these various groups were outside of the walls awaiting an order to search and destroy. We huddled in fear and imagined the various gasses the authorities discussed using to quell this riot. We have all heard tales about people who are about to die seeing their lives pass before them. This is what many of us experienced for over twenty-seven hours. It seemed as if it lasted for years.

The American inmates, for the most part, had a short time to serve, that they be Level 1, 2, or 3 (which are low security levels), not presently eligible for a camp, that they have no disciplinary reports, no Immigration and Naturalization detainers (in other words American inmates), and that they have basically all of the attributes of a "Model Inmate." At least this was the way it was presented by the individual institutions attempting to convince people that to volunteer would be putting themselves in favorable light with potential Parole Boards and associated hearings. Finally, we were assured that there would be no Cubans in Atlanta and, due to the makeup of the "work cadre" and its individuals' history of good behavior by virtue of the aforementioned qualifications, the institution would be run like an FCI and no as a Penitentiary. The realities of Post-Riot Atlanta USP are far removed from the expectations of the bulk of the present inmate population.

In their prior institutions, most of the present Atlanta inmates were reasonably comfortable, had established good work records, had perfect institutional reports, were either eligible, or close to being so, for camps and furloughs where they could visit their families, were receiving top grade pay, and most had private or semi-private, sanitary and well-lighted rooms, along with other privileges that they had earned through hard work, good performance, and seniority. In addition, many inmates were involved in continuing education and/or vocational training programs, committed to preparing themselves for their future and had access to books via their libraries and legal materials through their law libraries. In contrast, Atlanta was burnt, dilapidated, and filthy, the housing rat, bug, and asbestos infested, the lighting was grossly inadequate, many available fire escapes welded shut. Five floors of rooms with stairs that must be carefully negotiated and which would not be allowed in any public housing building due to their hazardous condition. There are no libraries (legal or otherwise), there are no educational programs and the administration will not allow inmates to enroll in accredited correspondence programs. The recreation program is in disarray and there are no visible signs of efforts to remedy these problems. These items alone represent a direct violation of the standards that have been established by the federal court system and are presently practiced elsewhere by the Bureau of Prisons, and various amendments to the U.S. Constitution.

On January 21, 1988, all the inmates of Atlanta USP were summoned to the auditorium with the understanding that finally the rumors would be put to rest and we would be able to speak with the warden himself. Instead of the warden, however, we were addressed by four associate wardens. The two (2) that primarily spoke on behalf of the warden were Garland Jeffers and T. Harrigan. Not only what they said, but also the manner in which they addressed us, was very inciteful in itself. One would get the impression that they were just trying to cause some kind of confrontation so they could justify whatever the repercussions might have been. They informed us that we not "volunteers," as we were led to believe, that we were not part of a "work cadre," that we would not be receiving any kind of consideration at all from the staff at Atlanta regarding special *good time* or enhanced wages for working under unsafe and unsanitary conditions, and they even went so far as to say that they would not even suggest to the Parole Board that we were volunteers or should receive any type of superior programming for our efforts. In short, we had been duped and, in the vernacular, "We had nothing coming." In addition, they informed us that soon the population would be 750+ inmates and in the near future we could expect approximately 1100 as the population. Mr. Harrigan took, what appeared to be great pleasure, in pointing out Atlanta is, was, and always will be a U.S. Penitentiary and that we would have to get used to that whether we liked it or not. Is this the reward one receives for trying to straighten his life out and go one step further than just following the rules by volunteering to do some arduous and undesirable task? Is this consistent with any principles of rehabilitation or even just plain decency?

Now as the process continues, we are still expected to work and clean up in cold weather inside of burned-out buildings, often working with hazardous materials such as asbestos, without the proper safety equipment, standing in eight to ten inches of water and freezing for 11¢ per hour, while staring into the face of belligerence and condescension. Although the bulk of the population are "model inmates," who are volunteers and not disciplinary problems, we find ourselves constantly harassed, agitated, and provoked by administrative policies that even the staff often times seem very apologetic about enforcing. We must remember that this is the same administration that seemed inept at controlling a disturbance that ended up costing millions of dollars to remedy because they did not, or would not, realize that they should keep the Cubans locked down. Isn't it a bit late and inappropriate to over-react now? They have managed to create another situation where tension is bilingual to a level where it is potentially explosive. It seems that the mind set of our "sixteen wise men" continues to prevail.

Although there are some important philosophical and social questions arising from the rubble of the riot torn Atlanta USP, there are also some of a more practical nature. What was the source of $20,000, in cash, that had been found in a safe during the riot? Why had there been no mention of the deaths that occurred in addition to the one that was made public during the riot? Why have the American inmates not been offered the psychiatric care that the staff seems to so urgently need? Why are inmates presently being transferred or placed in segregation, contradicting the principles set out in the First Amendment and Procunier vs. Martinez (416 US 396, 94 S. Ct.-1800, 1974), for attempting to contact the News Media with information critical to the Atlanta Prison and its administration? Why would the Bureau of Prisons intentionally mislead and disrupt inmates from their continued efforts toward self-improvement while struggling to maintain family ties and personal lives? Was this merely for the sake of justifying salaries and continued federal funding at the expense of "inmate rehabilitation"? Finally, why is the same arrogance and disregard for the lives and hopes of individuals, that was an integral part of the Atlanta riot, being allowed to continue?

In conclusion, this riot should never have occurred. It was 100% preventable. Estimates run as high as $150 million dollars for the repair and losses in Atlanta alone, with another $18 million dollars for the damage in Oakdale, Louisiana. Keep in mind these figures only reflect property damages.

When it is so apparent that the Administration finds their staff expendable in the face of crisis, perhaps, it is necessary to make retribution to retain their loyalty. The staff that were held hostage have been paid handsomely since the riot, as well as receiving countless thousands of hours of overtime pay, TDY pay, psychiatric care, and who knows what else? Could we consider this to be "hush money"? Certainly, the guards that were on duty at the inception of the riot, and many who subsequently became hostages, knew that the riot was going to occur. The administration had enough foresight to get all of the women, and themselves, out of the line of fire before it began. We think that the media has a responsibility to the American taxpayer to look beyond all the contrived answers delivered to them by career bureaucrats. We also feel that there should be some concern regarding the continued deception and manipulation of those American inmates presently being confined at the Atlanta USP. The American taxpayers are the source of the vast amount of money that will be necessary to put this institution back into operable condition and they should be demanding and certainly deserve the truth. At a time when the "sleaze factor" has become synonymous with government, we cannot fail to notice such an apparently avoidable waste of large sums of taxpayers' hard earned income and what has become a total disregard for the rehabilitative efforts of human beings struggling to better themselves and re-establish their niche in society.

Just a brief update on what has occurred at Atlanta since the Cuban riot. It didn't take long to find out why the Bureau of Prisons ask for "low level" inmates to volunteer to go to Atlanta until they were able to facilitate a make-shift factory in the old gym. Level one (1) inmates were issued gate passes so that they could work outside the wall in the UNICOR factory located in the minimum security camp. These inmates continued to work outside as well as two (2) shifts who worked in the old gym inside—which is without any running water—toilet facilities which are provided in the form of "porta-johns." Thus, there are no sinks so that you may wash your hands before eating. In mid-May we did finally get a limited law library and, after four (4) to six (6) weeks, a commissary. Several months after returning they finally opened the recreation yard so that the inmates could exercise.

All the damage done by the Cuban riot still lies in shambles as it was at the conclusion of the riot. There are still many problems which exist there. Some cells are shared by as many as seven (7) to eight (8) inmates, which are not large enough for four (4). This is against all federal codes and regulations. Showers that don't work half the time, inmates are without hot water most of the time because of constant repairs which must be made on the plumbing. The prison was ordered closed by a federal judge because of the horrendous condition it was in. Instead it was turned into a detention center for the Cubans. True, there are repairs currently underway with rebuilding in a number of the cellblocks. These repairs are far from finished, and the institution should have been kept closed after the riot until these repairs could be completed. Because the staff had to return to work, there had to be inmates, regardless of the conditions. They had to live under deplorable conditions because of some of the more serious conditions seemed to be put on hold for repair. Because of some of these serious conditions, the inmates at Atlanta staged a "peaceful food boycott" in hopes of after exhausting all other means to get the staff to listen and to try finally resolve some of the issues. The boycott lasted only for two (2) meals. Just long enough to get their (staff) attention. Everyone continued to report to work as usual. This occurred on June 13, 1988.

The morning of the 14th, Warden Truman issued an order for the lockdown of the entire prison. Inmates were not allowed to eat breakfast or report to their job details. Instead, they were removed from their cells, one by one, and taken to interview rooms downstairs and ordered by various staff members to eat. They were required to consume a full meal or either face serious disciplinary actions. All the inmates had been up since six (6:00) a.m.

CHAPTER 16

AFTERMATH

EVEN THOUGH IT HAS BEEN MORE THAN THIRTY YEARS
since the riot, life has not continued as it was. The riot brought many changes in my life. I still suffer the wide range of difficulties caused by PTSD. I still have nightmares and night horrors. I still wake up in the middle of the night sometimes looking to see where everyone else is. Prior to the riot, Vietnam vets would be charged with murder or other horrendous crimes and explain that it was a result of PTSD, and I would think that this was as good of an excuse as any. Once as a union representative, I represented an individual who had PTSD from 'Nam. I had no idea where he was coming from in his explanation. By the middle of 1988, I had realized that if I would have had any idea the consequences of being a hostage I would never have allowed it. I could have been killed or released, but I never would have stayed.

My union activities at work made it difficult for me to be accepted for reassignment. I was seen by management as a troublemaker. The bureau had an office set up in Washington to assist us. When I was unable to get an assignment, I called the individual in charge of this office to find out what was going on since the director of the bureau had promised that we would be assigned to any open position within the bureau to again get back to work. I put in for two open positions and was not accepted for either position. When he came to the phone, he said, "Mr. Lawson, I really need to talk to you."

My response was, "I have no idea why in hell I am talking to you. The director promised us that we could be re-assigned to any open position once we were going to be returning to work, but I have been unable to get reassigned." The conversation went downhill from there.

I went to Ashland, Kentucky, to see about an opening in their furniture department. I met the factory manager, Mr. White, who I knew from his employment in Atlanta several years earlier. I told him that I was going to apply for the job opening in the furniture department. He explained that he had another person in mind for the job. He knew that if I applied for the job, that he would have to accept me, but wanted me to understand that he did not want me there and would get rid of me as soon as he could. From there, I went to the personnel office to see about other vacancies in industries. I saw an opening that interested me in PA. Unlike other open postings, this did not have the salary on the announcement.

As I was leaving, I met the personnel officer in the sally port. I asked him about the salary of the open position and was told that he didn't know. I reminded him that such information was not on the information available on the board as usually posted. He shrugged his shoulders and responded, "I have only been in personnel for more than twenty years! I never knew that!" and walked off.

When I returned home, I wrote a letter to the director of the bureau and explained what had occurred. It explained that I was ready to return to work, and provided seven options. At the same time, I explained that, while I was ready to return to work, neither would I cause a problem or tolerate any more of the bullshit. A letter came back from the bureau, advising me of the date that I was expected to begin work at Ashland.

When arriving there, and before getting to the institution, I met an individual who was going to become the industries manager. He was just coming in to replace Mr. White, who had retired. He assured me that I would have no difficulty there, as his father had been held hostage and injured during the uprising in Oakdale, Louisiana. While in Ashland, I had constant flareups from the PTSD, resulting in hospitalization on several occasions. The sounds from the machines and the Cubans that were working with me, even though they were good workers and never presented a threat to me, kept the emotional issues and the PTSD active. Eventually, I took a medical retirement. Soon afterward, I converted the retirement to the Federal Workers Compensation Program. I then returned to Georgia. After becoming a little more emotionally stable, I started going to a group of retired employees from the prison, who met on the grounds of the Atlanta facility. This did not continue for any long period.

Recently, I returned to the Atlanta facility on a couple of occasions. Unlike the conditions when I worked there, retirees were no longer permitted to enter at will with retiree identification papers. I was recently advised that a request can be made to the institution to get a visit inside the institution. Not too long ago, there had been a larger retiree group that had toured the facility. I hope to join the next group to see some of the changes. I did learn of some of the changes that have taken place since the riot.

The facility was changed from a level-five, high security facility to a medium security facility that houses more than 2,000 inmates. While the walls around the institution go as deep as they are above ground and are much wider at the bottom, and escape is still a challenge for anyone wanting out, the original facility is more than 120 years old. The large cellhouses, A and B, held more inmates in each unit than most of the modern facilities. The officer in charge of the unit had three staff members working for him in the unit during his shift and was responsible for as many as 500 inmates. With the Cuban population, there were times when the day shift officer, a GS 8, would have as many as fifteen staff members and over 700 detainees in the cell house.

The newer institutions have fewer than 500 inmates in the facility with a warden and three associate wardens in charge.

The cell houses in Atlanta had also been split into two units, each with their unit managers and counselors as well as correctional staffing in each of the units. This provided for more hands-on staffing the area, rather than depending upon staff from other parts of the institution if a problem arose. When I went to work in Atlanta, sanitation was a concern because of rats and bugs. The floors were kept clean at all times, although a thick coat of wax and shining floors was never an issue. I once shined the main corridor using tooth powder and wax. One could see himself in the shine. I was highly criticized for it, and it took several weeks to get it removed. Should an emergency arise and the floor get wet, staff would be in danger of falling if they ran down the hall.

Inmates walking over the grass or shining their shoes was never a concern. As long as there were no dead bodies, it was a good shift. In the smaller institutions, it became more like a military barracks. Shoes lined under the bed, clothes hanging in lockers, and daily inspections. An incident report could be written if the officer was not satisfied. Most of the Atlanta staff were permanent residents of the Atlanta area and would not consider moving to another part of the country for a promotion. In corrections, to go from a GS 8 to a GS 9 supervisor position, and beyond that, the employee had to relocate into another facility. The counselor position, a non-supervisory position, was the only GS 9 position available without relocating to another facility.

Even though Atlanta is a medium security facility at this time, it is not without its problems. It still houses younger and more dangerous inmates. When I started there, it was mostly older and professional criminals. As I was told by one inmate who was there for bank robbery, "I would not be a bank robber today! These young kids want to go in with a gun and start shooting! I robbed a bunch of banks all over the country, but I would have never shot anyone. I believed in using finesse and my brains."

The average inmate was over thirty-four years of age and had the next thirty years planned for them. I have been told that the age for the inmates there today is younger and more prone to creating a problem.

The Mexican gangs that come into this country also represent a larger portion of the population today. Fights and assaults are more frequent. Many of the staff are more concerned with their personal safety than existed with the American population, even though there are more staff in the housing units. With the Cuban population, assaults on staff was a frequent event, but it was sudden and unexpected physical assaults with hands. One could be talking to a detainee with no signs of trouble and suddenly be in a fist fight with him. Atlanta was having almost as many assaults on staff by the detainees as the rest of the bureau combined. Yet staff was not being assaulted with weapons nor intent demonstrated to cause serious bodily harm or death to staff by the Cuban population.

The industries building which was burned by the Cuban population has since been rebuilt. I do not remember what they are building there now, but industries are an important part of the correctional setting. It occupies the time and energy of inmates as well as providing job training for skills outside the institution. It also provides an income, which allows the inmates money to purchase their cigarettes and other needs. The funds go onto the books, much like a local bank, and items purchased come off much like a debit card. Actual cash is never introduced legally into the institution.

For younger individuals seeking employment in the correctional setting, I will say that the Federal Prison System is not a bad place to work overall. Any federal correctional system is a small city within itself. Any job available in any city is also available within the prison system. Doctors, nurses, secretaries, and even the police (correctional staff) are there. The advantage to working there is that the physical element is out of the job. If I was going to have a room painted inside, I would have an inmate go with me to get the paint and brushes. I was not going to carry a can of paint or a brush. With the overpopulation of detainees in Atlanta and the need to keep them busy, I had more detainees working for me in the furniture factory than I could use. I had one assigned to keep fresh coffee made for me all of the time. It was a tough job, but it had to be done!

CONCLUSION

AFTER THE RIOT, THE FEDERAL BUREAU OF PRISONS acknowledged that communication had been a contributing factor. In Atlanta, it was not the lack of communication, but the nature of the communication. Beginning in the regional office and management officials in the institution, it was a combative communication. The relationship between the correctional staff and the detainees was much better than that between the labor and management.

There had been a change with the incoming warden. Prior to his arrival, there was an open battle between management, led by an associate warden, the late AW Ramos and me, as the outspoken union representative. He came in at a time of instability within the institution. Unlike what was reported by the bureau, it was not that there was poor communication between staff and management; there was no one on either side listening.

While the warden had opened the lines of communication and started a meaningful dialogue, we were not aware of his personal battle with cancer. His being set aside during the riot and the regional director, Mr. Gary Mckensie, doing the directing was misinterpreted by myself and some others as another assault on staff. While the conflict between labor and management was still in the forefront of many of our minds, the inmate (detainees) and staff relations were not as hostile. This was demonstrated by the lack of physical injuries to the hostages.

Overall, the detainees were much more accepting and forgiving of their plight than staff. The detainees accepted the fact that a large number had been given a release date which had come and gone while they were still there. Staff was not as accepting of the working conditions and hostile management approach of their representative from personnel and the AWO.

The announcement that the federal government and Cuba had reached an agreement to return some detainees to Cuba on the national news before offering any explanation to the detainees or staff was viewed as just another example of the contempt for everyone inside of the walls. By the hostages, it was seen as acknowledging that we were expendable. Every uprising of the past had brought financial benefits to the bureau.

After more than thirty years, constant PTSD symptoms, and a serious heart condition, there is still anger and hostility directed toward the bureau. In spite of the panic and the anxiety attacks, I have to acknowledge, God has been so good to me. While I have all of the pains and symptoms that come with old age, I thank God for giving me the time to acquire them!